ALTRINCHAM IN 50 BUILDINGS

STEVEN DICKENS

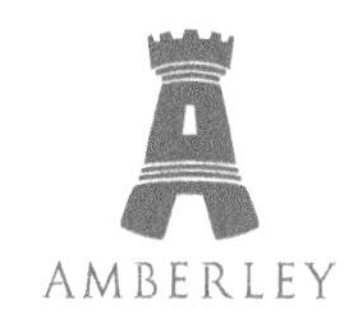

Dedicated to the memory of Barbara Dickens. Thanks for everything, Mum.

First published 2018

Amberley Publishing, The Hill, Stroud
Gloucestershire gl5 4EP

www.amberley-books.com

British Library Cataloguing in Publication Data.
A catalogue record for this book is available from the British Library.

ISBN 978 1 4456 7458 2 (print)
ISBN 978 1 4456 7459 9 (ebook)

Origination by Amberley Publishing.
Printed in Great Britain.

Contents

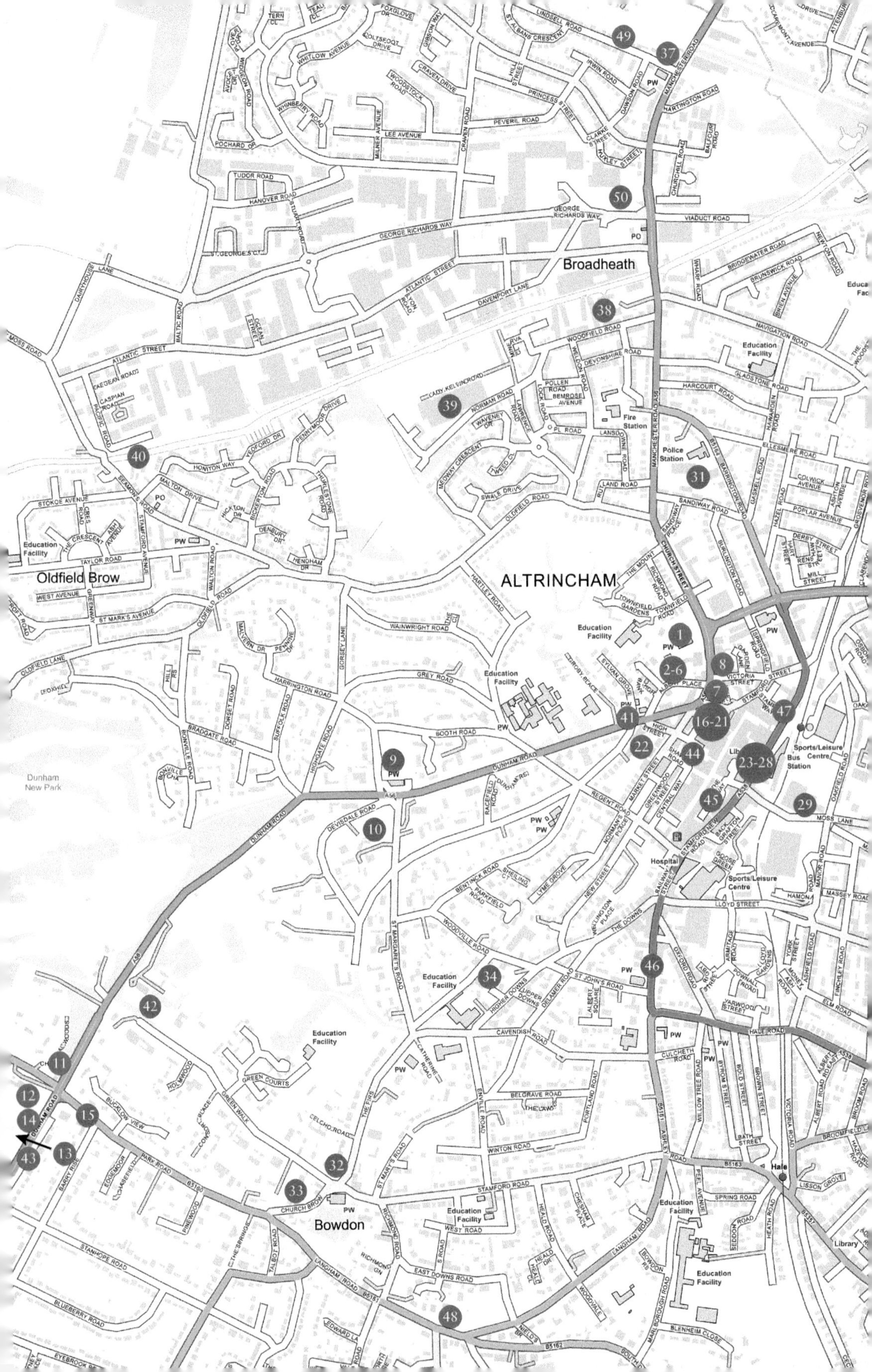

ALTRINCHAM
Broadheath
Oldfield Brow
Bowdon
Hale
Dunham New Park
Education Facility
Fire Station
Police Station
Hospital
Sports/Leisure Centre
Bus Station
Library
PW
PO
LINDSELL ROAD
ST ALBANS CRESCENT
MANCHESTER ROAD
DAWSON ROAD
IRWIN ROAD
PRINCESS STREET
HARTINGTON ROAD
PEVERIL ROAD
CLARKE STREET
HUXLEY STREET
CHURCHILL ROAD
BALFOUR ROAD
WHITLOW AVENUE
COLTSFOOT DRIVE
FOXGLOVE DR
GIBSON WAY
WOODSTOCK ROAD
CRAVEN DRIVE
CRAVEN ROAD
HILL STREET
WIDGEON ROAD
WHINBERRY ROAD
LEE AVENUE
MILNER AVENUE
POCHARD DR
TUDOR ROAD
HANOVER ROAD
STUART ROAD
GEORGE RICHARDS WAY
VIADUCT ROAD
ST GEORGES CT
ATLANTIC STREET
DAVENPORT LANE
LYON ROAD
DAIRYHOUSE LANE
BALTIC ROAD
OCEAN STREET
MOSS ROAD
CAEGEAN ROAD
CASPIAN ROAD
PACIFIC ROAD
BRIDGEWATER ROAD
BRUNSWICK ROAD
NEWTON ROAD
WHARF ROAD
BRIEN AVENUE
NAVIGATION ROAD
GLADSTONE ROAD
HARCOURT ROAD
HAWARDEN ROAD
ELLESMERE ROAD
COLWICK AVENUE
ASHTON AVENUE
POPLAR AVENUE
DERBY STREET
MILL STREET
HAZEL ROAD
GASKELL ROAD
GROSVENOR ROAD
WOODFIELD ROAD
DEVONSHIRE ROAD
WELDON ROAD
POLLEN ROAD
BEMROSE AVENUE
LADY KELVIN ROAD
NORMAN ROAD
WAVENEY ROAD
LAWRENCE ROAD
LOCK ROAD
LANSDOWNE ROAD
MEDWAY CRESCENT
SWALE DRIVE
TWEED CL
LAND ROAD
OLDFIELD ROAD
SANDIWAY ROAD
SANDIWAY PLACE
BARRINGTON ROAD
BURLINGTON ROAD
CHURCH STREET
THE MOUNT
RICHMOND ROAD
TOWNFIELD GARDENS
TOWNFIELD
HARTLEY ROAD
PENNYMOOR DRIVE
HONITON WAY
YEOFORD DR
MALTON DRIVE
BICKERTON ROAD
THURLESTONE ROAD
HICKTON DR
DENBURY DR
HENDHAM DR
SEAMONS ROAD
STOKOE AVENUE
THE CRESCENT
ASH AVENUE
TAYLOR ROAD
STAMFORD AVENUE
WALTON ROAD
WEST AVENUE
GREENWAY
ST MARK'S AVENUE
OLDFIELD LANE
FOXHILL
MALVERN DR
PENNINE DR
WAINWRIGHT ROAD
GORSEY LANE
HARRINGTON ROAD
GREY ROAD
SUFFOLK ROAD
DORSET ROAD
BRADGATE ROAD
BONVILLE ROAD
HIGHGATE ROAD
BOOTH ROAD
DUNHAM ROAD
A56
DEVISDALE ROAD
RACEFIELD ROAD
REGENT ROAD
SYLVAN GROVE
ALBERT PLACE
VICTORIA STREET
STAMFORD STREET
SPRINGFIELD ROAD
GARDEN LANE
HIGH STREET
SHAW ROAD
MARKET STREET
GREENWOOD STREET
CENTRAL WAY
NORMAN'S PLACE
STAMFORD NEW ROAD
BACK GRAFTON STREET
GOOSE GREEN
MOSS LANE
OAKFIELD ROAD
RAILWAY STREET
LLOYD STREET
HAMON
MASSEY ROAD
MANOR ROAD
BENTINCK ROAD
SHEILING CT
PARKFIELD ROAD
LYME GROVE
NEW STREET
WELLINGTON PLACE
THE DOWNS
WOODVILLE ROAD
ST MARGARET'S ROAD
OXFORD ROAD
ARMITAGE ROAD
LLOYD GARDENS
POWNALL ROAD
YORK STREET
ASHFIELD ROAD
FINCHLEY ROAD
ELM ROAD
YARWOOD STREET
HALE ROAD
A538
ST JOHN'S ROAD
DELAMER ROAD
ALBERT SQUARE
HIGHER DOWNS
UPPER DOWNS
CAVENDISH ROAD
CULCHETH ROAD
CATHERINE ROAD
BELGRAVE ROAD
THE LAWN
PORTLAND ROAD
ENVILLE ROAD
WILLOW TREE ROAD
BYROM STREET
BOLD STREET
BROWN STREET
VICTORIA ROAD
ALBERT ROAD
BROOM ROAD
BATH STREET
ASHLEY ROAD
B5163
B5161
WINTON ROAD
STAMFORD ROAD
CHESHAM PLACE
HEALD ROAD
WEST ROAD
PEEL AVENUE
SPRING ROAD
SEDDON ROAD
HEATH ROAD
LISSON GROVE
B5357
THE FIRS
CELCHO ROAD
ST MARY'S ROAD
GREEN COURTS
GREEN WALK
HOLMWOOD
BUCKLOW VIEW
CHURCH BROW
PARK ROAD
B5160
EDGEMOOR
BARRY RISE
PINEWOOD
THE SPRINGS
TALBOT ROAD
STANHOPE ROAD
BLUEBERRY ROAD
EYEBROOK RD
LANGHAM ROAD
RICHMOND GN
EAST DOWNS ROAD
EDWARD LA
B5162
WOODVALE
HEALD CL
BOWDON RS
MARLBOROUGH ROAD
BLENHEIM CLOSE
NIELD'S
1
2-6
7
8
9
10
11
12
13
14
15
16-21
22
23-28
29
31
32
33
34
37
38
39
40
41
42
43
44
45
46
47
48
49
50

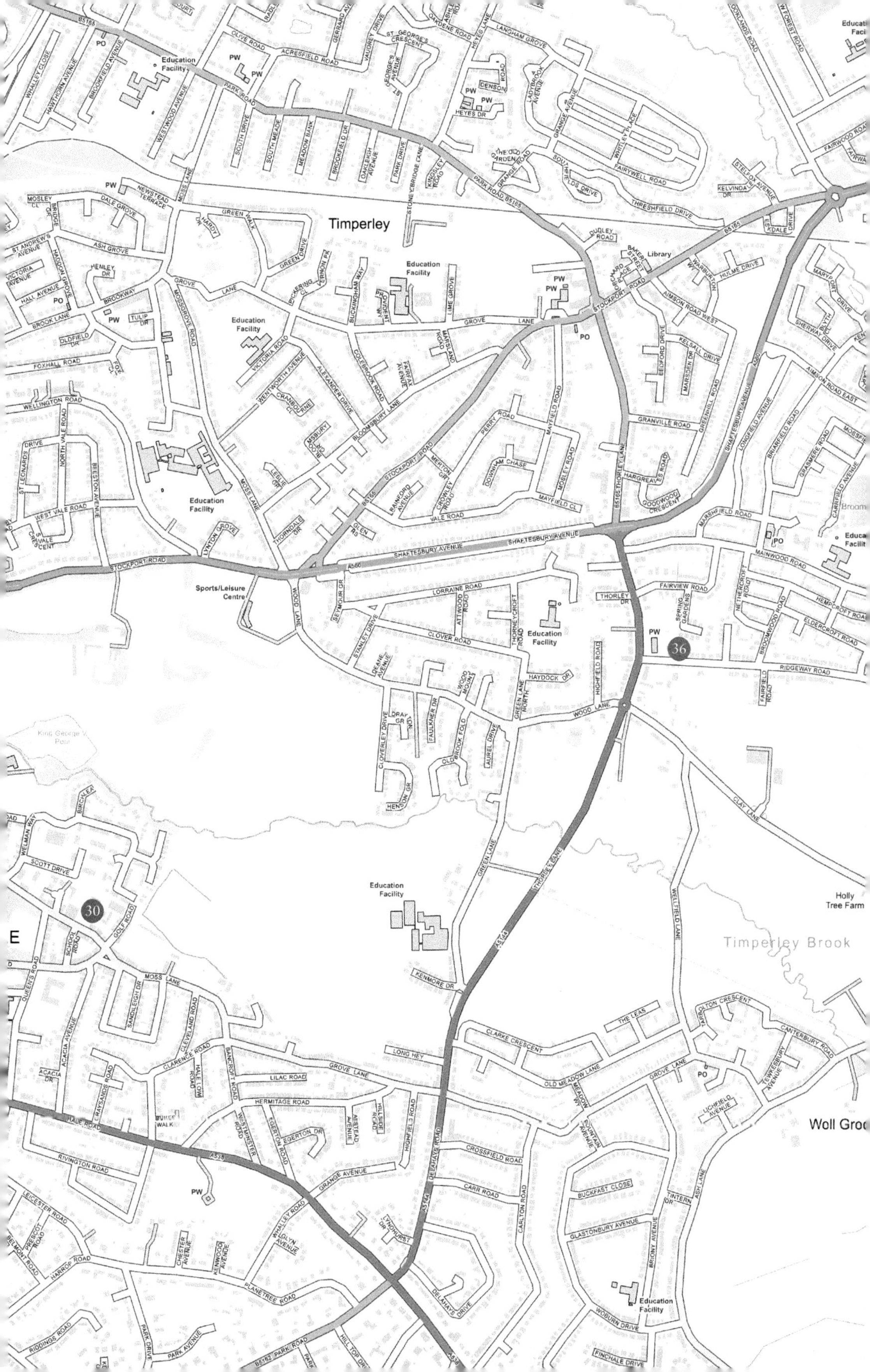

Timperley
Education Facility
Library
Sports/Leisure Centre
King George V Pool
Holly Tree Farm
Timperley Brook
Woll Gro
36
30
PARK ROAD
ACRESFIELD ROAD
STOCKPORT ROAD
SHAFTESBURY AVENUE
THORLEY LANE
GROVE LANE
MOSS LANE
WOOD LANE
CLAY LANE
WELLFIELD LANE
GREEN LANE
HALE ROAD
DELAHAYS ROAD
RIDGEWAY ROAD
MAINWOOD ROAD
MARSHFIELD ROAD
AIMSON ROAD EAST
AIMSON ROAD WEST
THRESHFIELD DRIVE
FAIRYWELL ROAD
GRANVILLE ROAD
MAYFIELD ROAD
VALE ROAD
CLOVER ROAD
LORRAINE ROAD
MOSS LANE
CLARKE CRESCENT
OLD MEADOW LANE
LONG HEY
LILAC ROAD
HERMITAGE ROAD
CROSSFIELD ROAD
CARR ROAD
CARLTON ROAD
GLASTONBURY AVENUE
BUCKFAST CLOSE
WOBURN DRIVE
FINCHALE DRIVE
PLANETREE ROAD
PARK AVENUE
PARK DRIVE
RIDDINGS ROAD
HARROP ROAD
RIVINGTON ROAD
GRANGE AVENUE
WHALLEY ROAD
QUEEN'S ROAD
SCOTT DRIVE
GOLF ROAD
SCHOOL ROAD
KENMORE DR
CANTERBURY ROAD
TARBOLTON CRESCENT
THE LEAS
WELLINGTON ROAD
NORTH VALE ROAD
WEST VALE ROAD
BEESTON AVENUE
FOXHALL ROAD
BROOK LANE
BROOKWAY
ASH GROVE
DALE GROVE
NEWSTEAD TERRACE
VICTORIA ROAD
WENTWORTH AVENUE
ALEXANDER DRIVE
BLOOMSBURY LANE
COLEBROOK ROAD
BUCKINGHAM WAY
LIME GROVE
MARSLAND ROAD
PERRY ROAD
MOBLEY ROAD
DOWNHAM CHASE
HARGREAVES ROAD
GOODWOOD CRESCENT
GREENHILL ROAD
KELSALL DRIVE
BEDFORD DRIVE
HULME DRIVE
SHERWAY DRIVE
MARYPORT DRIVE
BRIARFIELD ROAD
LONGFIELD AVENUE
GRASMERE ROAD
FAIRVIEW ROAD
SPRING GARDENS
HEMPCROFT ROAD
ELDERCROFT ROAD
BROOMWOOD ROAD
NETHERCROFT ROAD
FAIRFIELD ROAD
HIGHFIELD ROAD
HAYDOCK DR
STANLEY DRIVE
SEYMOUR GR
DEANE AVENUE
CLOVERLEY DRIVE
FAULKNER DR
LAUREL DRIVE
HENSON GR
B5165
A560
A5144
A538
B5162
PO
PW

Introduction

Altrincham has many historic locations, including Dunham Massey Hall and Park, established by the Norman Hamon (Hamo) de Masci (Massey) after the Norman invasion. In 1290, the town was awarded free borough status by charter and a weekly market was established at what is now Old Market Place, by Baron Hamon de Masci V. There is now a Market Hall on Market Street, which is included in this book along with many other nearby locations, some of Georgian origin. Dunham Massey Hall and some structures within the park are also included, as well as Old Market Place. Here, I have grouped some of the buildings together in order to identify its varied history. When the borough was established it was administered by a court leet and had an elected mayor since at least 1452. It kept the peace and regulated markets and fairs until it was abolished in 1886. There was a local court, prison lock-up and stocks, all used to keep order and located in Old Market Place. Around 1809 this location bore witness to an historic incident, when the sale of a woman by her husband in front of a large crowd took place. The importance of this locality continued post-1849 with the construction of a new town hall next to the Unicorn Hotel (Old Market Tavern). It was an important focal point of the town until new council offices were constructed on Market Street around 1900. George Truefitt's Cheshire 'black and white' still emphasises Altrincham's rural past in Old Market Place. The town was also the home of the Earls of Stamford until the death of the 10th Earl in 1976. Their influence is everywhere, even today, in the surviving buildings they constructed. The town's buildings were also influenced by the construction of the Bridgewater Canal, its infrastructure and the development of industry along its banks. Similarly, the railway saw the construction of Stamford New Road, now one of the many conservation areas around the town.

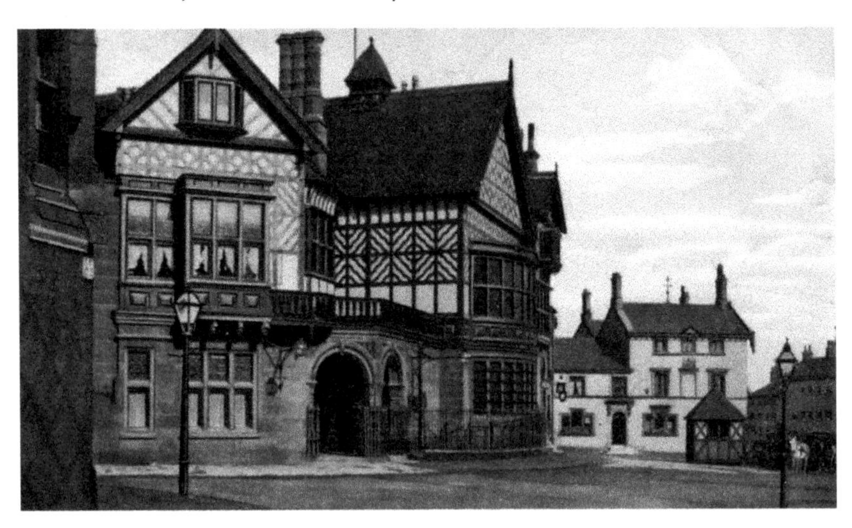

The 50 Buildings

1. St George's Parish Church, Church Street, Altrincham

St George is the Church of England parish church for Altrincham. It is a Grade II-listed building. Until the late eighteenth century Altrincham township had no church and lay in the large parish of Bowdon. Bowdon church came into existence in Anglo-Saxon times and as the population of Altrincham steadily grew, it became apparent that another ecclesiastical centre would be required for worship.

The original church was a chapel of ease to St Mary's Church, Bowdon, and was built in 1799. The tower and spire date from 1874 and the chancel from 1886. In 1896–97 the Lancaster architects Austin and Paley rebuilt the nave and aisles, with the tower remaining from the earlier church. The three lower stages of the tower are the oldest part of the church, from around 1829. The church contains stained-glass windows, dating from 1895 and located in the chancel, which were designed by Mary Lowndes. The first female glazier in the Arts and Crafts movement, Mary Lowndes was also an influential figure in the Suffragette organisation and designed many of their banners.

St George became a separate parish in 1868. The Revd Oswald Leicester, its first curate-in-charge (1799–1831), was influential in the founding of the church. There is a memorial to him in the chancel.

In 1873–74 J. Medland and Henry Taylor rebuilt the upper part of the tower. In 1886, the chancel was rebuilt and in 1896–97 the nave and aisles were rebuilt. The church is in red brick with terracotta, it has a slate spire, and clay tile roofs. It consists of a nave with a clerestory, north and south aisles, a chancel with a polygonal apse, vestry and chapel, and a west tower with a porch and spire. The windows have semicircular heads, and at the east end is a rose window. Between the years 1859–93 the population of the parish doubled from 2,800 to 5,600, with several schools built in the parish during this period. In 1868, the district was converted into a parish in its own right, with St George's as the parish church.

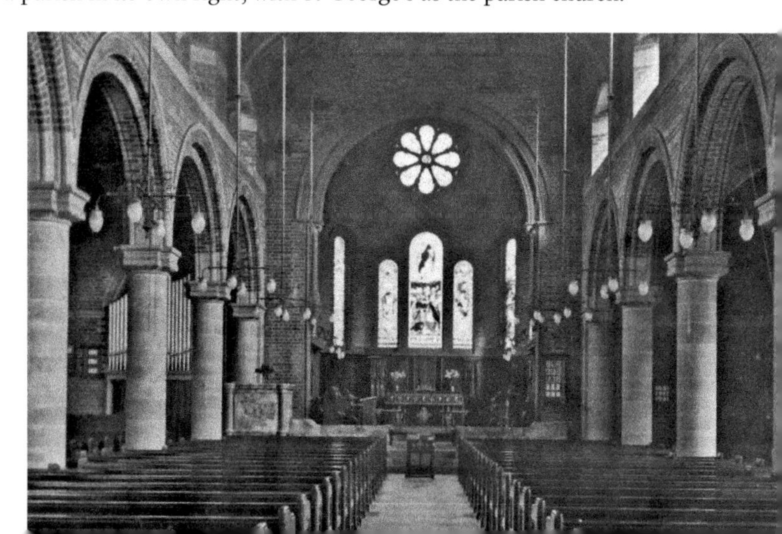

The interior of St George's in 1907.

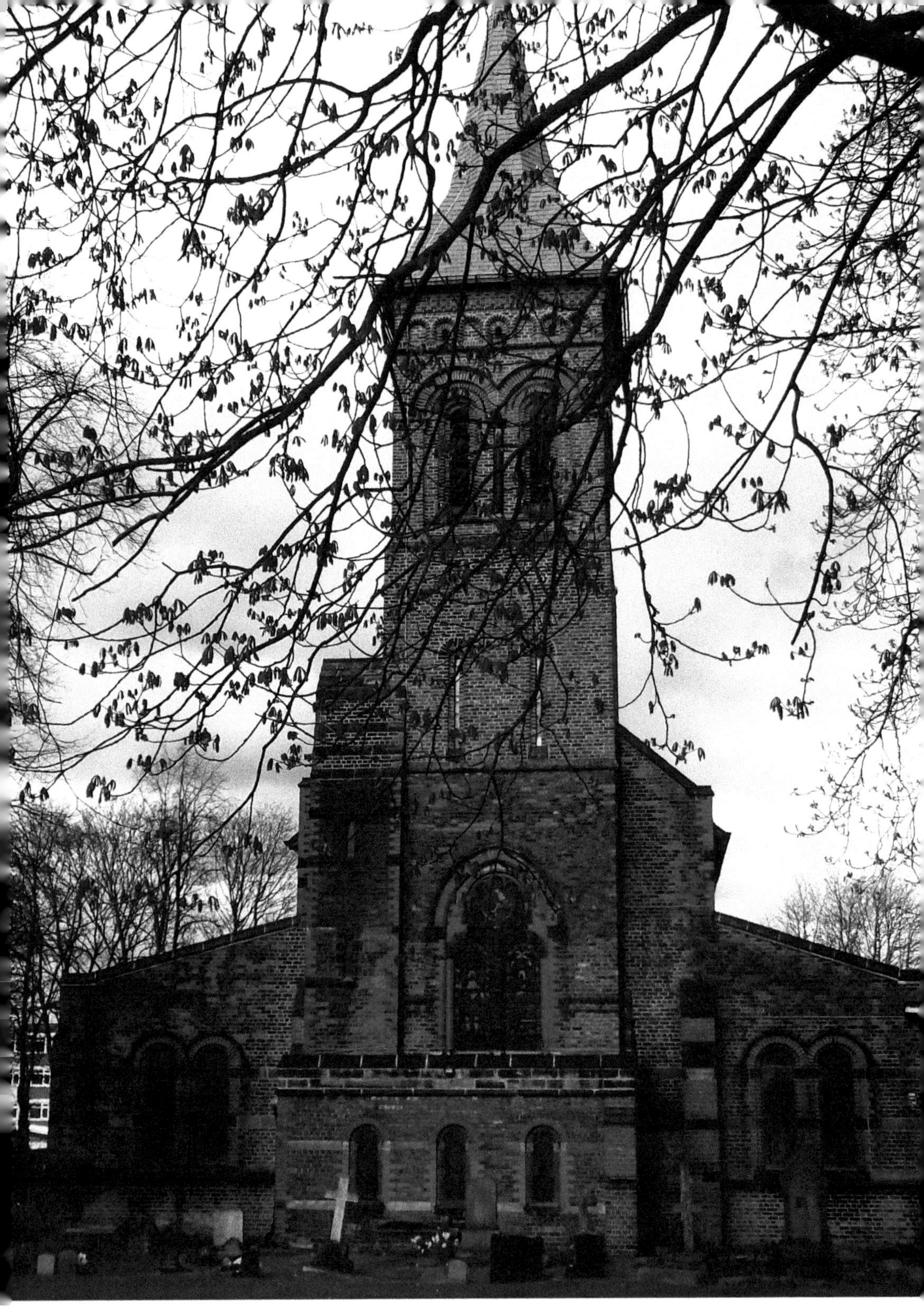

St George's Church from Church Walk.

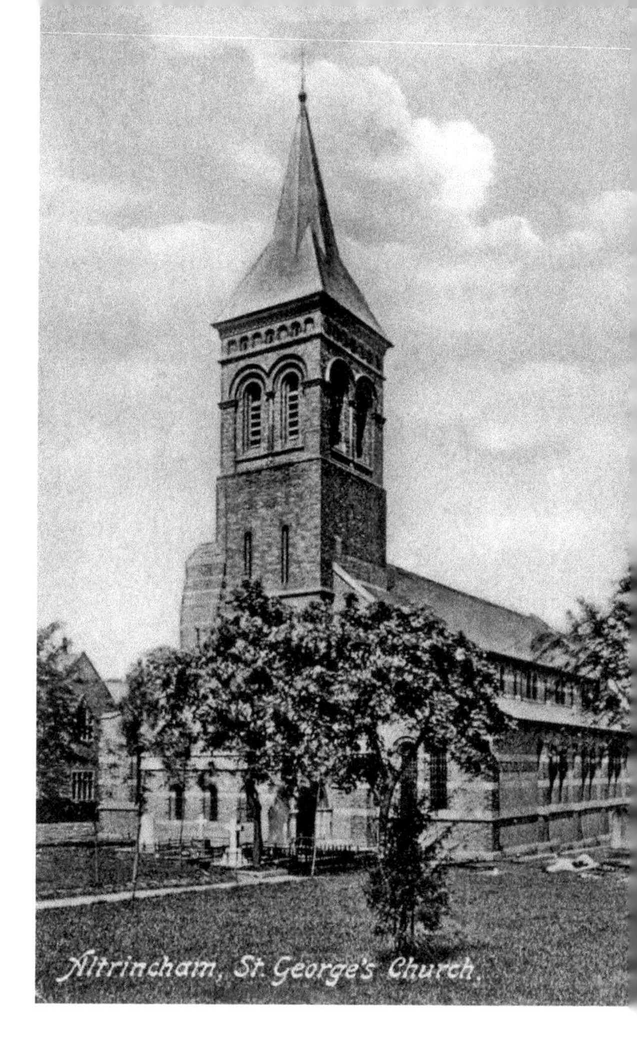

St George's Church, *c.* 1900.

2. The Unicorn Hotel (Old Market Tavern) and First Town Hall, Old Market Place, Altrincham

In 1814, Thomas de Quincey (1785–1859) wrote about Old Market Place in *Confessions of an English Opium Eater* while travelling from Manchester to Chester: ' ... and the bonny young women of Altrincham were all trooping about in caps and aprons coquettishly disposed' (after Nickson, p.30). A drawing of Old Market Place (No.4) shows it is still as hectic today. This print of an original engraving *c.* 1826 shows the market hall, dungeon, Unicorn Hotel and Roundabout House at the centre of the market. The Butter Market stood here from the seventeenth to the late nineteenth century. The Unicorn Hotel was adjacent to the old town hall from 1849, until the new town hall was erected around 1900. Local justice was administered from the Unicorn Hotel, hence the presence of the dungeon and stocks in Old Market Place. The Unicorn Hotel (Old Market Tavern) dates to the early nineteenth century, with the old town hall then incorporated into the hotel, later a public house when it closed.

The building is in brick, mainly rendered, on a stone plinth, with stone dressings and slate roofs. The hotel has three storeys, and on the east front there is a porch with Tuscan columns and two gables with pierced bargeboards. The former town hall has a carriage

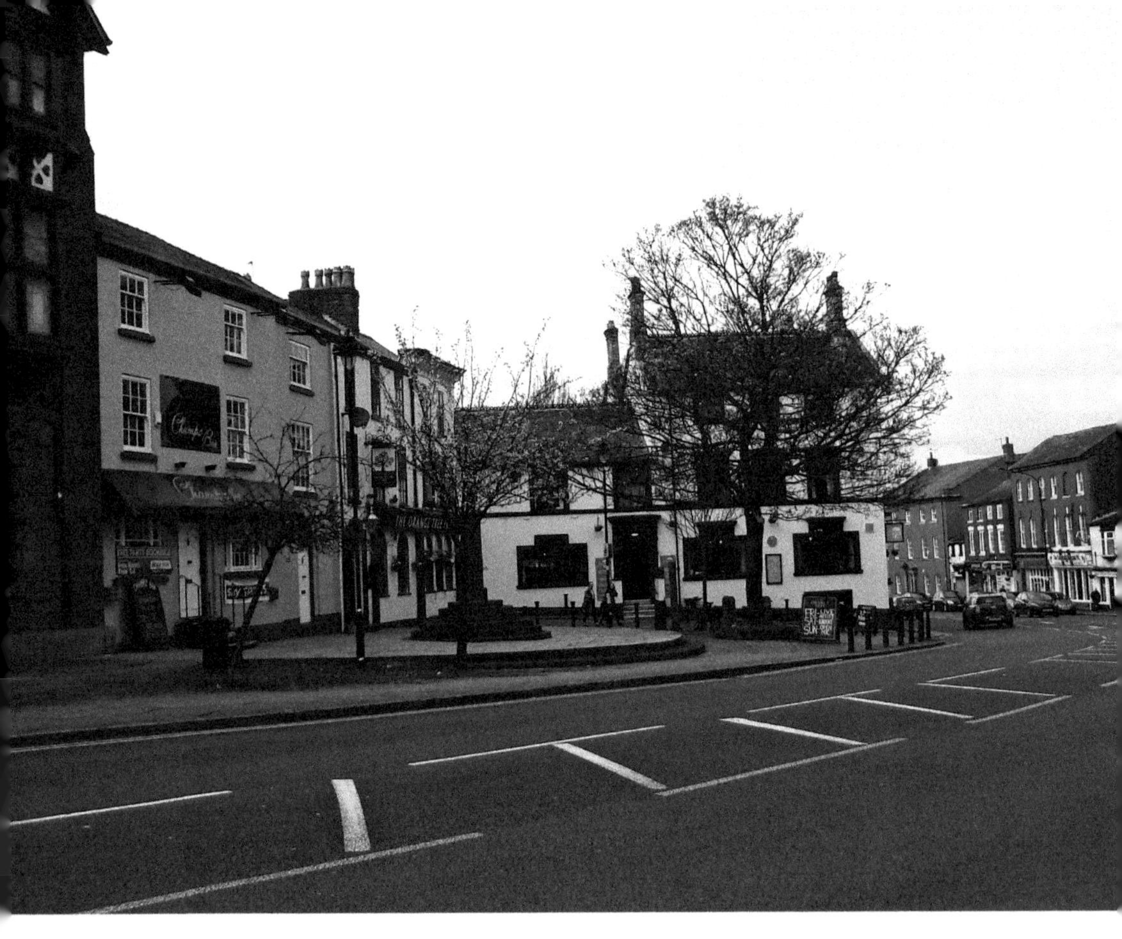

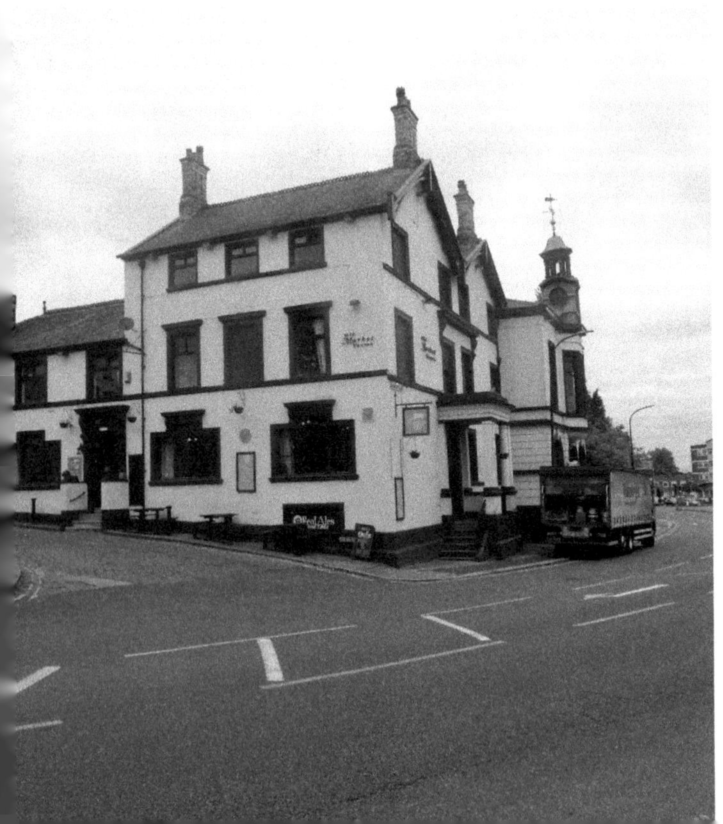

Above: Old Market Place, with the former Unicorn Hotel (Old Market Tavern) in the centre.

Left: Old Market Tavern and the first town hall, showing porch and bell cote.

The first town hall, showing bell cote and weathervane.

entry, an oriel window to the upper floor and a clock tower above it, with a bell cote and a weathervane. The court leet, held here, saw the election of court officers at the Michaelmas Assize (September–December) for the barony of Dunham Massey, before the burgesses and aldermen. Court officers legislated regarding the collection of rents and other services due to the lord of the manor. In ancient times tenants were required to grind their corn in the lord's mill. Rubbish collection and building repairs were also part of the court's remit. It was the responsibility of the court leet to ensure that constables, bailiffs, overseers of the poor, surveyors of the highways and other court-appointed officers were doing their duty. Trade was protected by the court leet, which ensured that weights, measures and prices were regulated and that produce was of the required standard.

3. Unicorn Hotel (Old Market Tavern) Blue Plaque and Buildings in Old Market Place, Altrincham

George Massey, the hotel's proprietor, set up Altrincham's first gas-making plant in 1844, in order to light the frontage of the hotel. There is a blue plaque located here that reads, 'Near this site George Massey, proprietor, manufactured gas for the first time in Altrincham to illuminate the Unicorn Hotel 1844.'

Other buildings of interest in Old Market Place include No. 16, which is Grade II listed and located on the east side of Old Market Place. It has been a house and offices and is of early nineteenth-century construction. The building is of roughcast brick, with

Below left: Blue plaque on the Old Market Tavern, Old Market Place.

Below right: Nos 2–4 Old Market Place, showing central recess and balcony (left).

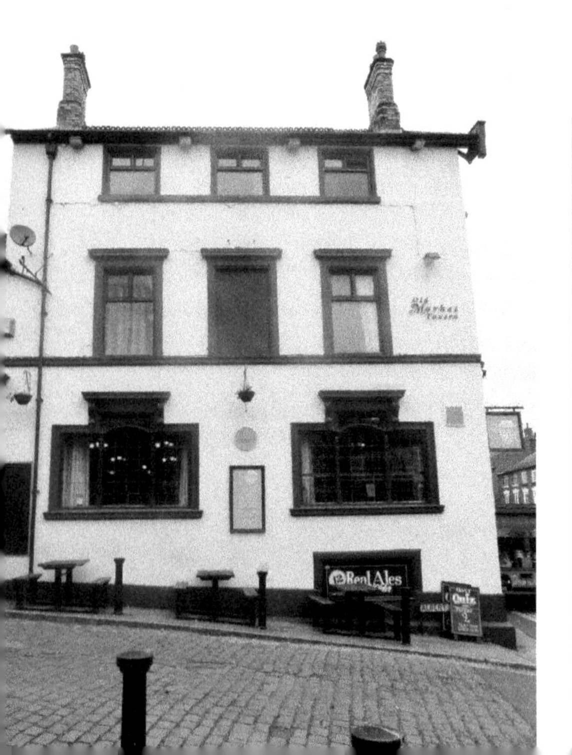

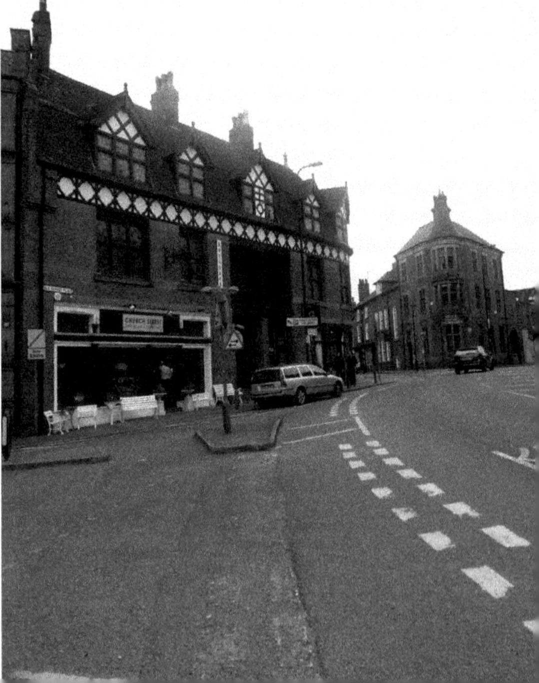

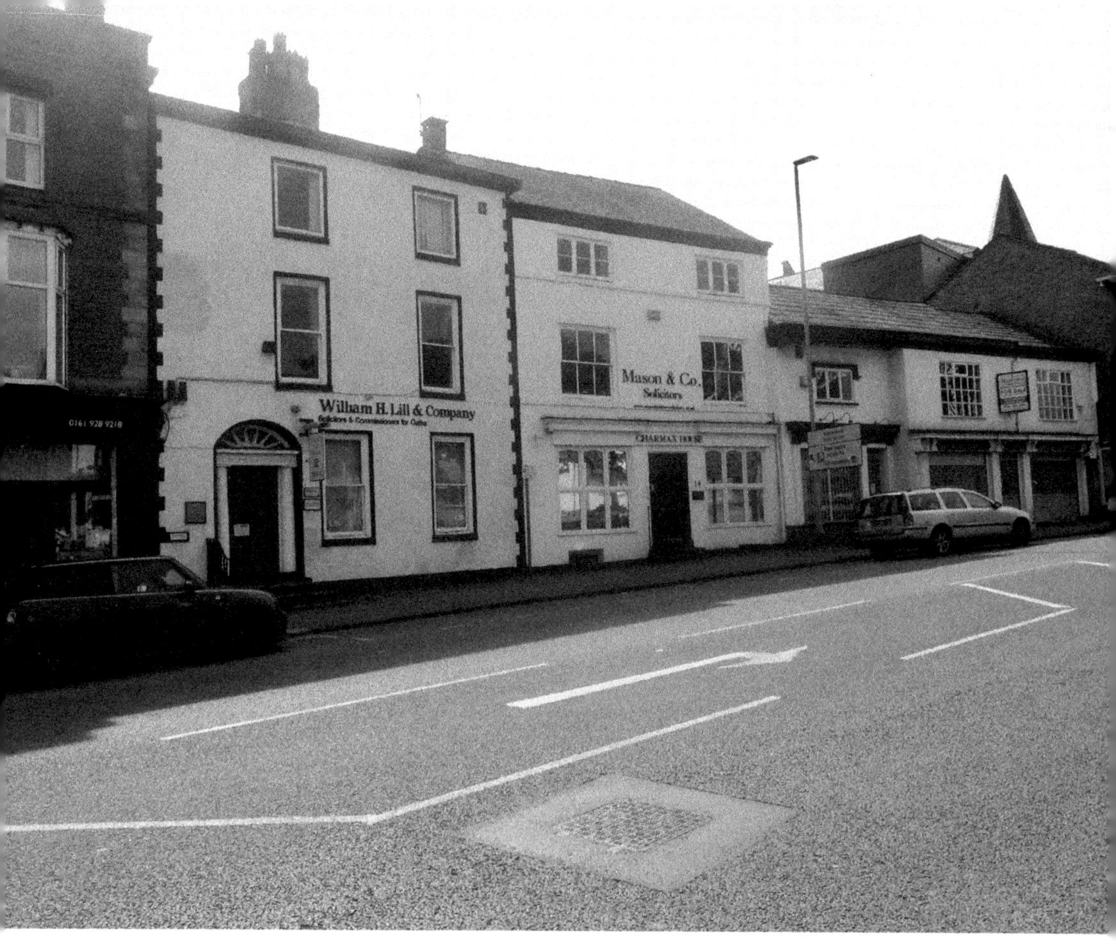

No. 16 Old Market Place (white building, near left).

stone dressings and a slate roof. It has three storeys and among its features are a four-panel door with fluted Doric three-quarter columns, a segmental fanlight with radiating bars and four steps with a cast-iron handrail. Nos 2, 2a, 4a and 4 Old Market Place are all Grade II listed and are located on the south side of Old Market Place. They were commercial premises originally and have been in use as restaurants and offices. They were built in the 1890s for Sir William Cunliffe Brooks, probably by George Truefitt. The building is constructed in header-bond brick and there is decorative timber framing, eaves and bargeboards, with a clay tile roof. The façade of five bays 'sweeps gracefully' into Post Office Street, where there are two further bays. The building has two storeys and attics, and it is described as 'Romantic in manner and yet almost symmetrically composed'. The entrance to Nos 2a and 4a are in a central recess with a balcony above. The outstanding feature of this building is the style of its windows. The shopfronts have two and three light mullion and transom windows above, five windows with decorative bargeboards, finials and timber-framed gables. All the windows have leaded lights except for the ground floor. There was originally a weathervane on the roof, which recorded the initials of the patron. The building complements Cunliffe Brooks' other buildings: the former Lloyds Bank and Nos 1, 1a and 3 Market Street, which are described elsewhere.

4. The Orange Tree Inn and Old Butter Market, Old Market Place, Altrincham

The building of the Orange Tree Inn dates from 1679, and the location of an inn here is indicative of the need for stagecoach accommodation for travellers before the age of the railway and motor car. The real character of Old Market Place is evident here. The Orange Tree is reportedly haunted and the restored stocks, where floggings were administered until the early nineteenth century, are also to be seen. The restored old market cross remains in Old Market Place too, probably originally erected in the fifteenth century. This is close to the Old Market Tavern (Unicorn Hotel), and the adjacent former town hall.

Old Market Place is thought to stand on the site of the original Saxon settlement and is now a conservation area, the cobblestone paving dating from 1896. The Butter Market stood here from the seventeenth to the late nineteenth century, in a central location. This was the dominant feature of Old Market Place, erected in 1684 by Henry, Lord Delamer, who was Lord of the Manor and owner of the rights to the market. An old drawing of the building shows a turret in the centre of the old Butter Market, which would appear to mirror the turret on the old town hall of 1849, built by the Earl of Stamford. The turret of the old Butter Market contained a bell, which bore the inscription 'Delamer 1684 Donum pr. Nobile Henry Domine. Cast at Little Budworth.' When the town hall of 1849 was built this bell was hung in its turret, and a clock was added by the Earl

Old Market Place, former Red Lion Hotel (left) and Orange Tree Inn (right).

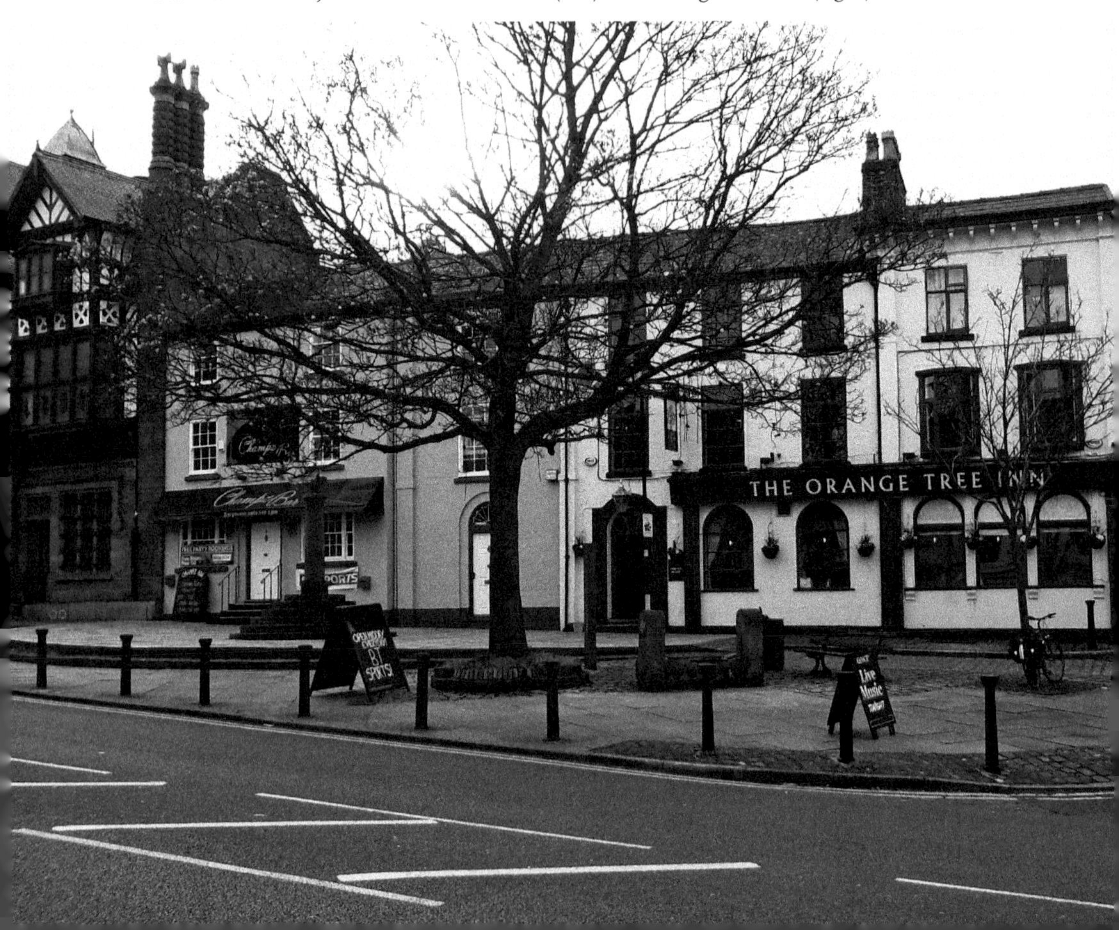

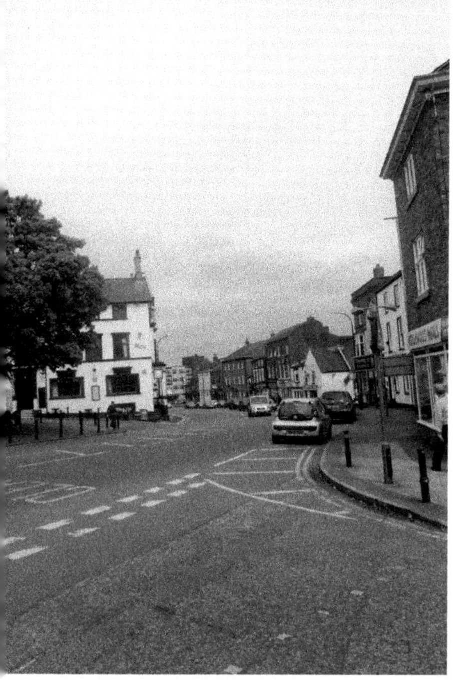

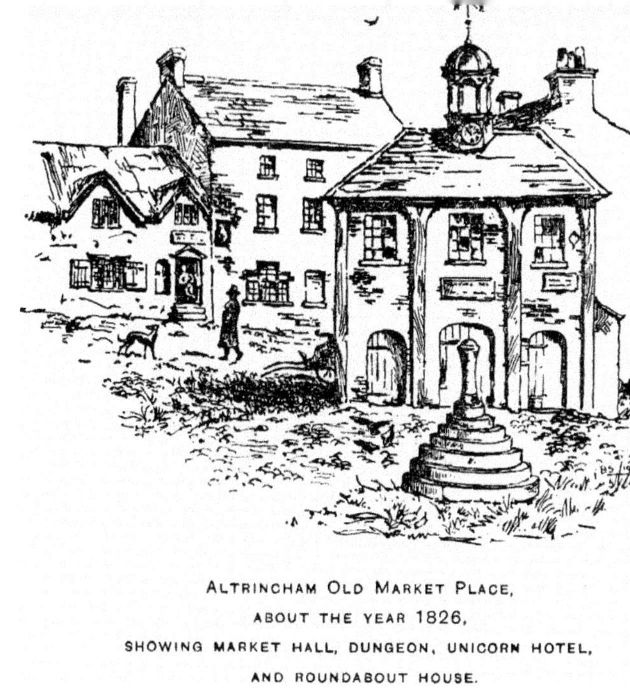

Above left: Site of the former Butter Market (centre), Old Market Place.

Above right: Drawing of 1901, showing Old Market Place in 1826.

of Stamford, with the bell then used to strike the hours. The Butter Market was a six-sided building surrounded with palisades and constructed on two floors. The upper floor was used as a courtroom and the lower floor accommodated the butter-sellers. There was also a lock-up, or, as it was more commonly called, the 'Dungeon'. This probably accommodated felons prior to their appearance in the courtroom on the upper floor of the Butter Market, or housed the drunk and disorderly overnight, or until they were well behaved enough to be released!

5. Former Red Lion Hotel, Old Market Place, Altrincham

The former Red Lion and Unicorn hotels were built on what was originally a Saxon settlement. The hotels became a staging post for coaches travelling between Manchester and Chester. Some of these coaches can be seen in the original photograph from around 1900. The Red Lion was used as a billet by the troops of Bonnie Prince Charlie when they came to Altrincham in 1745. The Unicorn Hotel was built by Lord Delamer and became contiguous with Altrincham's first town hall in 1849. This was the original nucleus of the market town centre, with a market cross, stocks and market hall of the sixteenth century located in the very centre of Old Market Place.

Altrincham was the principal centre for business in the locality and so tradesmen built their shops around the perimeter of Old Market Place, trading with the farmers who came to market once a week. They would sell butter, eggs, cheese and poultry to local people and occasionally trade their surplus stocks of cattle, sheep and pigs to other local farmers. Old Market Place at this time was a rather haphazard development, with the houses around it at the end of the eighteenth century and the beginning of the nineteenth century

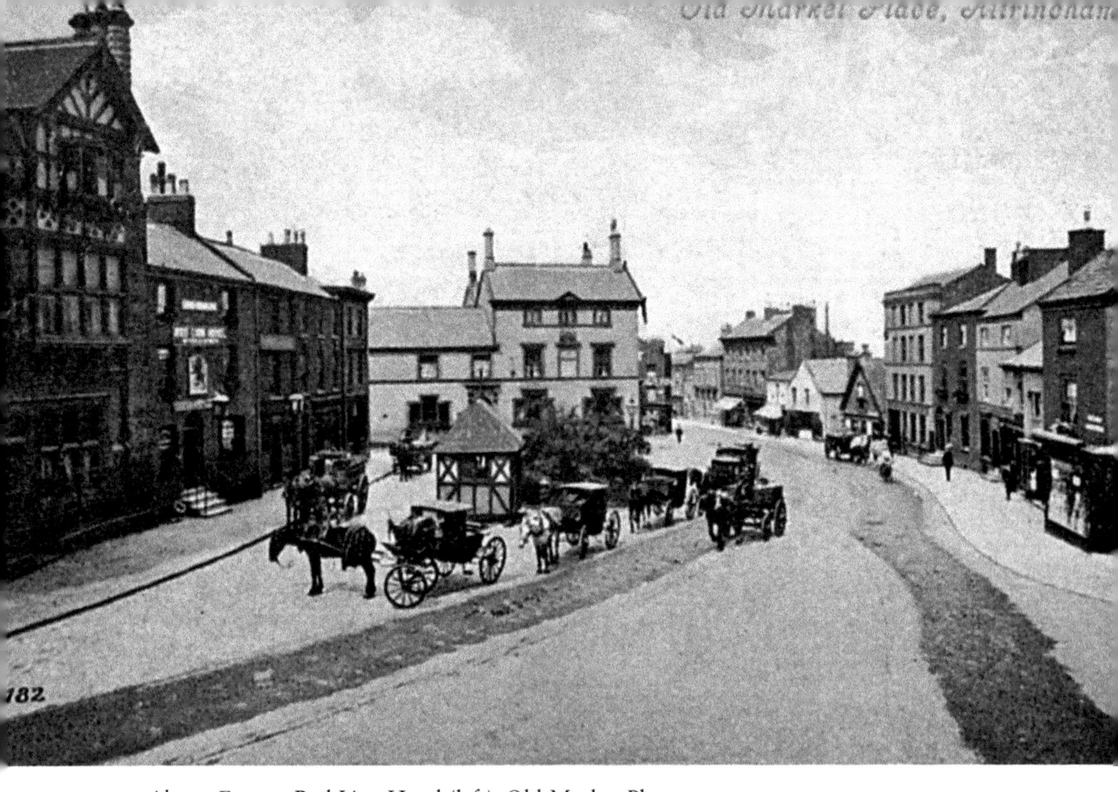

Above: Former Red Lion Hotel (left), Old Market Place.

Below left: Former Red Lion Hotel (centre), showing stocks and Market Cross.

Below right: Former Red Lion Hotel (left), Old Market Place.

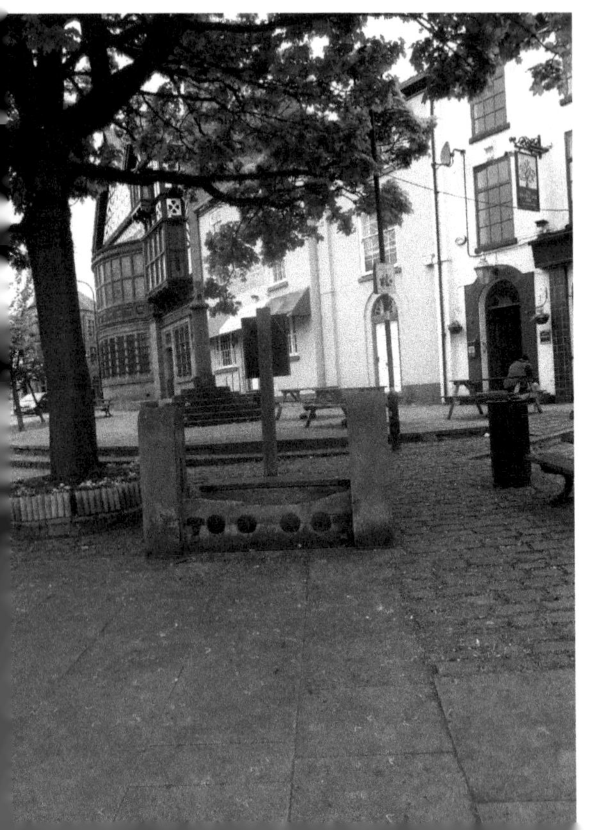

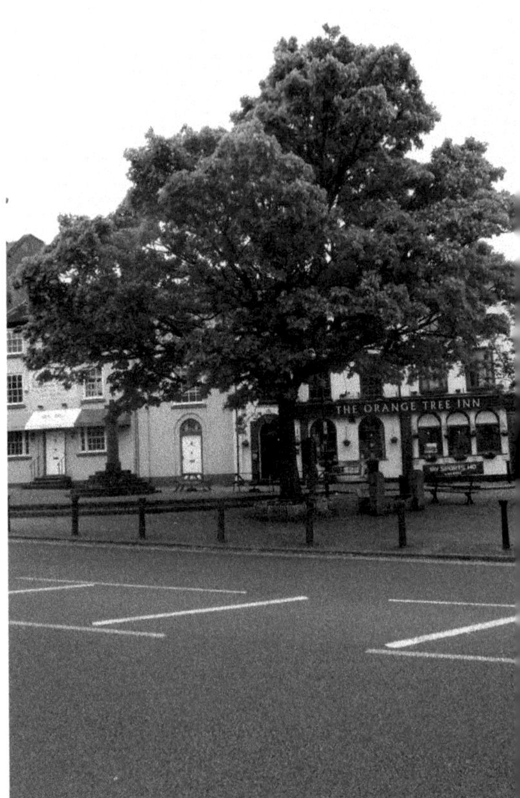

constructed with red brick and slate roofs, like the Red Lion Hotel and the Orange Tree Inn. Slotted between these developments in equally haphazard fashion were a number of half-timbered cottages dating back to the fifteenth century. The last was not demolished until well into the twentieth century. These formed the original dwelling places of the old market town centre, around a tight hub. It is thought that Old Market Place probably traces the boundaries of the original Saxon stockade, with new buildings of brick replacing what were once wattle and daub structures. Every morning the stagecoach would pass along the Manchester–Chester road, past the Red Lion Hotel via Church Street and into Old Market Place, bringing daily newspapers and mailbags. Market day was a Tuesday, with stalls in the old square and the old market hall. It steadily grew in importance and size since De Quincey first wrote about market day in the early nineteenth century.

6. The Old Bank, Old Market Place, Altrincham

In 1851, James Byrom established a drapery business in a shop which is now covered by the former Lloyds Bank. In 1868, the business was moved to new premises in Stamford Street, later renamed Kingsway. When the new Turnpike route, known as Dunham Road, was linked to Old Market Place, the old shop, together with the Waggon and Horses Inn, were taken down. The extension of Dunham Road made available a large area of prime building land.

The former Lloyds Bank was built by George Truefitt for the local banker Sir William Cunliffe Brooks *c.* 1880 and continues as commercial premises into the twenty-first century. The whole of the west side of Old Market Place was occupied by houses and included the Waggon and Horses, all demolished to make way for the construction of the bank and the opening of the Turnpike route. Carriages used to line up along here awaiting business.

The old bank was known as Bank House and originally as Brooks's Bank, built for Sir William Cunliffe Brooks, whose decorative initials adorn the building in stone. It curves around a corner and has a red sandstone ground floor with timber framing above and a clay

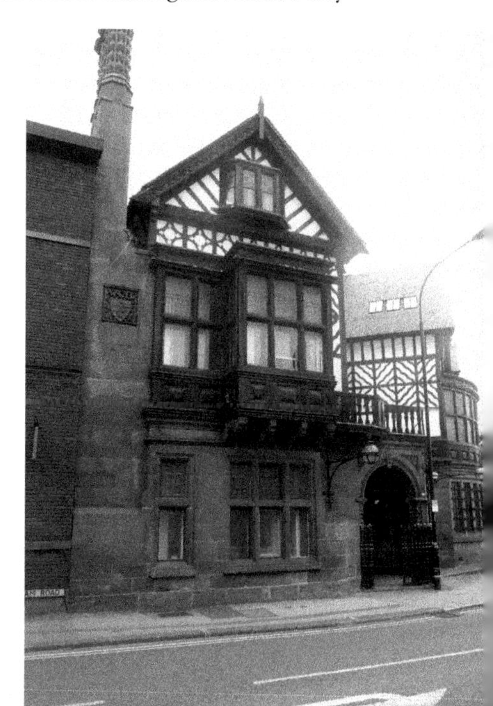

The Old Bank, Old Market Place, showing stonework detail and 'WCB' plaque.

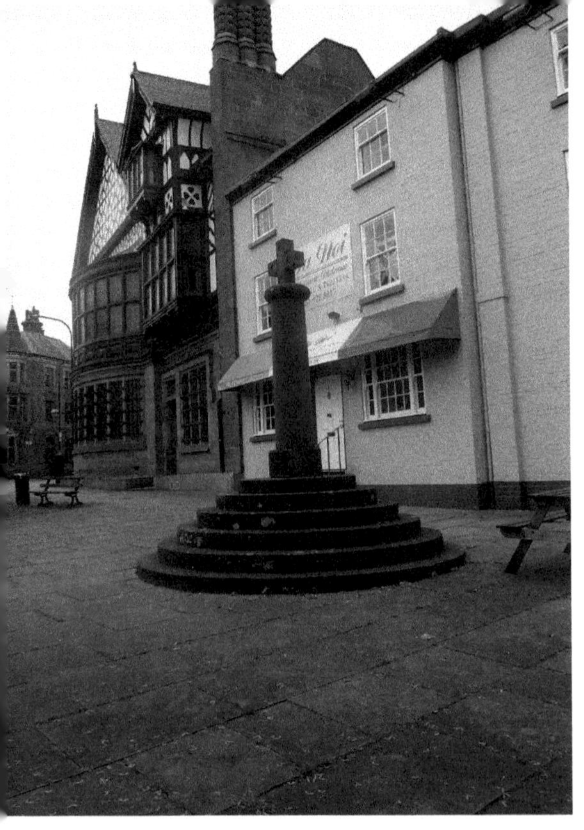

Left: Detail of the Old Bank from the Market Cross, Old Market Place.

Below: Former Lloyds Bank, Old Market Place, showing its Cheshire 'black and white'.

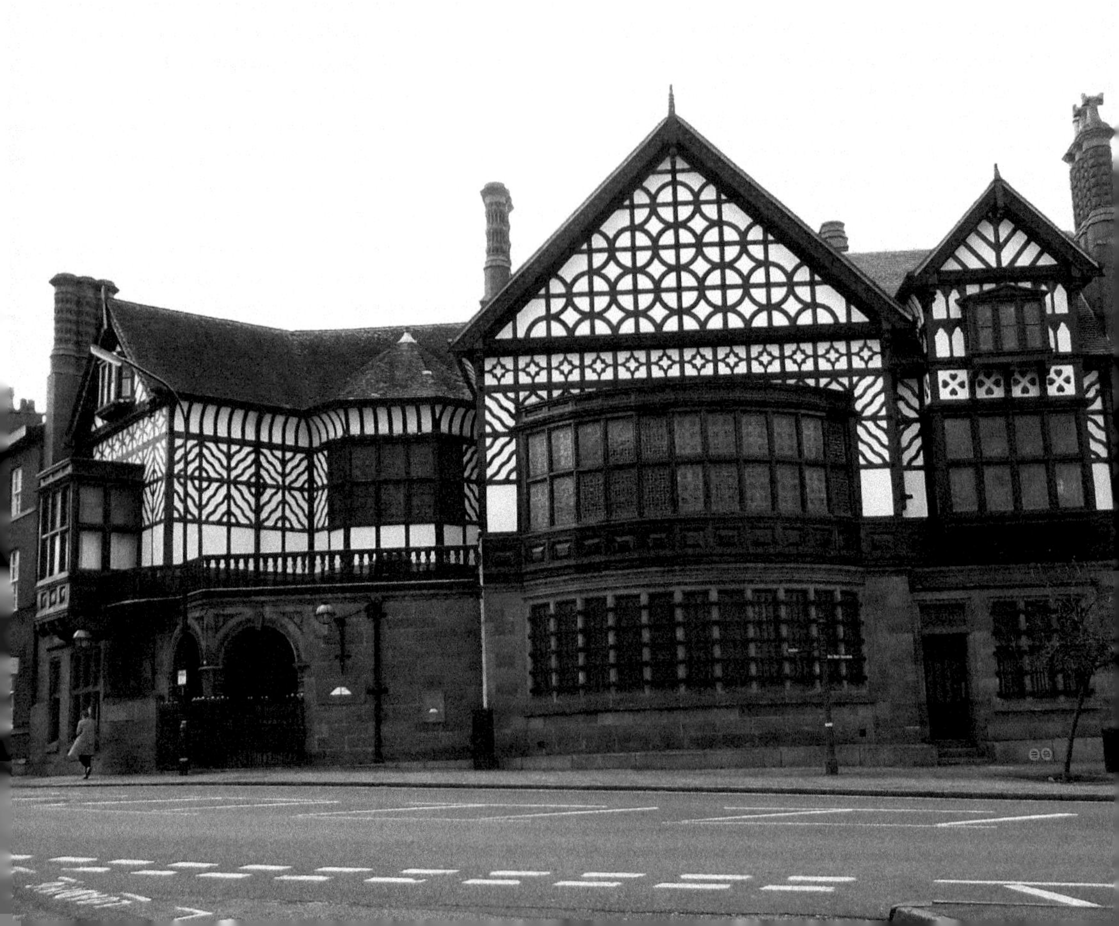

tile roof. The building has two storeys and attics, with four bays and three unequal gables, with decorative bargeboards and finials. In the second bay is a double-arched entrance with a balustrade and a balcony above. The third bay contains a large, two-storey curved bay window with eleven lights. On the roof are Tudor-style chimney stacks and a lead bell cote. It is an impressive building, being a mix of red sandstone and traditional Cheshire 'black and white'. The mullioned windows of stained glass are 35 feet high. On the south side of the Old Market Place is a set of late nineteenth-century brick-built shops and offices, constructed with stone plinths, decorative stone bands and timber framing, which were also built by Cunliffe Brooks and complement well the architecture of the adjacent bank. There are also a number of shops and offices of the 1870s on nearby Kingsway, which are built of red sandstone.

7. Nos 1, 1a and 3 Market Street and No. 2 Post Office Street, Old Market Place, Altrincham

These buildings are located on the south-west side of Market Street. Morrison's Central Auction Galleries, which are now commercial premises, were once located here. The name of Morrison will be familiar to many residents of Altrincham, especially those interested in local history, the author of *Looking Back at Altrincham* (1980) being Basil D. Morrison. These buildings were built in the 1890s for Sir William Cunliffe Brooks and were constructed in header bond brick, with stone dressings, decorative timber framing and a clay tile roof. In this respect they are very similar to Cunliffe Brooks' other buildings located in Old Market Place. The overall plan of the building sees four bays overlooking Market Street and two plus the former Auction Hall behind it overlooking Post Office Street. Again, there are two storeys plus an attic and a corner entrance, which is curved on the original plan and remains curved today. The entrance has a stone surround and is

Former Morrisons Auctioneers, as seen from the Old Bank, Old Market Place.

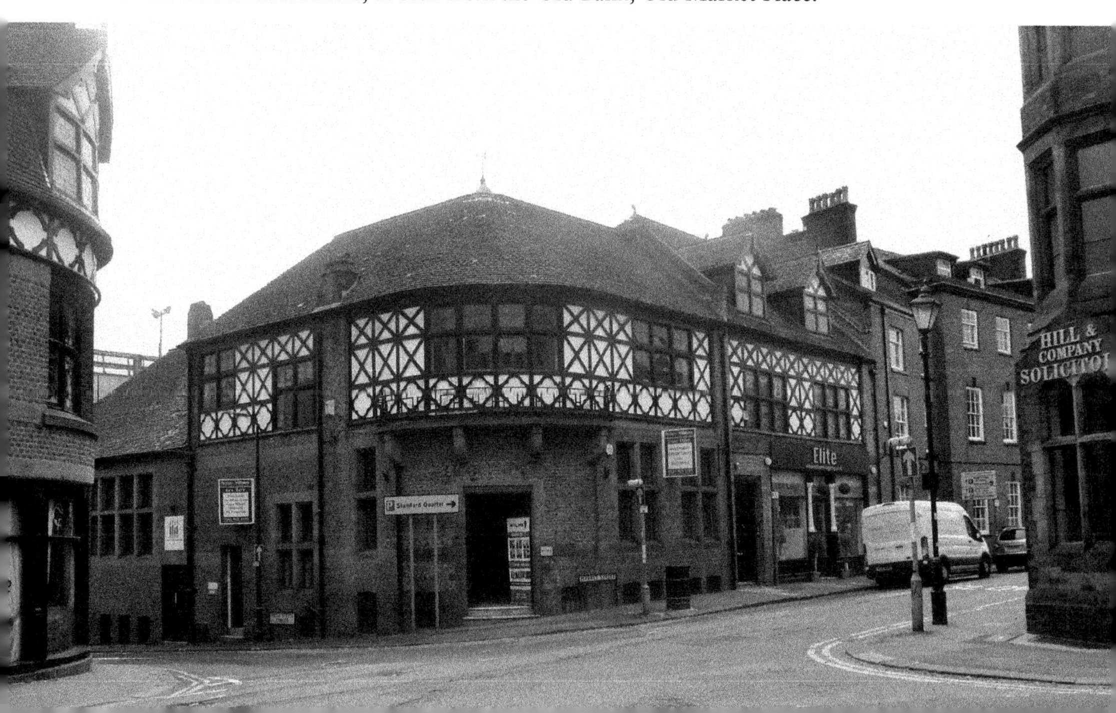

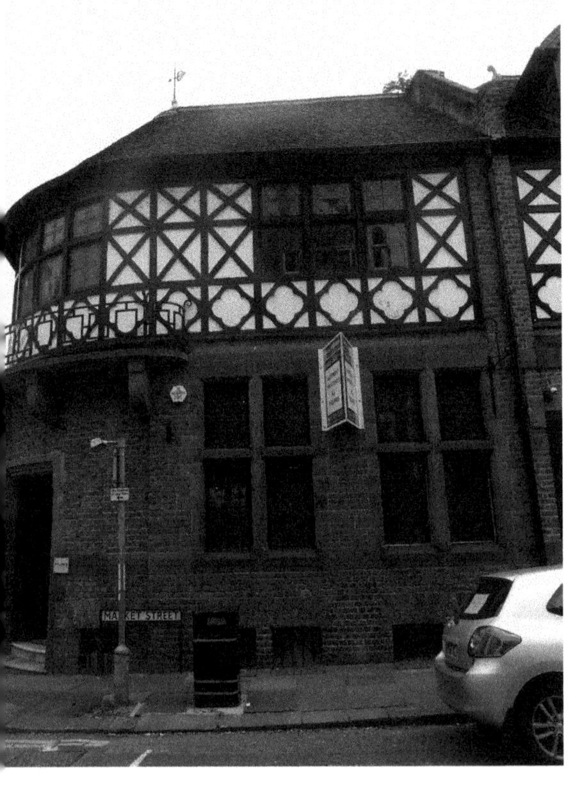

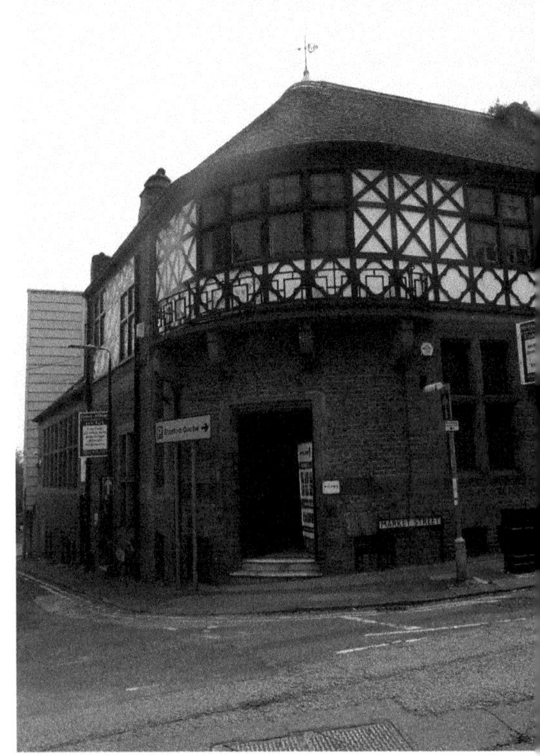

Above left: Former Morrisons Auctioneers, showing detail of the Market Street frontage.

Above right: Detail of the curved entrance and old auction hall (left), Post Office Street.

further enhanced by a balcony being positioned above it, complete with cast-iron railings and large stone brackets. The first floor continues the overall theme of decorative timber framing, which follows the building round onto Market Street. This is also the case with the windows, with a curved, four-light mullion and transom window. The ground floor facing onto Market Street has two-light mullion and transom windows. There are also doorways and a shopfront, with three-light mullion and transom windows above and two dormer windows above that, while the former Auction Hall on Post Office Street has one eight-light and one six-light mullion and transom window and a hipped roof. The building's main roof follows the sweep of the construction around the junction of Market Street and Post Office Street and a weathervane with the initials 'WCB' record the original patron of the buildings. The overall effect of this set of buildings is to initiate the style of medieval Cheshire 'black and white' while producing some magnificent leaded glazing in the process.

8. Byrom's Men's Shop, Nos 6, 8 and 10 Kingsway, Altrincham

This was one of the oldest family businesses in Altrincham, established in 1851 by James Byrom, who was the Mayor of Altrincham in 1880. The original shop once stood on part of the site later occupied by Lloyds Bank in Old Market Place and then moved across the road and lower down Kingsway. In 1867, on the south side of Stamford Street, James Byrom

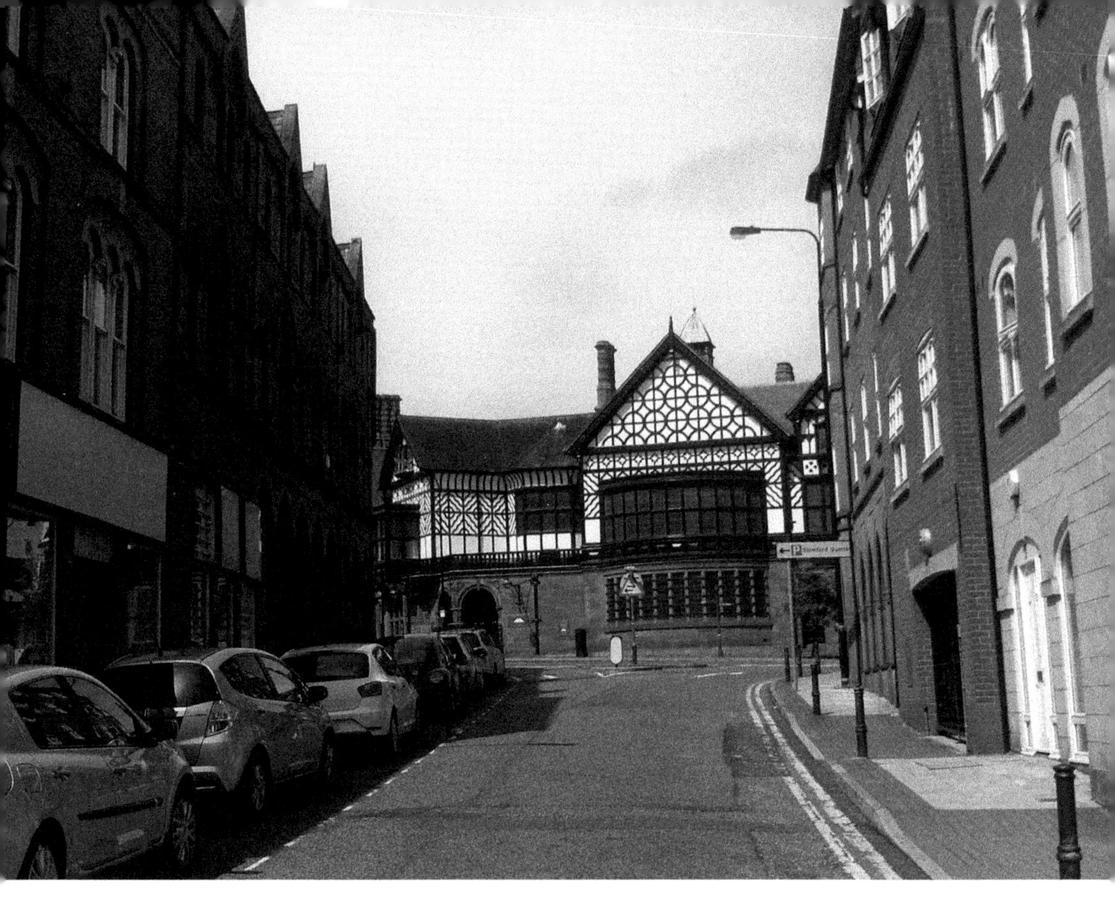

Above: Former Byrom's premises (left), Kingsway, and Old Bank (centre), from Stamford Street.

Below left: Lower Kingsway, as seen from Old Market Place.

Below right: Kingsway (left), Post Office Street (right), Nos 2–4 Old Market Place (centre).

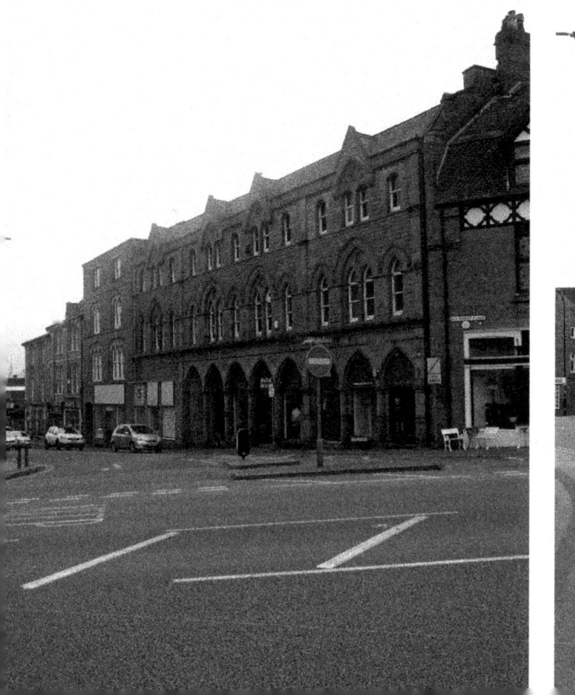

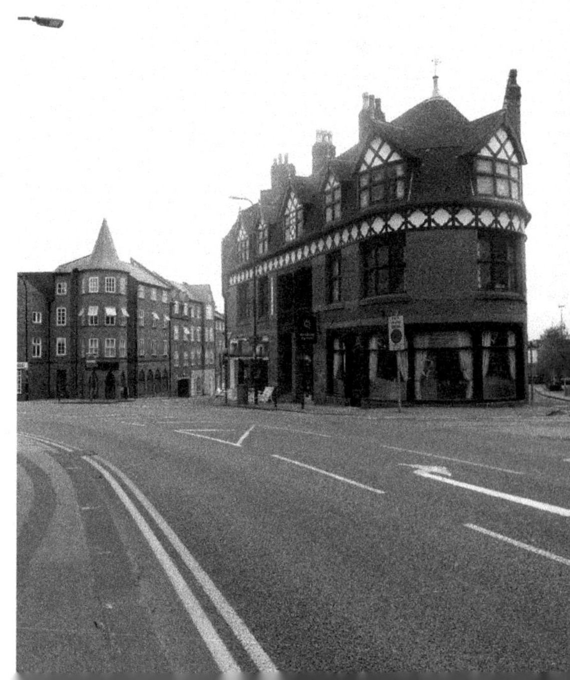

built a large shop, with the whole of this side of the street eventually appropriated for the erection of business premises. In 1886, J. W. Byrom, who was Mayor of Altrincham in 1901, succeeded to the business. He was followed by his son, Jack Byrom, who was influential in the Altrincham Garrick Society. Closed around 1970, it was the first Altrincham store to display electric lights. An advert of 1946 for Byrom's of Kingsway, Altrincham, tells us of the 'newest arrivals at Byrom's Mens Shop. Ready to wear hand woven Harris Tweed Sports-Coats; Simpson tailored riding macs; Union and cotton Gaberdine raincoats; Fine grade lamb's wool linen tan cape gloves; Good quality winter weight pyjamas; Medium weight underwear by Jaeger. Customers say: - "It's a pleasure to shop where everyone is so polite and helpful. That's what I like about "Byrom's." You too, will be a welcome visitor at Byrom's.'"

Around 1881 Stamford Street was extended to the railway station, with the extension named Station Road. In August 1908 shop owners and residents presented a request to the district council asking for the road names to be changed to Kingsway along the entire length of the thoroughfare. Several other road names in the district included the name of Stamford, and so the change was agreed to by the council. They were of the view that the road was of some historical significance and that the title suited the business character of the district. It was the principal one used by the King and Queen, when the Prince and Princess of Wales were on their way from Tatton Hall, where they were guests of Earl Egerton of Tatton, to open the Manchester Exhibition on 4 May 1887.

9. St Margaret's Parish Church, Dunham Road, Altrincham

On 11 April 1855 St Margaret's became the district church for parts of the township of Dunham Massey and Altrincham, which were previously served by St Mary's, Bowdon. It later included the chapel of Dunham Massey, All Saints. On 5 November 1867 St Margaret's boundaries were reduced when part of the township of Dunham Massey was transferred to the new district of Altrincham, St John the Evangelist.

St Margaret's was consecrated on Wednesday 13 June 1855 by the Bishop of Chester. It is entirely built of stone, the style of architecture being Perpendicular, which was popular in the fifteenth and early part of the sixteenth centuries. Today the church includes such activities as a Sunday school, organised children's worship and a youth group. The church was constructed in 1853–55 by William Hayley (architect) of Cross Street, Manchester, and is a Grade II-listed building. It was extended westward from 1923–25 by Walter Tapper, part of this scheme remaining incomplete. The two-stage central tower had a steeple until 1927, when it became unsafe and was removed.It was 210 feet high. It is a typical example of the Gothic Revival period. The church has a very elaborate canted Gothic panelled ceiling and tall crossing arches. There are carved screens, an organ chamber, pulpit and a selection of stained-glass windows. The building is in stone with a slate roof, and consists of a nave with a clerestory, north and south aisles, a south porch, north and south transepts, a chancel with a chapel and a vestry, and a tower at the crossing. The tower has two stages, angled buttresses, a clock face, and an embattled parapet. Nickson (p. 43) tells us that 'Perhaps the most prominent feature of the new (Dunham) road was that of St. Margaret's church which, with its soaring spire, crowned the summit of the hill.' The church was built by the Earl of Stamford and Warrington. It occupies the highest point of Dunham Road, and when first constructed commanded some wide panoramic views.

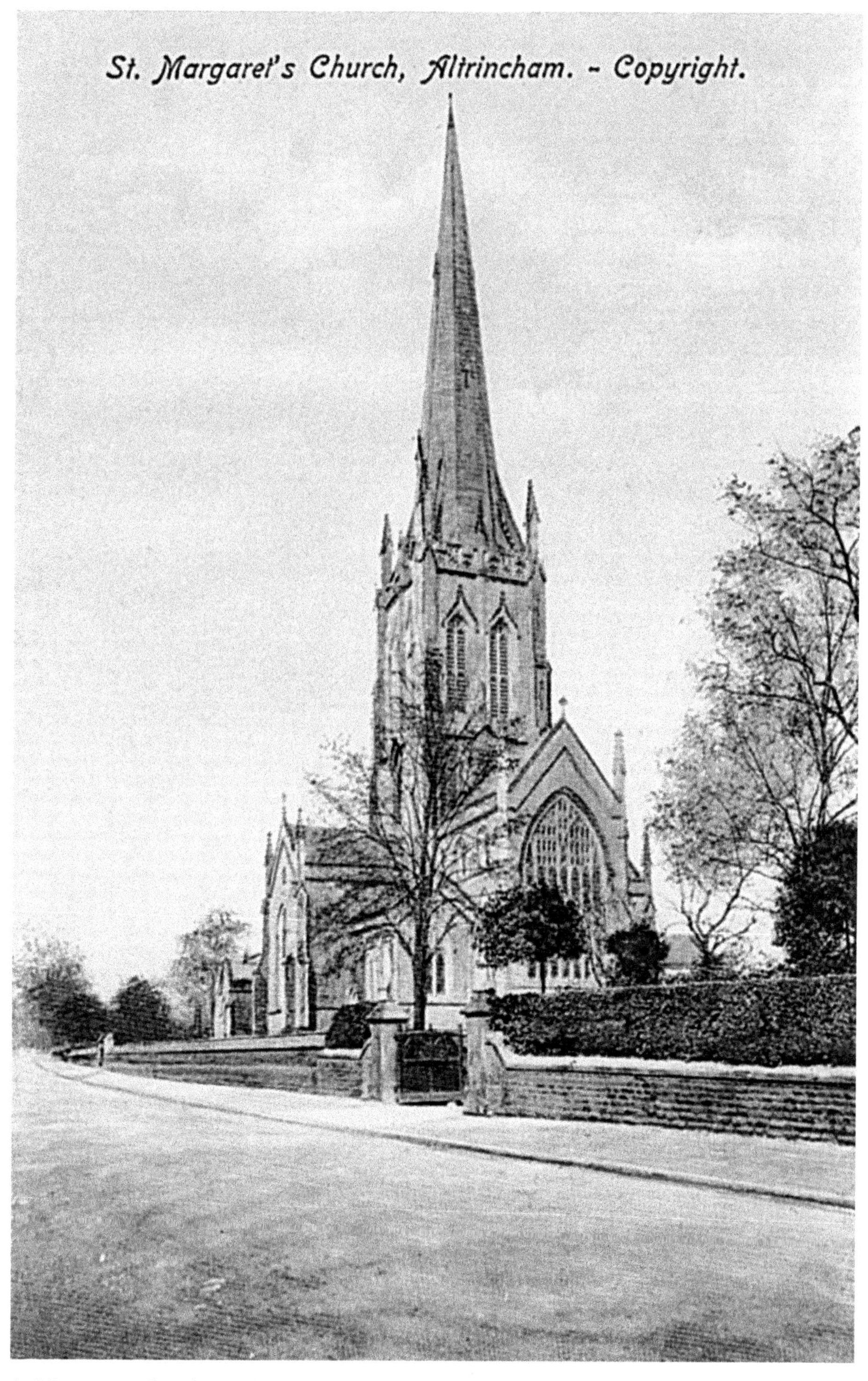

St Margaret's Church, Dunham Road, showing its spire in 1916.

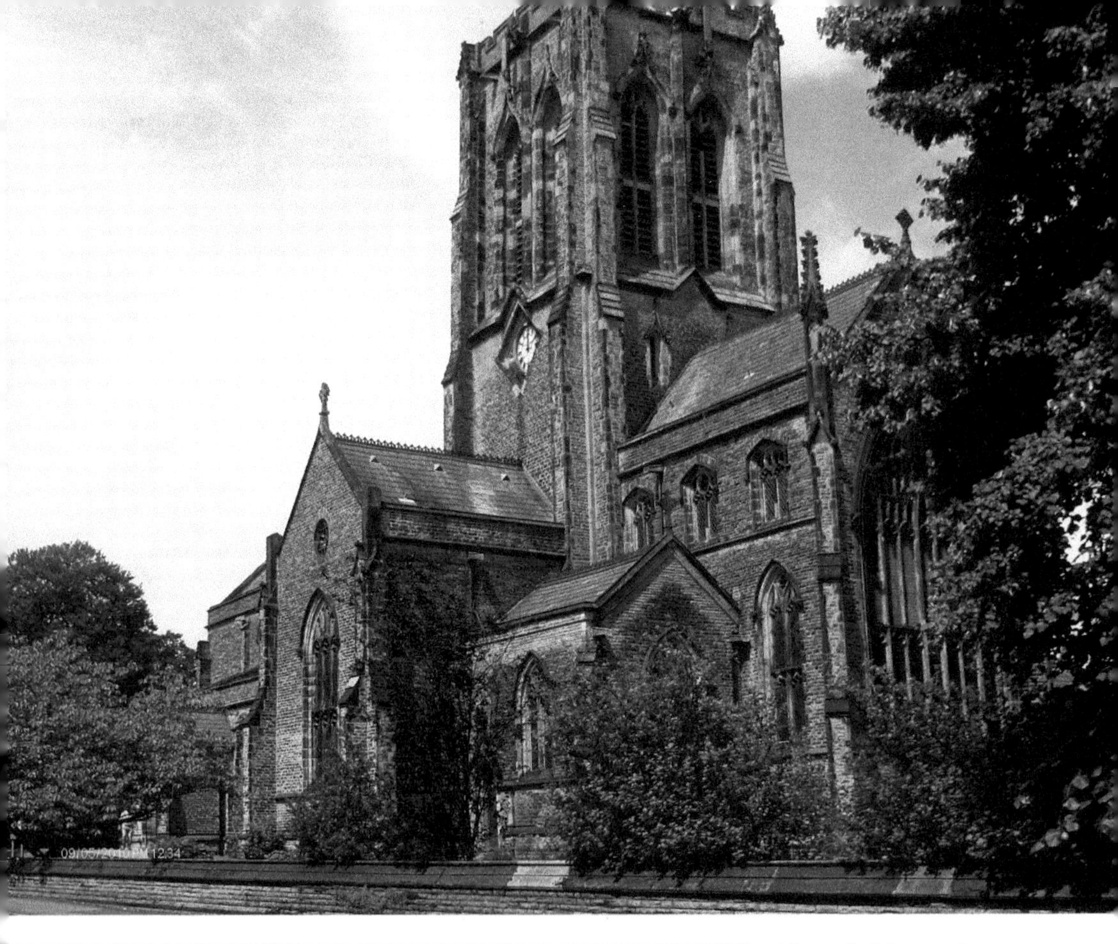

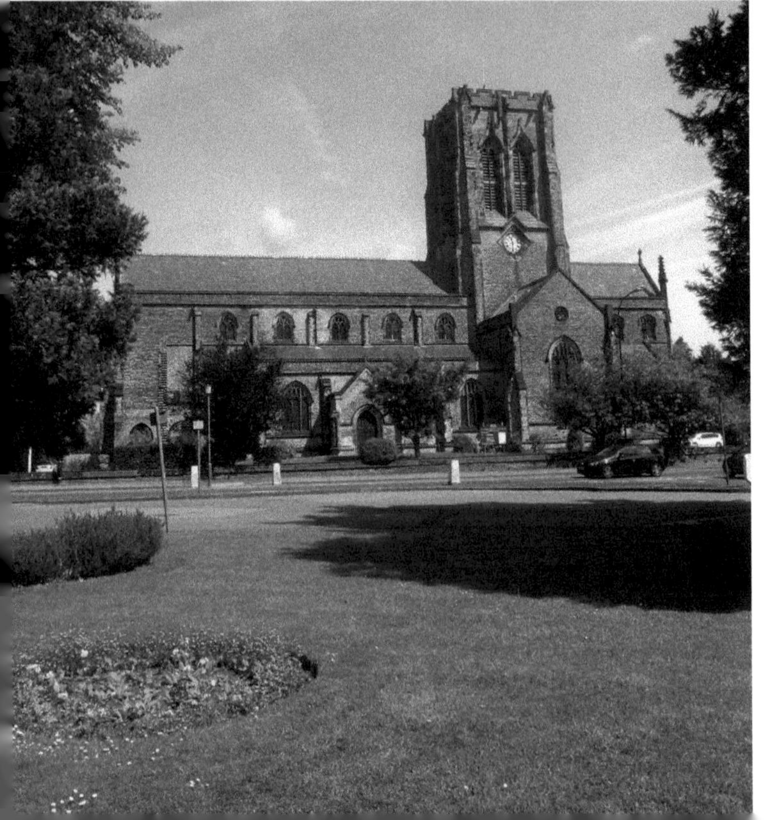

Above: St Margaret's Church, Dunham Road. The same view today.

Left: St Margaret's Church, Dunham Road, from the Memorial Gardens, junction of St Margaret's Road.

10. Altrincham and Dunham Massey War Memorial, Junction of Dunham Road and St Margaret's Road, Altrincham

Unveiled on 13 November 1920, Grade II listed and costing £1,500, the war memorial, honouring those lost in both world wars, is of Portland stone. It was dedicated by the Bishop of Chester, witnessed by relatives and friends of the fallen and consists of a Celtic cross on a stepped plinth, resting on a wide octagonal dais, from the designs of George Faulkner Armitage. The dais has a surrounding low wall on six sides and two flights of steps with ramped balustrades leading up to it. On the inner face of the wall are seats, and there are two lanterns on slender shafts. On the wall copings are engraved bronze plaques listing those 396 men of Altrincham and Dunham Massey who gave up their lives in the First World War. There are carved interface decorations of a flat interlacing design on the faces of the cross shaft, and at its foot are two inscribed bronze plaques. The height of the cross from ground level is 25 feet, and the main shaft, rising from a broad base and forming a seat, is fixed on a dais, having an octagon plan 22 feet in diameter.

Land for the memorial garden was donated by the Earl of Stamford in 1948. Early in 1927 numerous fractures were discovered in the stonework of the spire of St Margaret's Church. The cross on the summit of the spire was only affixed with iron clamps; therefore the safest course of action was a partial demolition, in order to avert a potential collapse onto the war memorial below. The war memorial was eventually

Below left: Altrincham and Dunham Massey war memorial: close-up of Celtic cross design.

Below right: Altrincham and Dunham Massey war memorial looking towards St Margaret's Road.

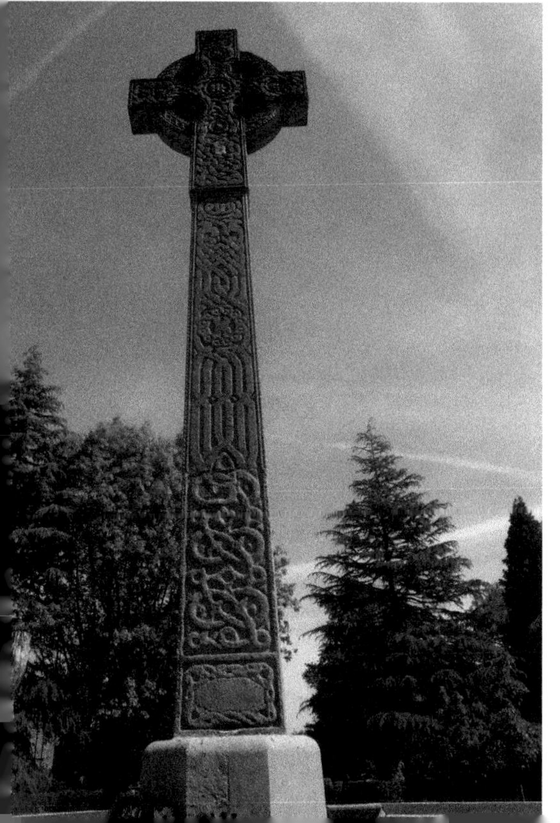

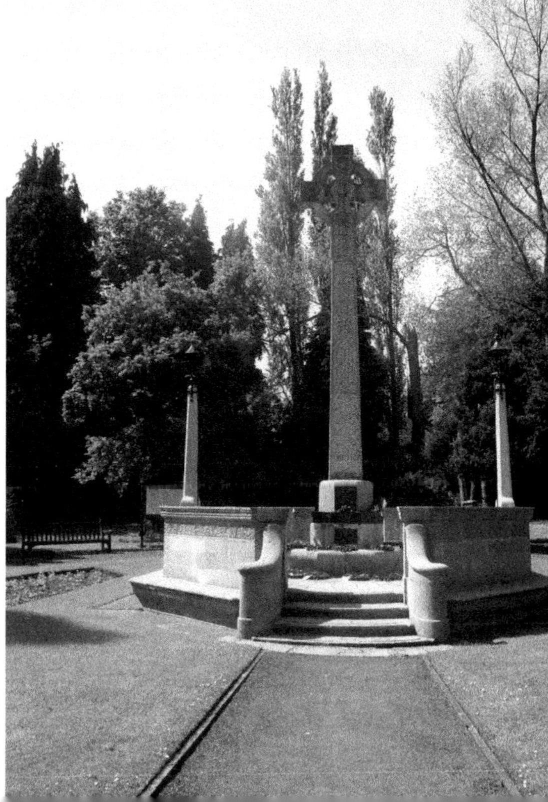

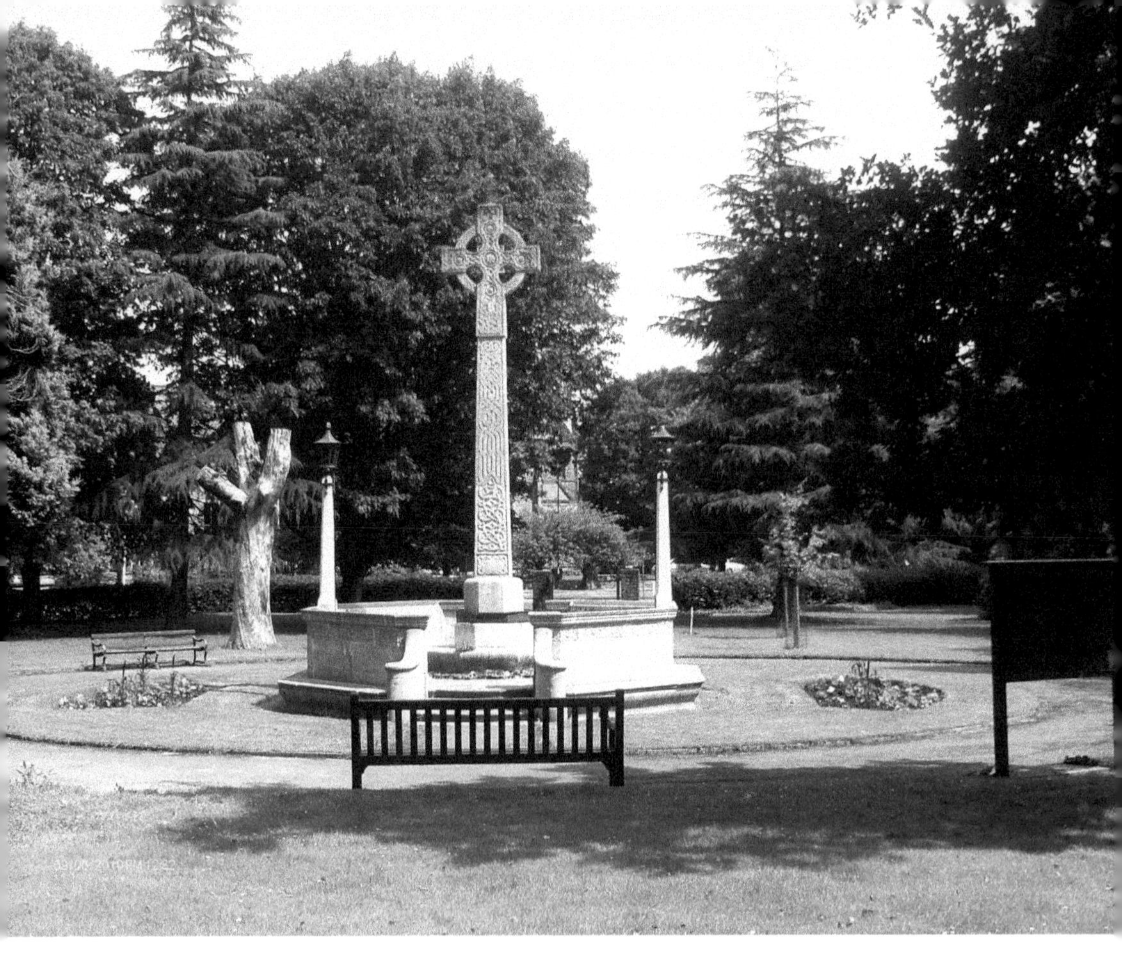

Altrincham and Dunham Massey war memorial looking towards the church.

moved to an area with its own memorial gardens in 1948 due to heavy traffic. The decision to remove the spire came about despite the launch of an appeal fund for the new spire's construction. Ongoing maintenance costs and the fact that the church was still undergoing repair and renovation works at the time also influenced the decision. In July 1923 an extension was proposed as a memorial to those members of St Margaret's parish who fell in the First World War. However, much of the work of Walter Tapper remained incomplete.

11. Shepherd's Cottages, Dunham Hill, Dunham Road, Bowdon

In the latter part of the nineteenth century the junction of Charcoal Lane and Dunham Road was known as Shepherd's Brow/Brue, with Shepherd's Cottages on the north side of Charcoal Lane at its junction with Dunham Road. The 'milepost' shown in the image of *c.* 1900 was mid-nineteenth century and constructed of cast iron, with a curved sign stating 'Dunham: to Altrincham 1 mile, to Northwich 11, Knutsford 6 miles.' The post was circular with a hemispherical cap. To the left of this view are the grounds of Parklands, a large Victorian mansion belonging to William Berry, whose boot polish company was involved in the launch of Cherry Blossom boot polish in 1906.

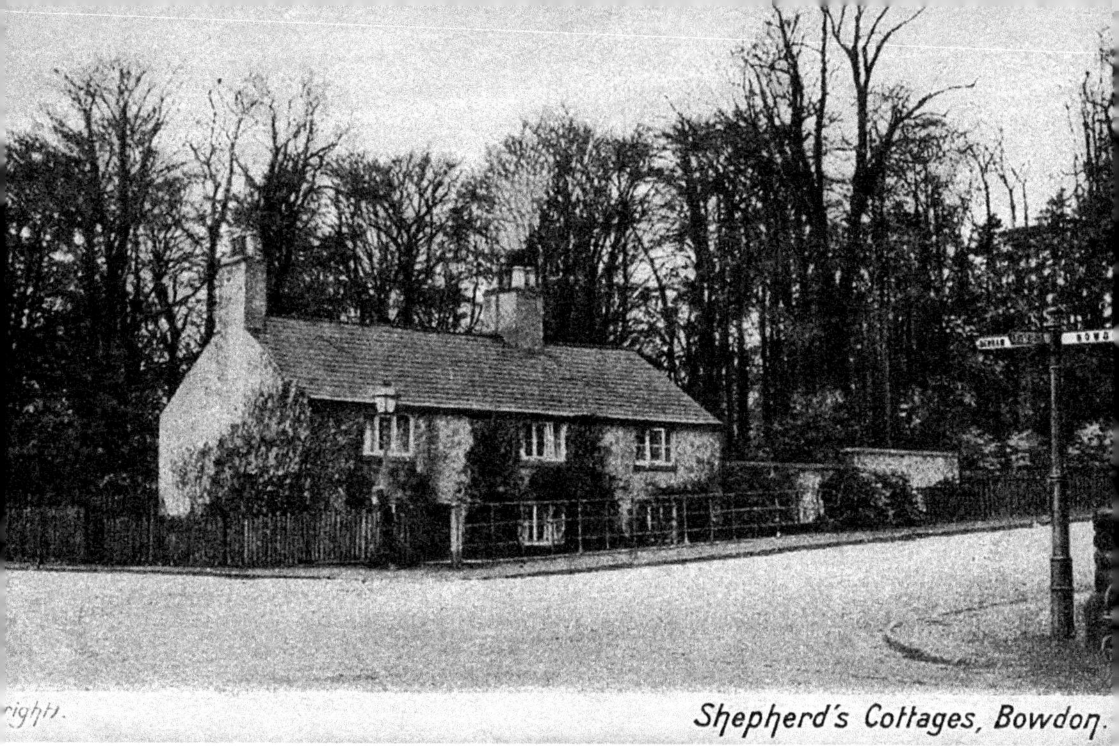

Above: Shepherd's Cottages, Dunham Hill (Shepherd's Brow), junction of Dunham Road and Charcoal Lane, *c.* 1900.

Below left: Shepherd's Cottages, Dunham Hill (Shepherd's Brow), junction of Dunham Road and Charcoal Lane, 2018.

Below right: The same location in 2018, with Shepherd's Cottages behind the tall hedge.

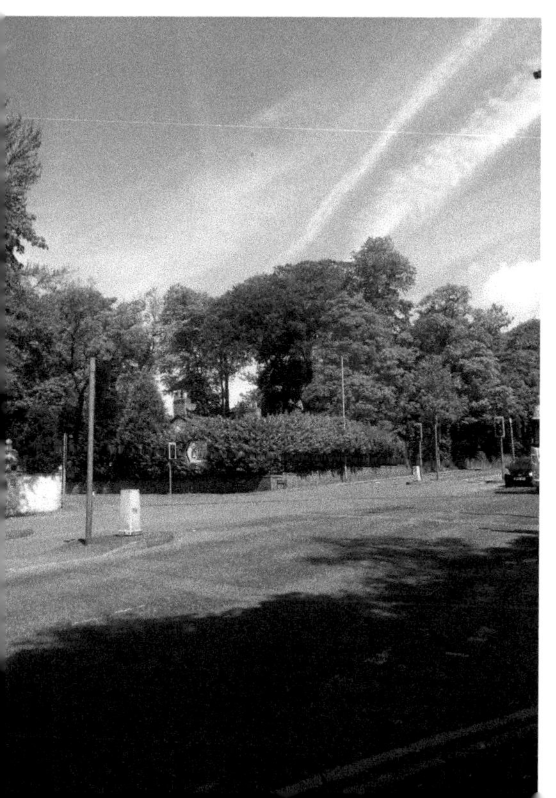

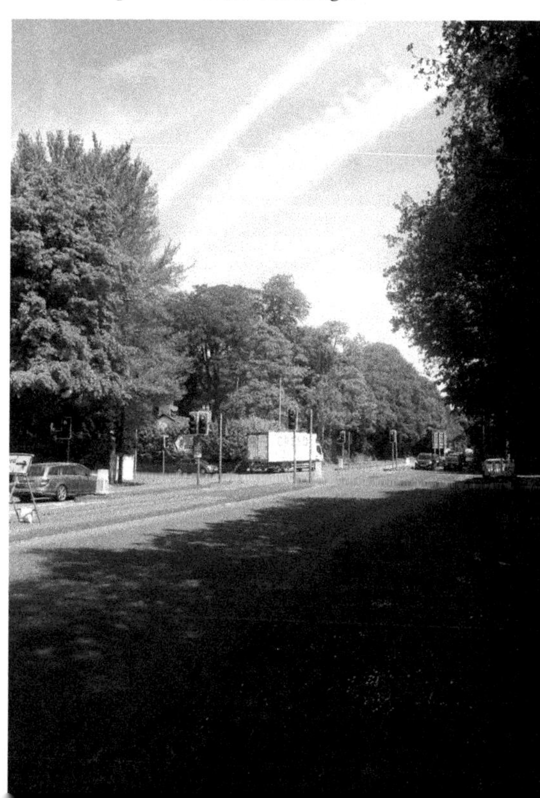

In 1913, William Berry Ltd were bought out, but they continued to be influential in the area, building commercial developments on Stamford New Road and in Hale. The Berry family continued to live at Parklands until 1963, when the house contents were auctioned off and the property sold. It was William Berry who was responsible for the family's relocation to Parklands, at Dunham Massey. He is named on a conveyance dated 13 December 1887, which also included Arthur Frederick Payne, and The Right Honourable Catherine Countess of Stamford and Warrington. The mansion house was constructed in 1888, the same year that William Berry's properties in Hale were built. The land conveyance focuses on two fields located on the south side of Charcoal Lane, near its junction with Dunham Road and Shepherd's Brow, which until 1851 at least were a part of the Earl of Stamford's estate. The first plot, which forms the bulk of Parklands grounds, was originally known as Nursery, with the second field known as Horse Pasture, both owned and occupied by the Earl of Stamford. A portion of Horse Pasture was part of Home Farm in 1838, which was originally called New Bridge Farm and later Dunham Farm. In the seventeenth century it was tenanted by the Tipping family, who were bailiffs to the Booth family until 1671, with another branch of the family stewards until 1663.

12. Parklands, Dunham Massey

One view shows the former main gate to Parklands at the junction of Charcoal Lane and Dunham Road, where there are now traffic lights at these busy crossroads. Located here is a fine Victorian mansion of red brick and stone. Built in 1887–88 by William Berry, a Manchester businessman who had made his fortune in the wholesale blacking trade, it remained in the family until its sale in 1963. Until 1994 it was the base of the Institute for the Study of Hierological Values. It is now a private residence.

The mansion was built by William Berry, beginning with a land conveyance of 13 December 1887, and involved property belonging to the Stamford Estate at a time when the hall itself was not occupied. The history of the house follows a course which is not dissimilar to that of many Victorian mansions of the same ilk; that is, one of initial affluence followed by a slow and steady decline and the eventual adoption of a business and multi-occupation use. Wealthy people came to the higher parts of Altrincham, particularly Bowdon, attracted by the healthier climate that the prevailing winds created. This meant that Altrincham was rarely affected by the sort of smoke-laden fogs that ruined the air quality in Manchester and the other towns and cities of northern England. William and Thomas Berry, to the west of Altrincham, at Dunham Massey – although they preferred to refer to the location as Bowdon for reasons of ostentation – would have benefited from this prevailing westerly wind and from the social and economic changes that radically affected the area in the 1880s and 1890s. Nickson (1935) tells us that Stamford New Road was first developed in 1880 (p. 94). This decade coincides with the Berry family's construction of Parklands at Dunham Massey and their developments at Peel Causeway (Hale) in 1888. The 1880s witnessed the Berry family's economic influence in the area, leading also to the construction of shops and offices, which very quickly transformed what were once orchards and vegetable plots along Stamford New Road.

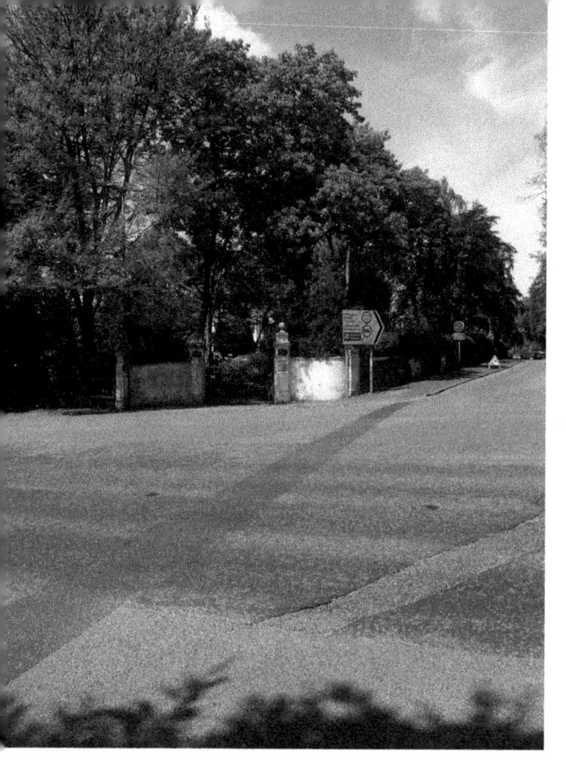

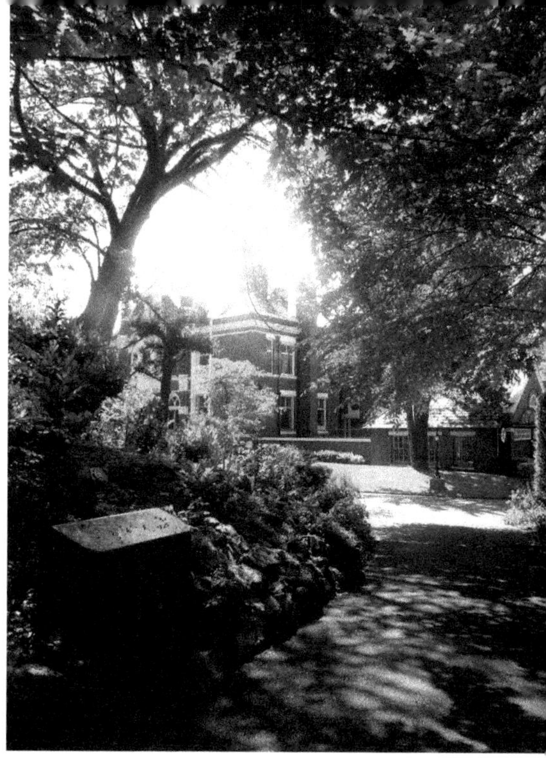

Above left: Parklands, former main gate onto Dunham Road.

Above right: Parklands, house and lodge, Charcoal Lane, Dunham Massey.

Below: The house from Charcoal Lane, Dunham Massey.

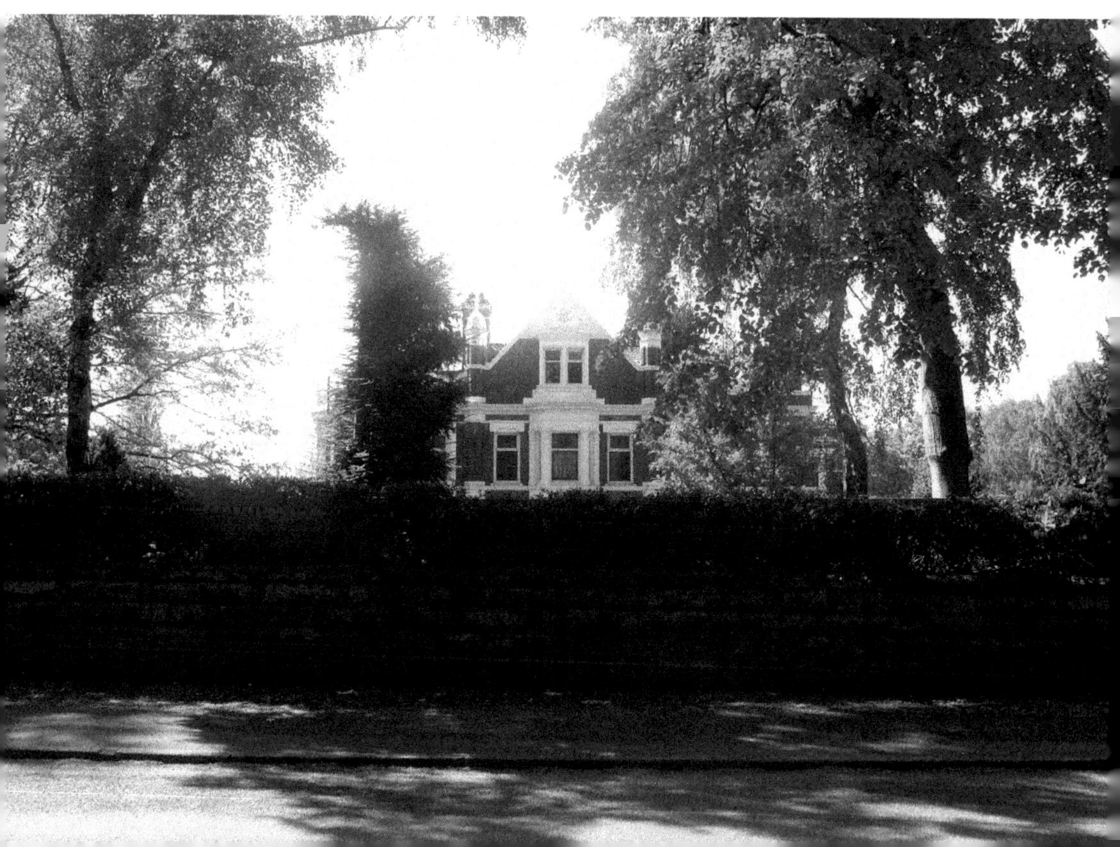

13. Lodge and Entrance to Dunham Park, Dunham Massey, 1908

The lodge and entrance are located at the junction of Charcoal Lane and Main Drive. The photograph of 1908 shows us the view from Main Drive looking towards Charcoal Lane and heading into Altrincham on the right. Behind the photographer, Main Drive stretches through the woodland of the National Trust-owned Dunham Park, towards Dunham Hall. Coach and horse teams of the Earls of Stamford would have used this gateway on their way to and from church and official functions. The original site of Dunham Hall was probably a wooden motte-and-bailey castle. This moated location was later probably rebuilt in stone, when it was occupied by Hamo de Masci (Massey) and his family at the time of the Domesday Book in 1086. The castle may have been built on the site of a fort constructed by Alfward. Dunham Hall and park was to be the home of six generations of the de Masci family, Hamos I–VI, until 1342. Shortly after the de Mascis arrived, a park around Dunham Castle was enclosed as a hunting lodge for deer and other animals.

The hall stood empty for around fifty years at the end of the nineteenth century, until the 9th Earl moved to Dunham in June 1906. The 10th Earl, Roger Grey, remained unmarried and arranged, before his death, for the property to go to the National Trust as his nephew did not want it. He died on the 18 August 1976 and the hall and gardens opened to the public in April 1981.

Dunham Hall is surrounded by a deer park, which covers 192.7 acres. It features formal avenues, pasture-woodland, and parkland, occupied by a herd of fallow deer that have been resident since the Middle Ages. The deer are very tame and tolerant of visitors. It is also home to an impressive collection of ancient trees, some giant oaks dating from the seventeenth century. Owned by the National Trust, it is considered a site of national importance. In 1917, Penelope, Lady Stamford, transformed Dunham Hall into an auxiliary hospital. Two hundred and eighty-one patients passed through Stamford Military Hospital in almost two years.

Lodge and entrance to Dunham Park, Dunham Massey, in 1908.

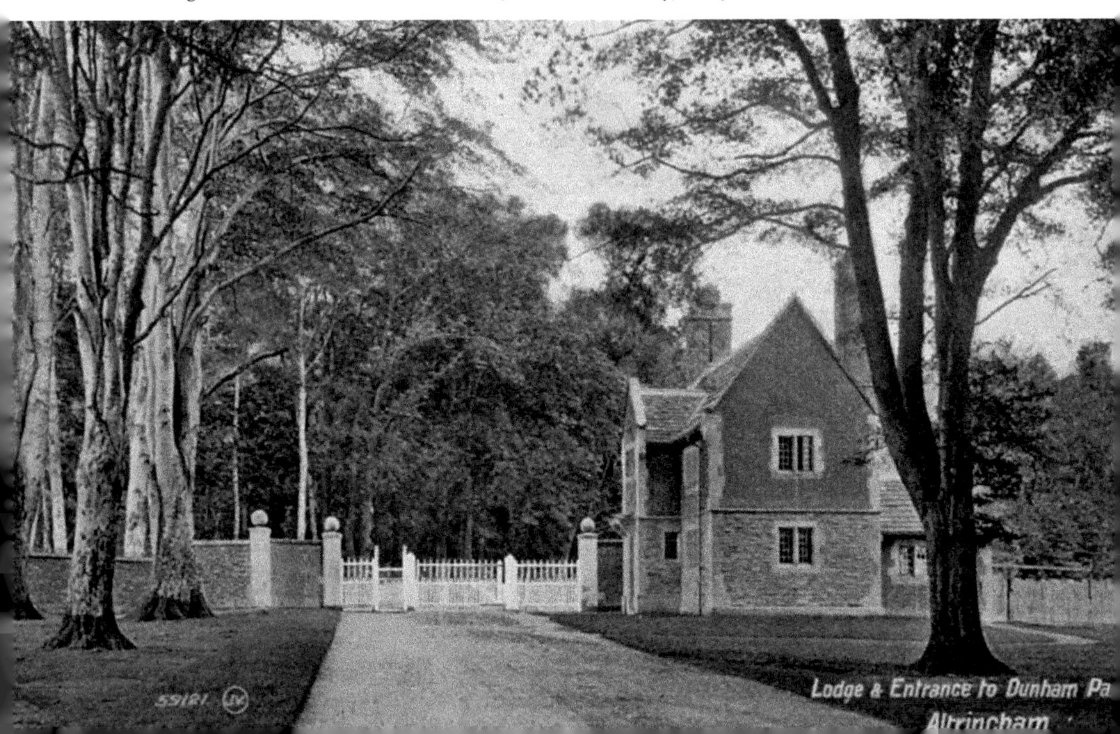

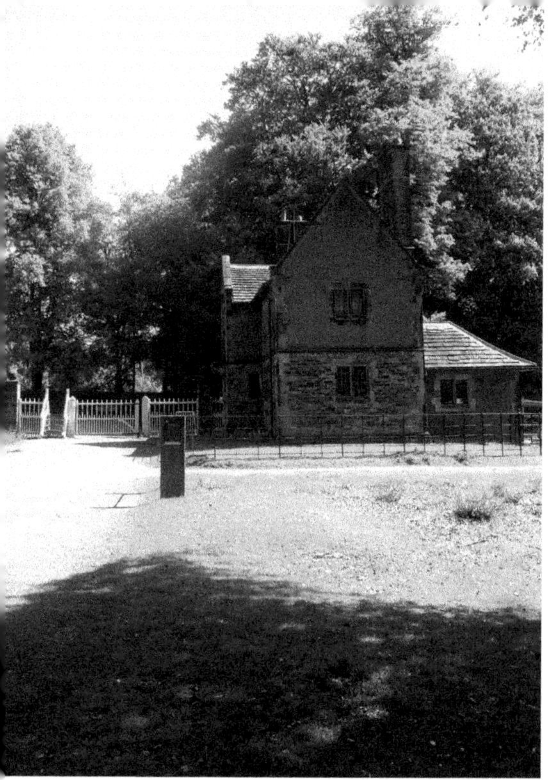

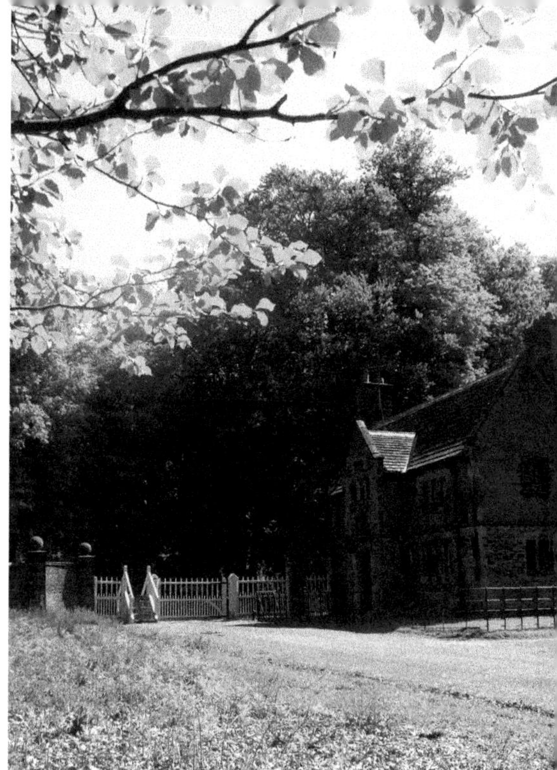

Above left: Lodge and entrance to Dunham Park from Main Drive towards Charcoal Lane.

Above right: Lodge frontage and entrance to Dunham Park from Main Drive, showing gate and stile.

14. The Hall, Dunham Massey

There was once a Norman castle on the site and a chapel was known to have existed as early as 1307. The first record of the park dates to 1362, but it is also recorded that wild deer and boar were hunted through the woods for many years before the deer park was established. Sir George Booth (1566–1652) built a house around a courtyard in the early seventeenth century, although little of this now remains. The 2nd Earl of Warrington turned the estate's fortunes around by planting hundreds of trees throughout the park. Many of these remain in the deer park today, providing an important haven for wildlife. With debts of £50,000, these trees provided the estate with a profitable source of timber for the future.

The main house was remodelled by John Norris between 1732 and 1740, in the time of George, 2nd Earl of Warrington, with minor additions by John Shaw in 1822. Further alterations were made by Joseph Compton Hall in the Edwardian period.

The most significant event connecting the occupants of Dunham Hall to the people of Altrincham took place in 1290, when Baron Hamon de Masci granted his tenants a charter. This made Altrincham a free borough and granted to the burgesses a Guild Mercatory, or a Society of Free Traffic, as well as freedom from tolls throughout the Barony. By a charter granted by Edward I in the eighteenth year of his reign, Baron Hamon de Masci was granted a market on Tuesday and a fair of three days' duration. Later, another fair was held in the month of April. The charter proved a very popular introduction, as many of the previous hardships suffered by the villagers were removed and serfdom was almost

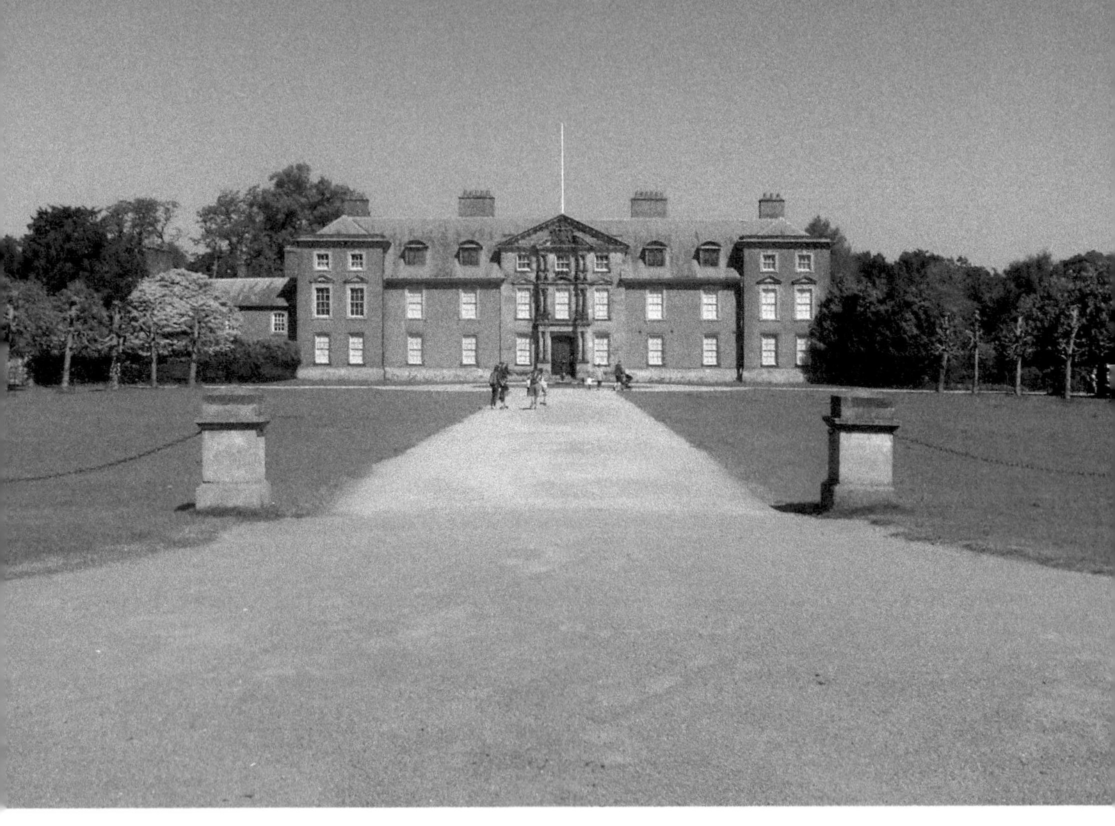

Above and below: Dunham Hall, Dunham Massey.

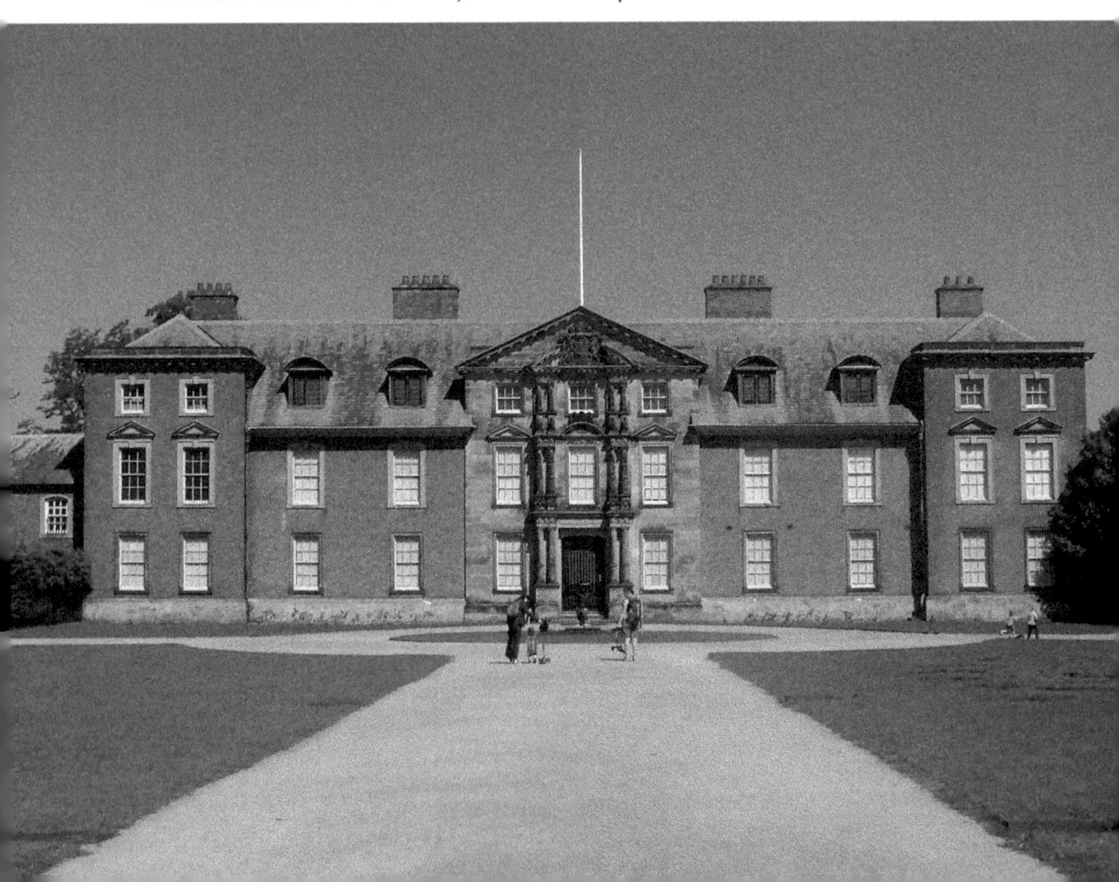

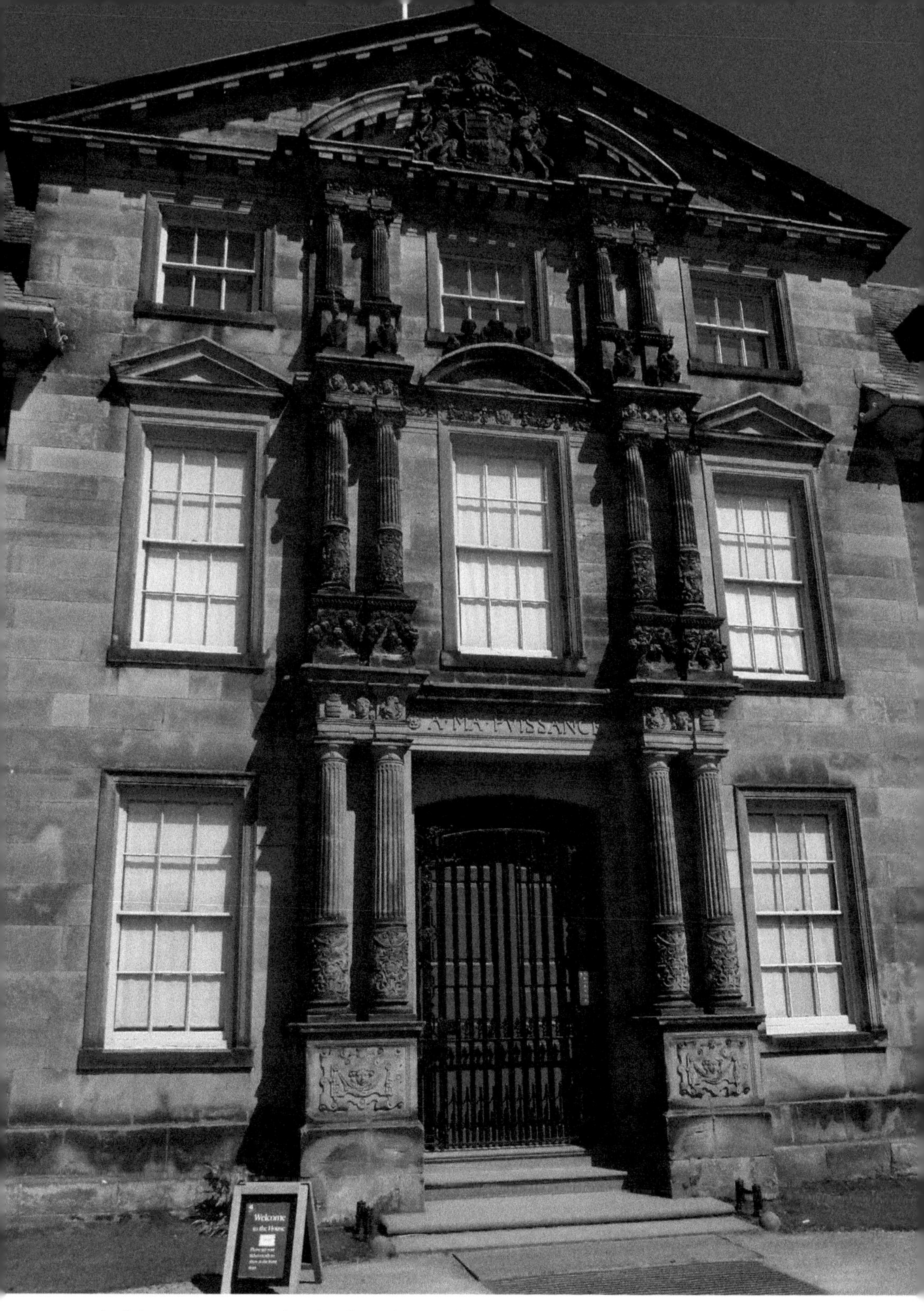

Detail of the main entrance façade of Dunham Hall.

entirely eliminated. The previously divided Saxon and Norman populations now began to integrate more freely. In 1976, the 10th Earl of Stamford left the entire estate to the National Trust. The 3,000-acre estate and the house, with all its contents, made Dunham Massey the largest bequest in the National Trust's history at the time.

15. The Old Mill, Dunham Park, Dunham Massey

The sawmill (originally a corn mill) was Grade II listed on 12 July 1985 and was probably built in 1616 (definitely pre-1697), in the time of 'old' Sir George Booth. It is a rare working example of a seventeenth-century watermill, which was restored, with machinery reconstructed around 1980. On the ground floor is the reconstructed overshot waterwheel and a lathe. On the first floor is the carpenter's shop, frame saw, wood boring machine and circular saw. The attic was formerly a granary.

Until around the thirteenth century access to common pasture for cattle and freedom to cut peat, known as turbary, were important privileges for the local community and were freely allowed at the de Masci estates in Dunham. Strip farming was also a common practice in medieval times, and it was expected that grain would be grown on burgage plots, with the proviso that it had to be ground at de Masci mills, which were located along the River Bollin. One eighteenth of the grain ground was then exacted as a toll, with all the bread made having to be baked in the lord's bakehouse. It is with this practice in mind that we can see the Old Mill on the Dunham Park estate. Although built at a much later time and converted to a sawmill, it gives us a good indication of former medieval practices.

Old Saw Mill, Dunham Park, Dunham Massey, *c.* 1905.

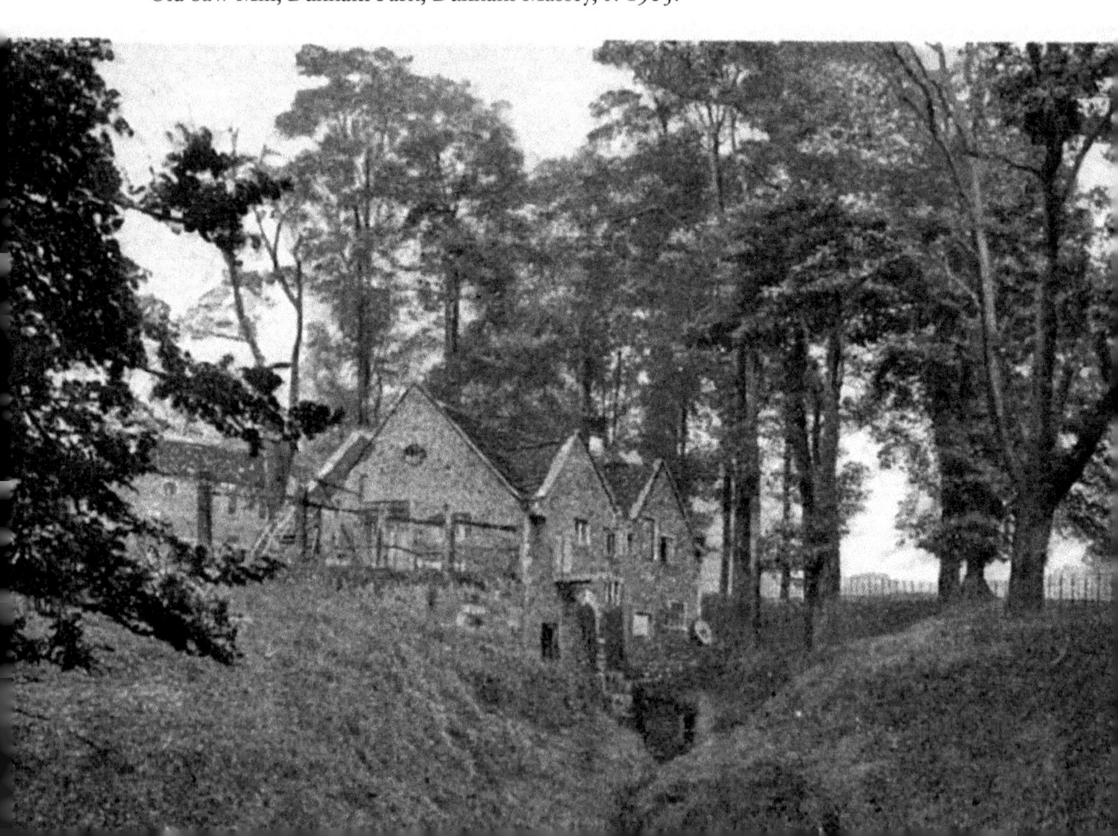

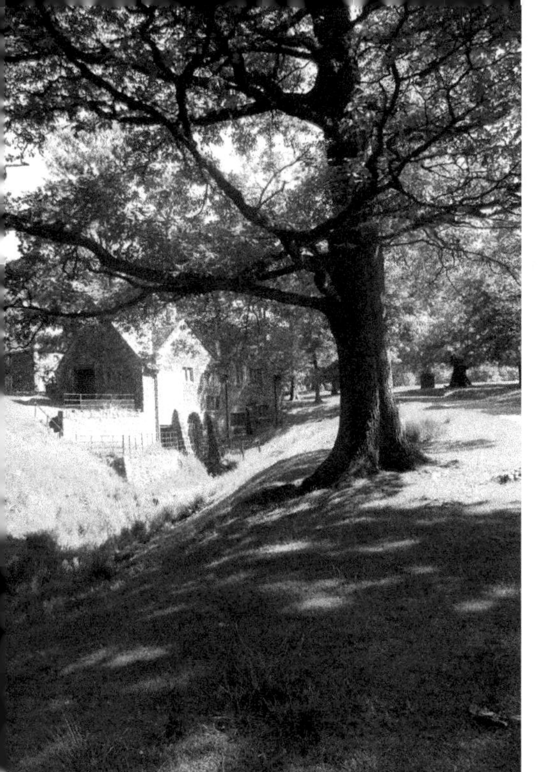

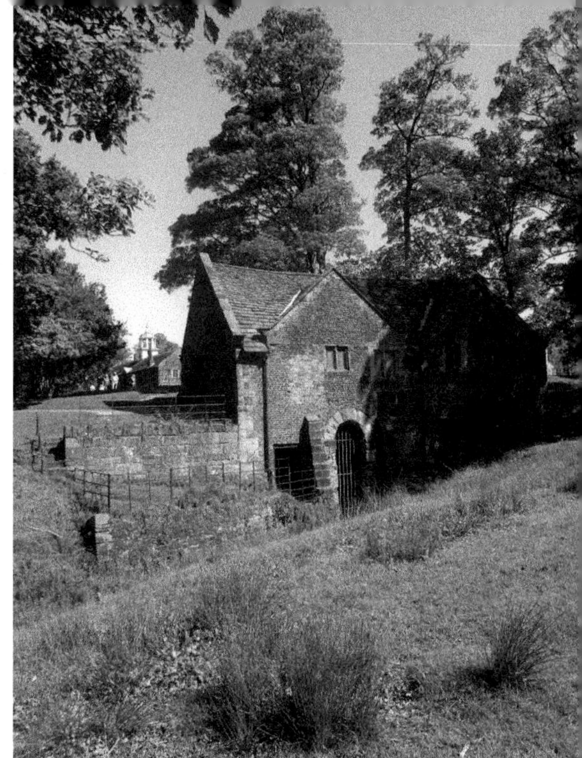

Above left: Old Saw Mill, Dunham Park, Dunham Massey, 2018.

Above right: Old Saw Mill, Dunham Park, with the stable block behind.

The baronial dynasty of the de Masci family, as the Lords of Dunham Massey, lasted from 1070–1342. Hamo (Hamon) was a common Norman name, although this was not always a quiet corner of Cheshire, with Dunham being recorded as having been garrisoned by Henry II, when the Earl of Chester supported the claims of Prince Henry for land in France against his father during the Angevin dynastic wars. Hamo was fined for his actions and castles erected without authority demolished by Henry. It was also rumoured that one child, Hamo VII, the son of Hamo VI, having died in infancy (or at a very young age), actually drowned in the moat at Dunham Castle at the age of nine.

16. No. 16 Market Street, Altrincham

No. 16 Market Street was the home of Helen Allingham (1848–1926), an accomplished Victorian watercolour artist. Shown are a pair of houses, Nos 16 and 14, which are Grade II listed and constructed in the early nineteenth century. They were later converted into offices. They are built in brick on a stone plinth, with a moulded eaves cornice, and a roof of slate and stone-slate. There are three storeys. No. 14 has two bays and No. 16 has four, the first two bays being slightly recessed. The doorway to No. 14 has fluted pilasters, a fanlight and a wedge lintel, and the doorway to No. 16 has a semicircular head, three-quarter Tuscan columns and a fanlight. The windows are sashes with stone sills, those in No. 14 with wedge lintels and those in No. 16 with cambered brick lintels. The blue plaque attached to No. 16 Market Street reads, 'Helen M.E. Allingham (1848-1926) Watercolour

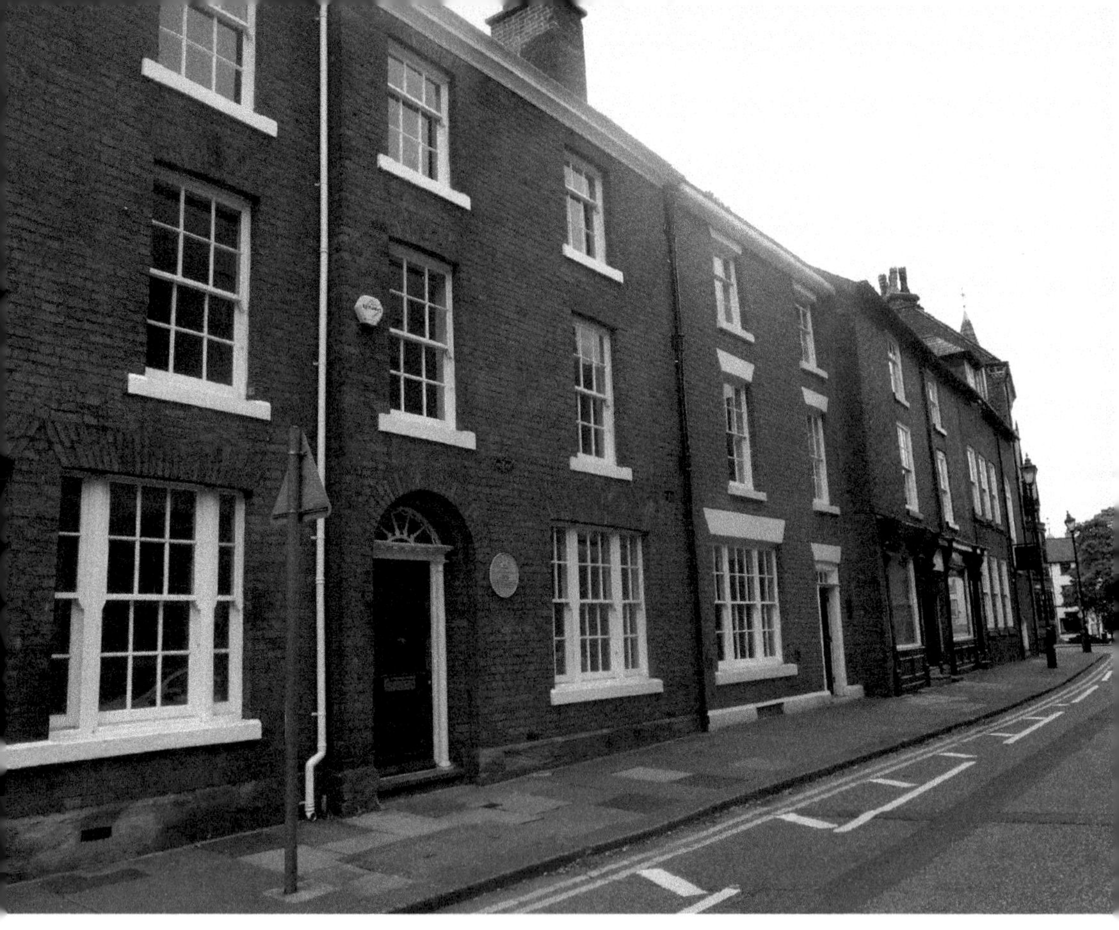

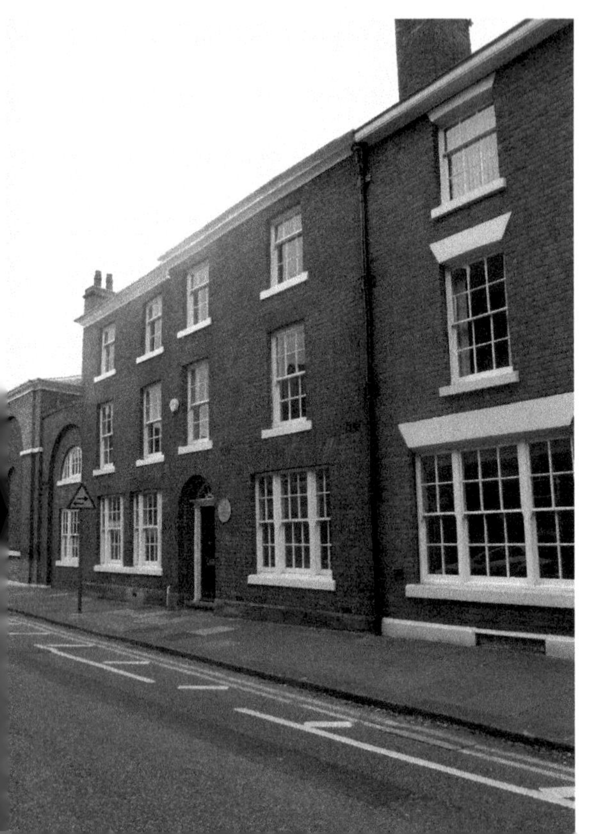

Above: No. 16 Market Street (near left) and No. 14 (far left), Altrincham.

Left: No. 16 Market Street looking towards High Street, Altrincham.

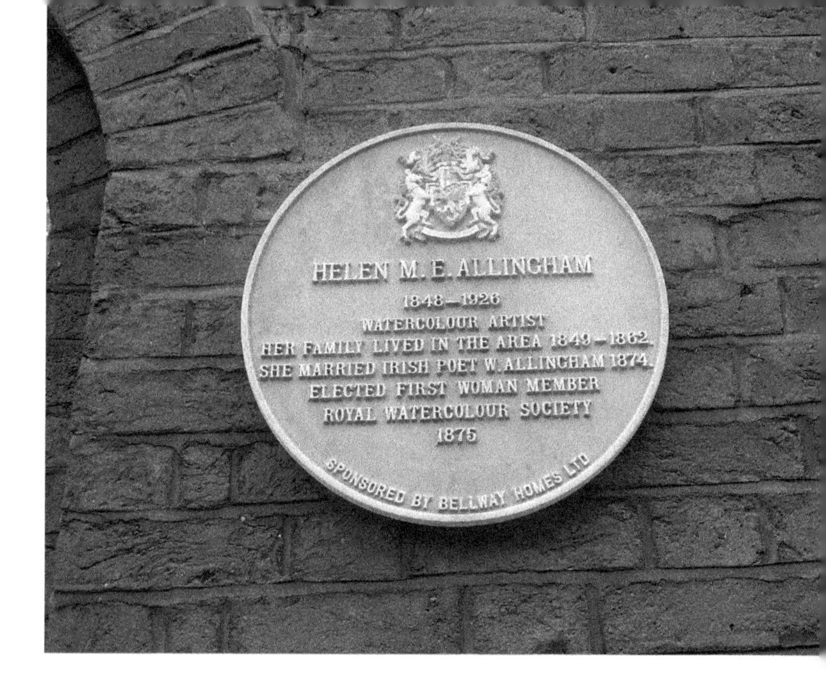

Blue plaque for Helen M. E. Allingham on No. 16 Market Street.

artist. Her family lived in the area 1849-1862. She married Irish poet W. Allingham 1874. Elected first woman member Royal Watercolour Society 1875.'

Helen Mary Elizabeth Paterson was born 26 September 1848 in Swadlincote, a small village near Burton-on-Trent in Derbyshire. She was the eldest of seven children born to Alexander Henry Paterson, a rural physician, and Mary Chance Herford, daughter of a Manchester wine merchant. Within the first year of her life the Patersons moved to Altrincham, where Helen's father set up a medical practice. The young family prospered in their new surroundings. It was during these years that Helen's interest and talent in art developed – both her maternal grandmother and her aunt were accomplished artists of their day. However, at the age of thirteen Helen's father died. While treating local victims of a severe diphtheria epidemic, Dr Paterson fell victim to the disease himself, in May 1862, along with Helen's three-year-old sister Isabel. The Paterson family moved to Birmingham shortly after, where Paterson aunts helped provide for them.

17. Former Altrincham Council Offices and Town Hall, Market Street

In 1849, the first town hall was established adjacent to the Unicorn Hotel. This was replaced by the town hall shown overleaf, which was built in 1900. It was home to the Altrincham Urban District Council, which was formed in 1894 and occupied an old private dwelling house in Market Street, using it as its headquarters until the construction of the new building. The new building included a fire station, the residence of the chief officer of the fire brigade and a public mortuary, at a total cost of £7,000. The town hall was built from the designs of C. H. Hindle of Manchester. It was constructed in red brick, with stone dressings and windows with stone mullions, in the Jacobean style. The council offices included a council chamber, which was well designed and functional, with windows decorated by the arms of the Earl of Chester, the Earl of Stamford and other influential county families. The town hall also had integral committee rooms and suites of offices for the use of the clerk, surveyor, sanitary inspector, medical officer of health, chief financial officer and other council officials.

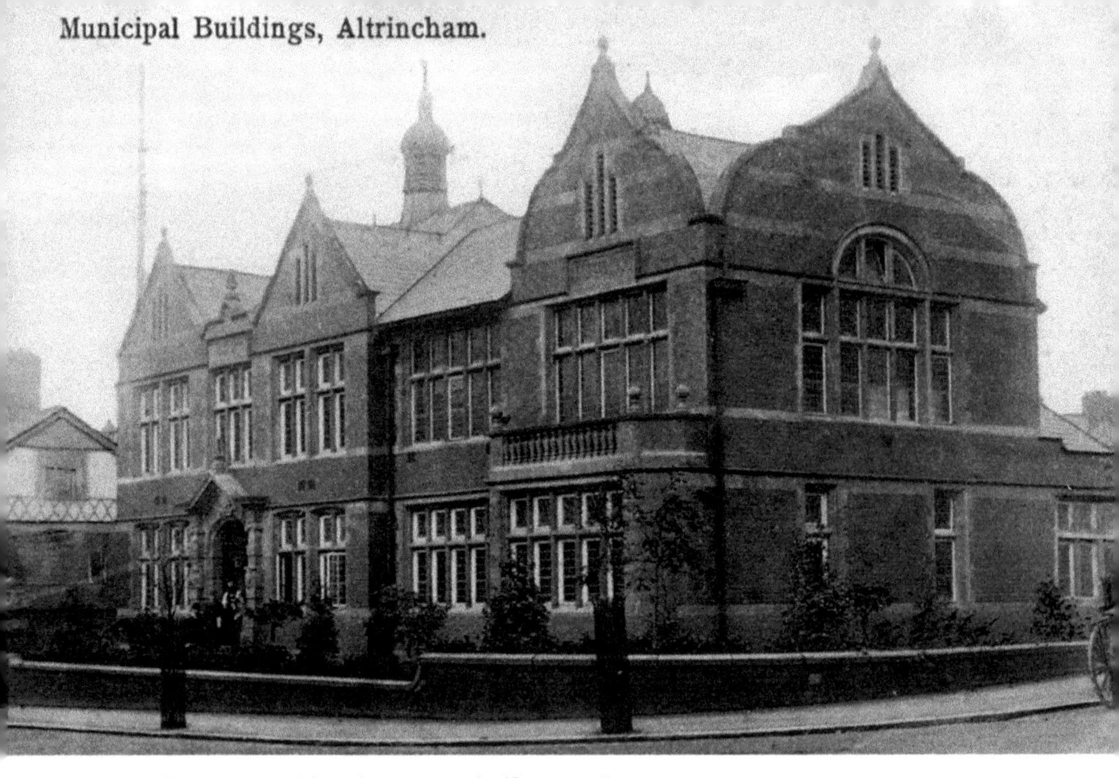

Above: Former Altrincham Council offices, Market Street, in 1917.

Below left: Entrance to the former council offices on Market Street, Altrincham.

Below right: The former council offices on Market Street from High Street.

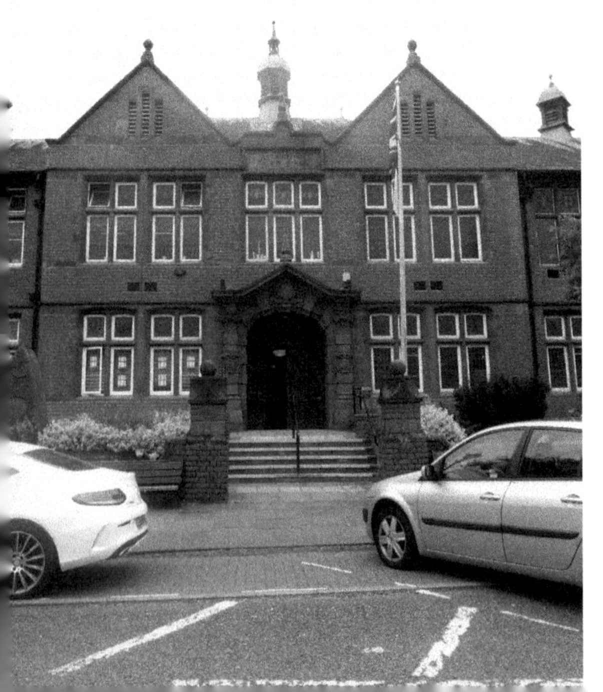

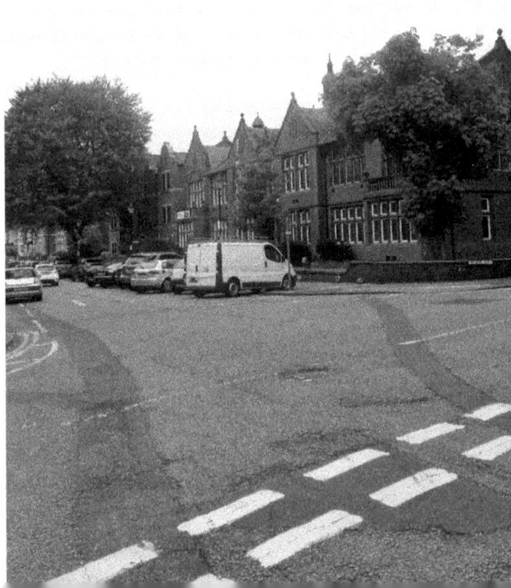

In 1930, an extension was added to the building in order to provide additional working space for the growing number of council departments in the UDC. This was caused by Altrincham's rising population, leading to an additional workload. The original architect, C. H Hindle, initially prepared these plans, but his subsequent death meant that the responsibility for completing the task was now passed to F. H. Brazier, a responsibility he duly discharged.

In 1974, Altrincham became a part of Trafford Metropolitan Borough Council and in 2004 Altrincham town hall was refurbished, creating a community facility and venue for meetings. The Victorian exterior of the building has been retained. The former council offices stand as a reminder of Altrincham's status as an Urban District Council and a borough pre-1974. It shows how the town has grown and developed both in population and status throughout the nineteenth century, with the town hall in Old Market Place, and the twentieth century, with further development on Market Street.

18. Altrincham Market Hall, Market Street

In 1290, Altrincham was granted a royal charter by Edward I, in the eighteenth year of his reign, enabling the establishment of a market. At the same time Baron Hamon de Masci granted his tenants a charter, making Altrincham a free borough. Baron Hamon de Masci

Altrincham Market Hall, Market Street.

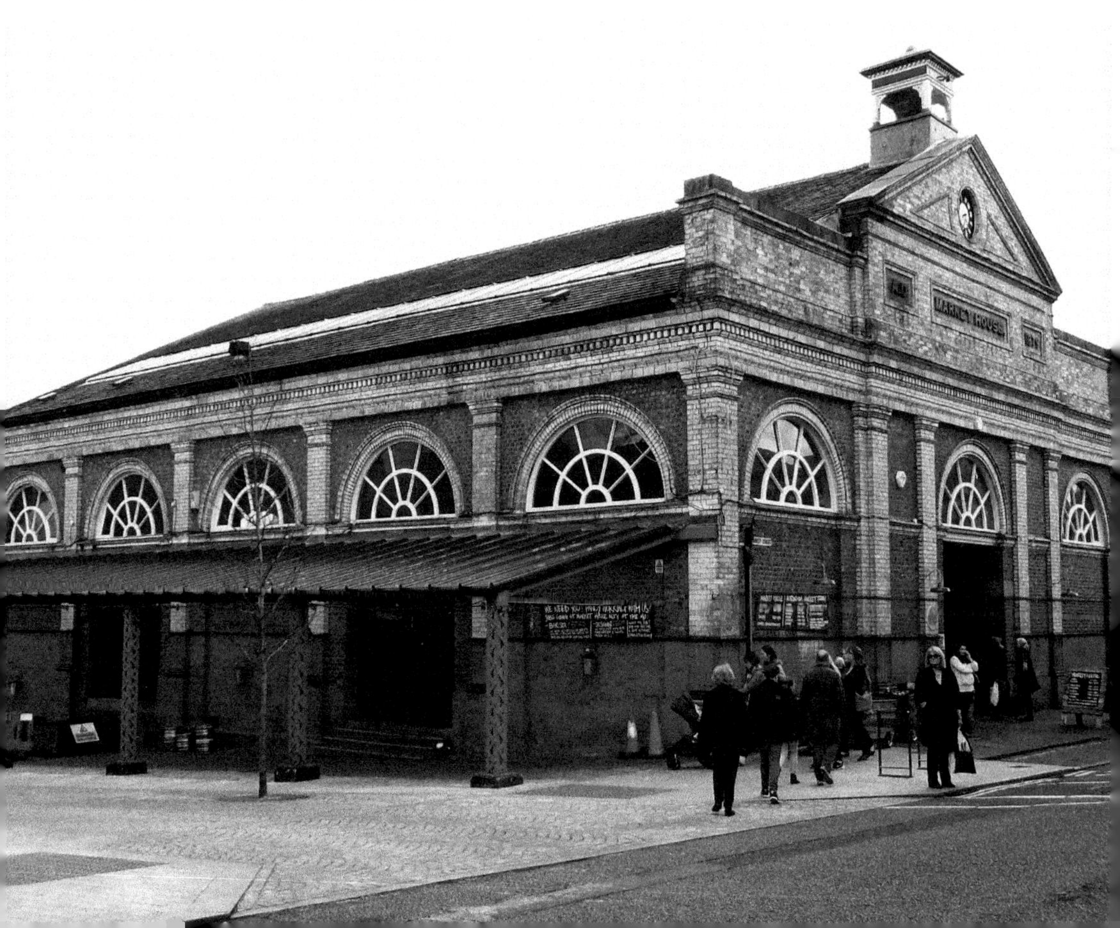

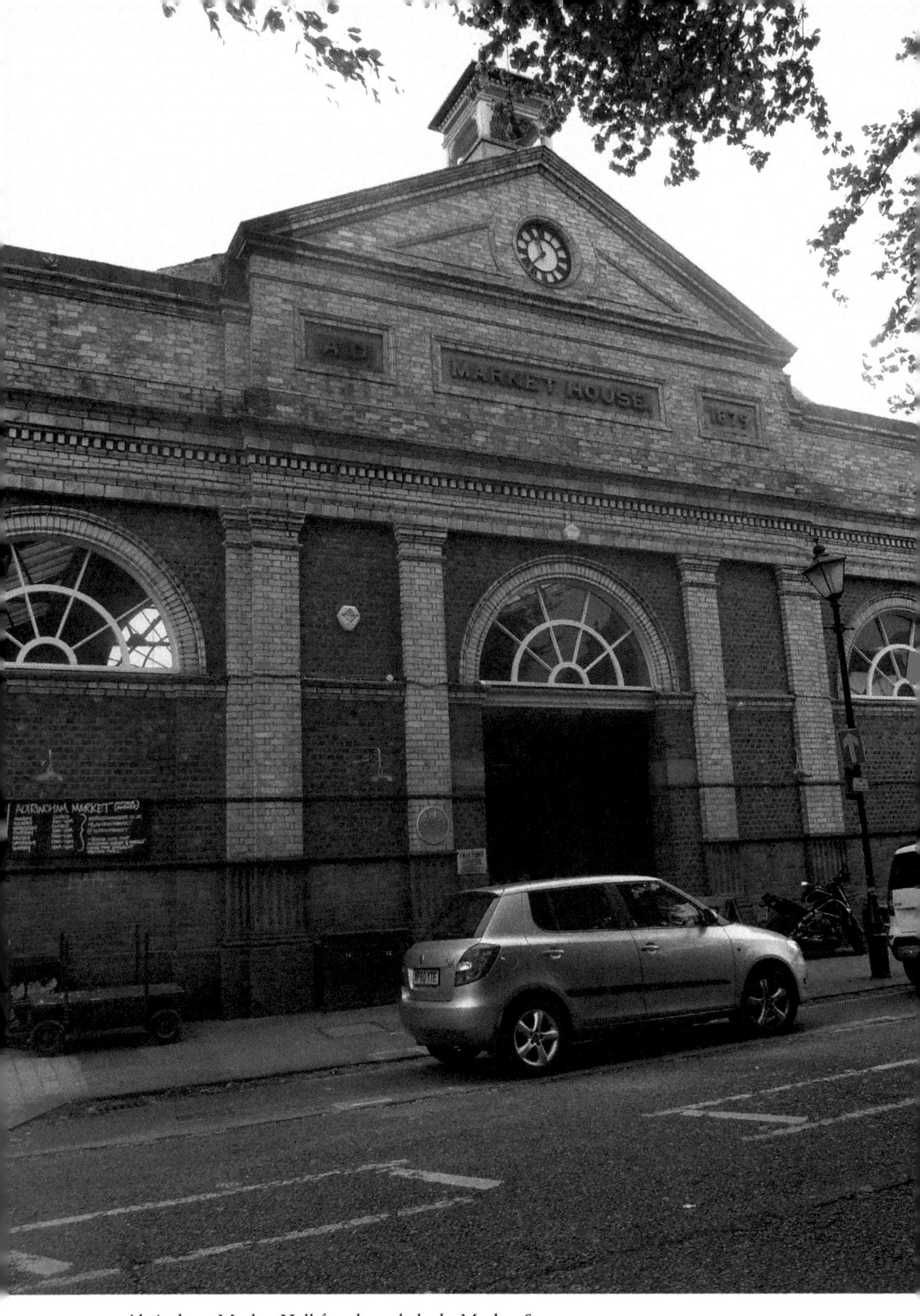

Altrincham Market Hall façade and clock, Market Street.

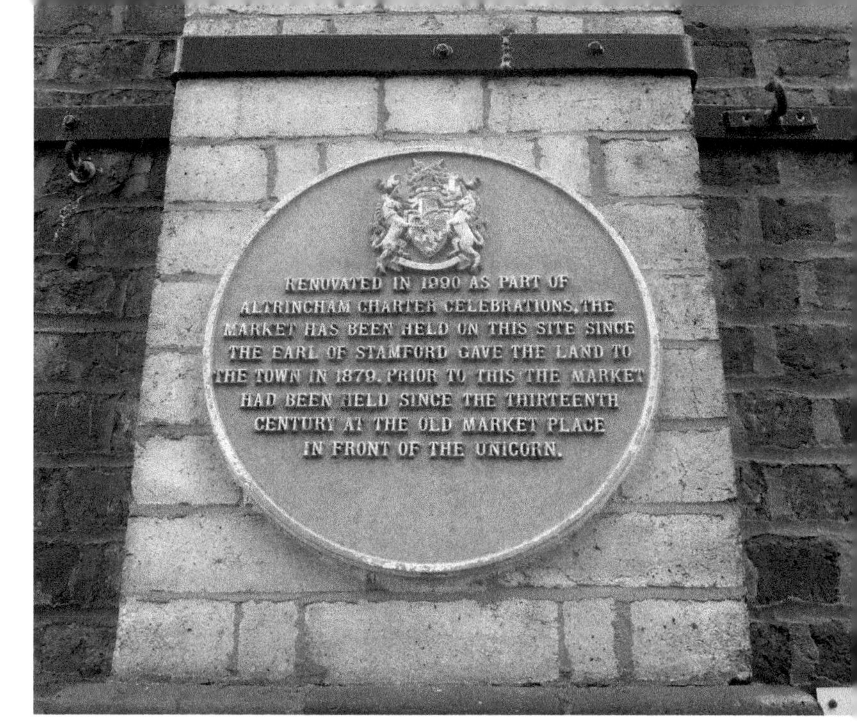

Blue plaque on Altrincham Market Hall, overlooking Market Street.

was granted a market on a Tuesday, and a fair of three days on the Feast of the Assumption of the Blessed Mary. However, in 1319, by a charter from Edward II, the date of the fair was changed to the feast of St James the Apostle. Later, a fair was also held in April.

In 1730, the old market cross was rebuilt by the Earl of Stamford, as a focal point for the market's activities. The court leet became the recognised ruling power immediately on the granting of the charter and up to the middle part of the nineteenth century. It was the main instrument of power for the administration of the law, regulating Altrincham's markets and fairs. In 1879–80 the present market hall was erected, at a cost of just over £5,000, and in 1930 the whole of the adjacent land was covered with a glass roof and iron pillars. The market hall is in pink and yellow brick and has a dentilled cornice, a slate roof, and fronts of three and five bays. The three-bay entrance front has a pediment over the central bay containing a clock face, and the outer bays have parapets. Along the sides are pilasters with fluted bases and in the upper parts are lunette windows. It is constructed in yellow Flemish bond brickwork. There is also a blue plaque overlooking Market Street and telling us that the market hall was 'Renovated in 1990 as part of Altrincham Charter celebrations, the market has been held on this site since the Earl of Stamford gave the land to the town in 1879. Prior to this the market had been held since the thirteenth century at the Old Market Place in front of the Unicorn.' Today, the market hall is home to many diverse traders, and there is also an outdoor market.

19. Former Altrincham General Hospital, Market Street

The former General Hospital building was located at the junction of Market Street and Regent Road. As the nineteenth century progressed, Altrincham developed from a market town into a commuter suburb of industrial Manchester. It became an area of great contrasts between the mansions of Manchester's cotton merchants and working-class housing situated at the lower end of Altrincham.

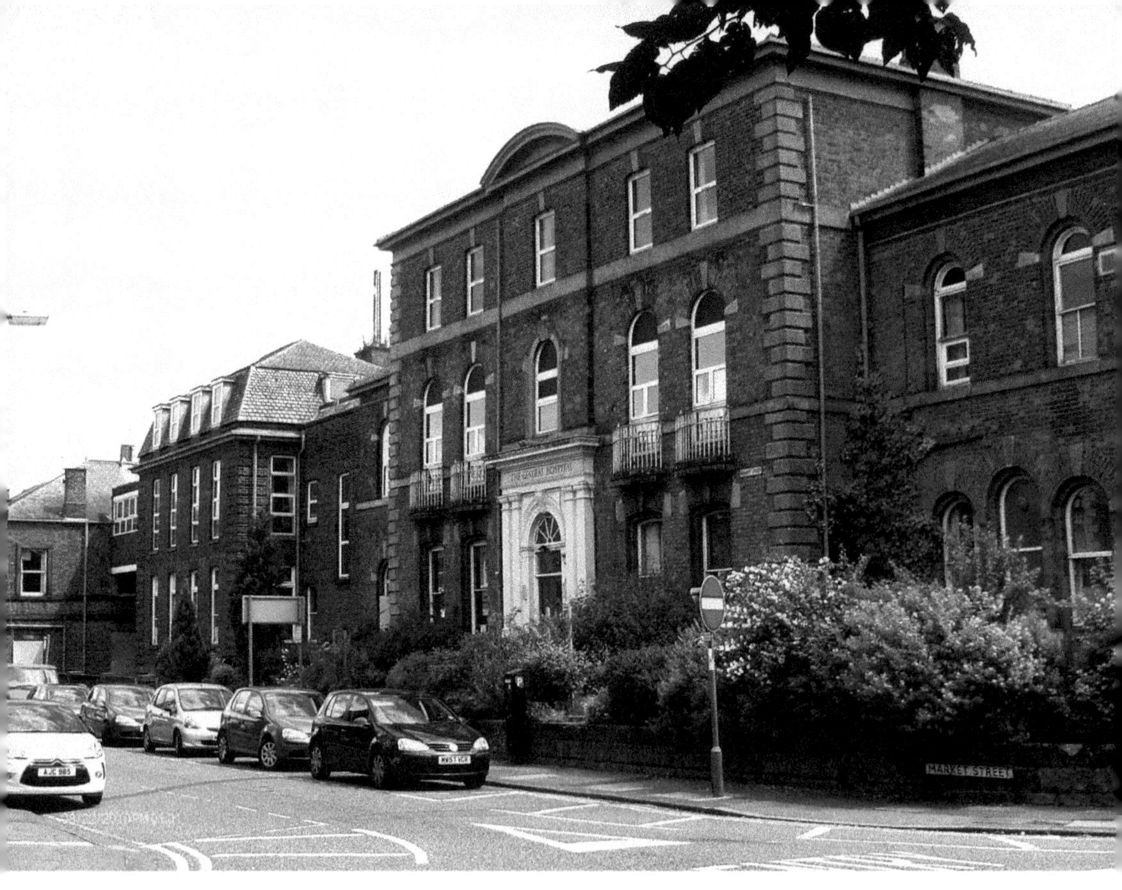

Former Altrincham General Hospital, junction of Market Street and Regent Road.

A Board of Health report on the housing conditions of the poor led to the construction of a new hospital (now replaced) along Lloyd Street, on land donated by the 7th Earl of Stamford. Altrincham's first hospital, built in 1840, was a wooden building on Hale Moss, near today's junction of Beech Road and Stamford Park Road, Hale. It was known as the Altrincham Smallpox and Cholera Hospital and was maintained by the township. Poor sanitary conditions and inadequate drainage in many of Altrincham's properties led to a rise in epidemics, with the hospital becoming obsolete. In 1850, the widow of Edward Jeremiah Lloyd, of Oldfield Hall, gave £300 towards the building of a new hospital. With the help of public subscription Lloyd's Hospital was built on an acre of land in Lloyd Street, given by the Earl of Stamford and Warrington in 1853, at a cost of £600. Those resident in Altrincham and Bowdon who contracted a contagious or infectious fever, or those who were poor or destitute and suffered an accident, could access the hospital. However, conditions were basic, with no medical staff, patients being attended by their own doctors.

In 1870, the Altrincham Provident Dispensary and Hospital was built on an old drill ground of the Rifle Volunteers at Bowdon Road (Market Street), and included any treatment required for eyes and teeth. Lloyd's Hospital was managed by the governors of Altrincham Provident Dispensary and Hospital, with both hospitals sharing the same medical staff. However, the new hospital had its own domestic staff and dispenser. An epidemic in 1877 caused the administration of Lloyd's Hospital to be transferred to the control of the local Board of Health. Lloyd's Hospital fell out of use in 1911. There is now a new hospital on Railway Street and redevelopment on Market Street.

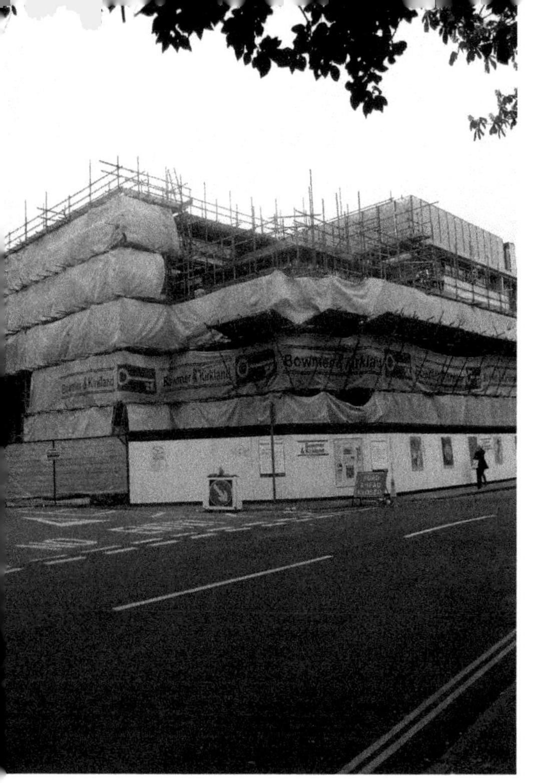

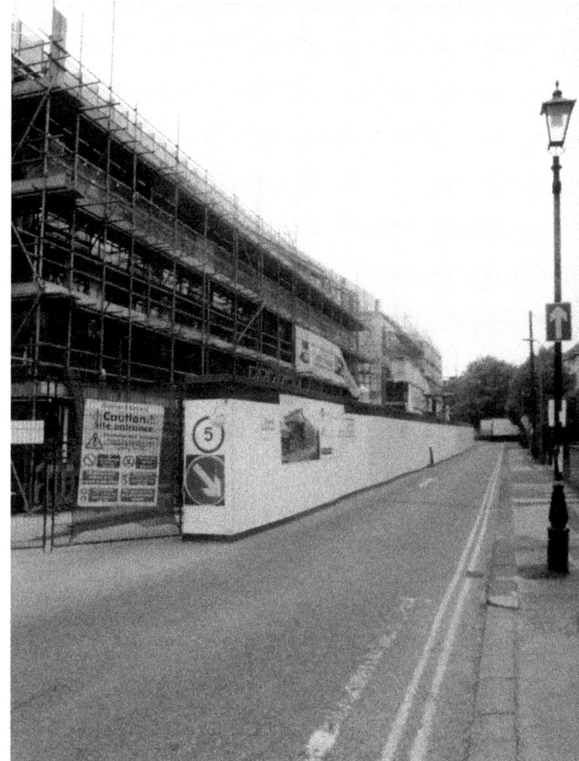

Above left: The same junction in 2018.

Above right: Redevelopment of the hospital from Market Street, 2018.

20. Former Woolworth's Store, George Street, Altrincham

George Street was designated a conservation area on 12 March 1987 and is considered 'at risk' as a result of changing shopping trends. Historically, George Street was at the centre of the medieval Lower Town, where artisans, workers' houses and workshops were located. The boundaries of some existing properties trace medieval burgage plots. These properties have varying styles of construction, including Georgian, Victorian and twentieth-century design.

George Street was essentially a residential area in the mid-Victorian period but is now a commercial district. The number of late Victorian commercial properties on George Street shows us the rapid development of Altrincham in this period. The ground floors of most of the Victorian properties along George Street have been developed as retail or commercial outlets today. Architectural detail is retained on first- and second-floor levels, where the historic character of these buildings is displayed. Building materials from the local area have been used in their construction, creating a 'uniform and harmonious appearance'. There were old cottages on George Street, which dated to 1690, with the last being removed in 1886. What was originally a winding lane of cottages has now become a busy shopping street in the twenty-first century.

One of the main features of George Street was that several of its old cottages stood high above the road. Some of them were approached by seven or eight steps, which allowed for the construction of cellar dwellings below the cottages. Today modern retail and commercial premises have been constructed in their place. In 1860, just prior to the

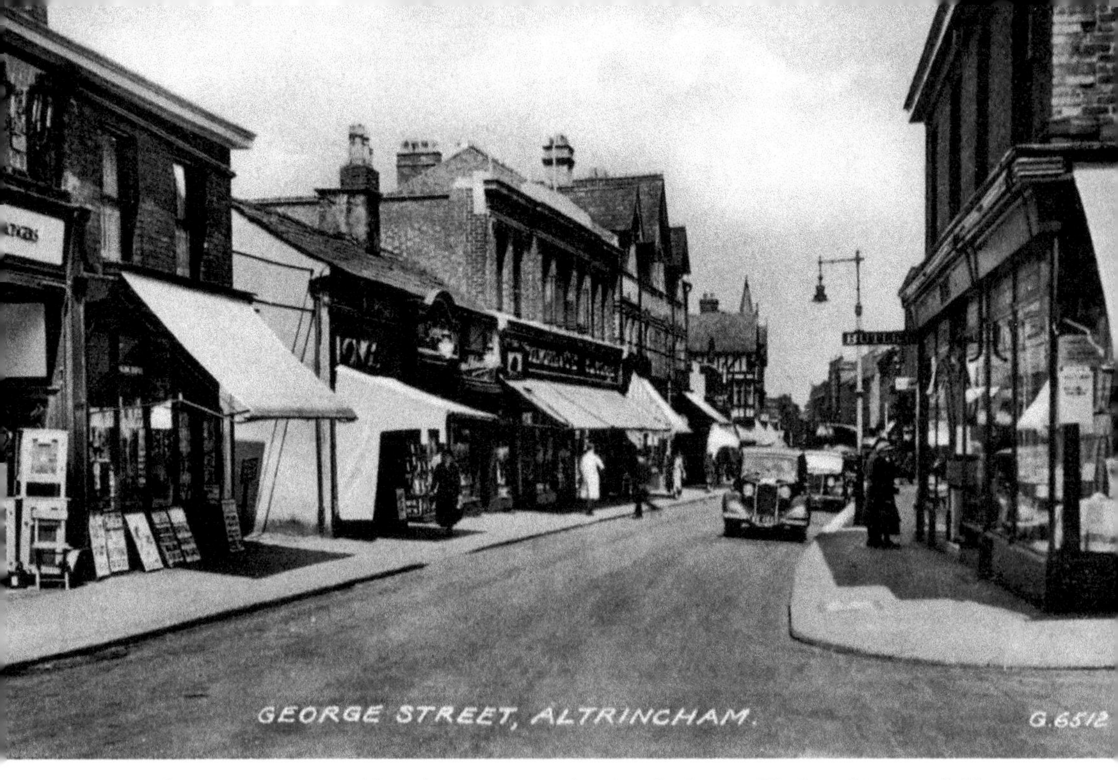

Above: George Street, Altrincham, in 1950, showing the former Woolworth's store (left).

Below left: George Street looking towards Regent Road with the former Woolworth's store on the right.

Below right: George Street with former Woolworth's store on the left.

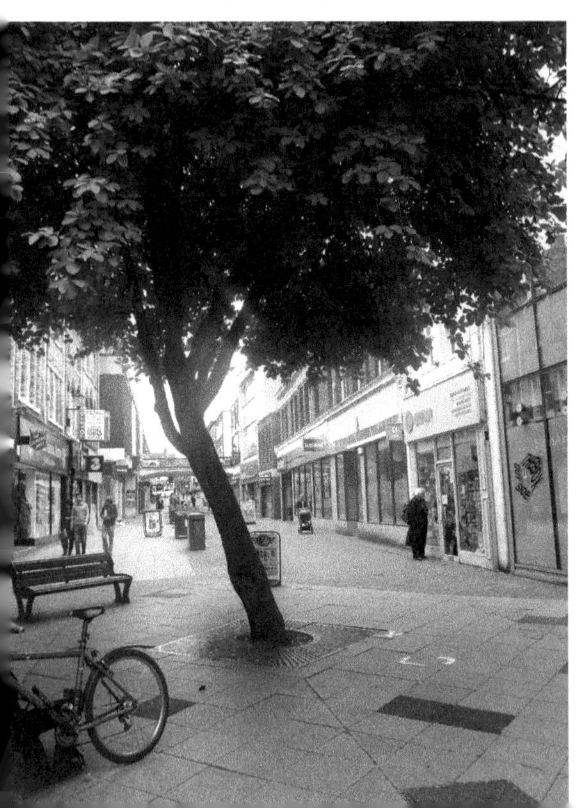

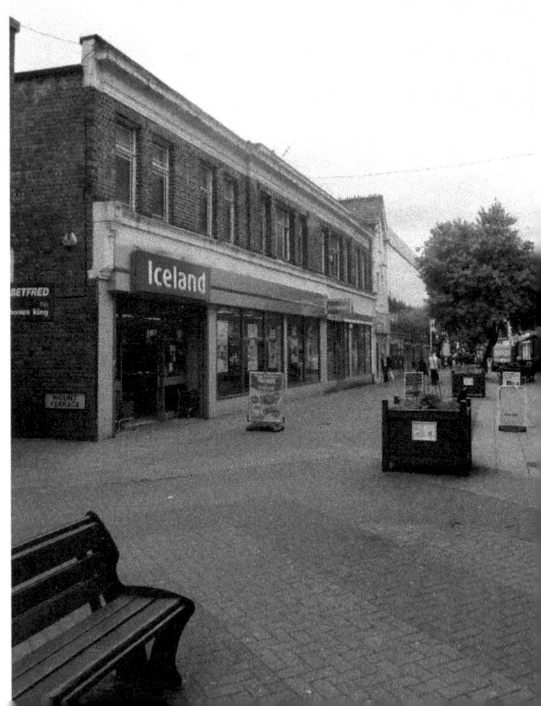

start of the demolition of these cottages, George Street was characterised by dwellings with thatched roofs and overhanging eaves. The street was no more than a country lane, although its importance as a business centre was still recognised and substantial rows of shops began to appear along it. The former Woolworth's store shown here is still a retail premises, although the Woolworth's Group entered into administration in January 2009. They began in the United Kingdom as F. W. Woolworth & Co., in 1909. The venture was initially very successful, expanding rapidly in the 1920s.

21. Chapel Street Memorial, Regent Road, Altrincham

One hundred and sixty-one men enlisted from sixty houses on the street. At the end of the First World War many public celebrations took place throughout the country and the mood of jubilation to mark the Armistice and ultimate peace was continued in Altrincham. Old Market Place was filled with people tightly packed along every road and approach to Altrincham's town centre. These celebrations were also reflected in nearby Chapel Street. The festivities were very particular to this historic street. Like the rest of the town, Chapel Street was decorated with flags and there was singing and dancing. In the evening there were fireworks in Hale and Bowdon and later there was the sound of a canon. The Borough Band also gave two concerts in Old Market Place.

Throughout the following year the people of Altrincham continued to honour the men of Chapel Street who, at the outbreak of war, volunteered for active service. A memorial was erected by public subscription as a tribute to their bravery. The memorial was unveiled by the Earl of Stamford on 5 April 1919 before a large gathering of townspeople. His words

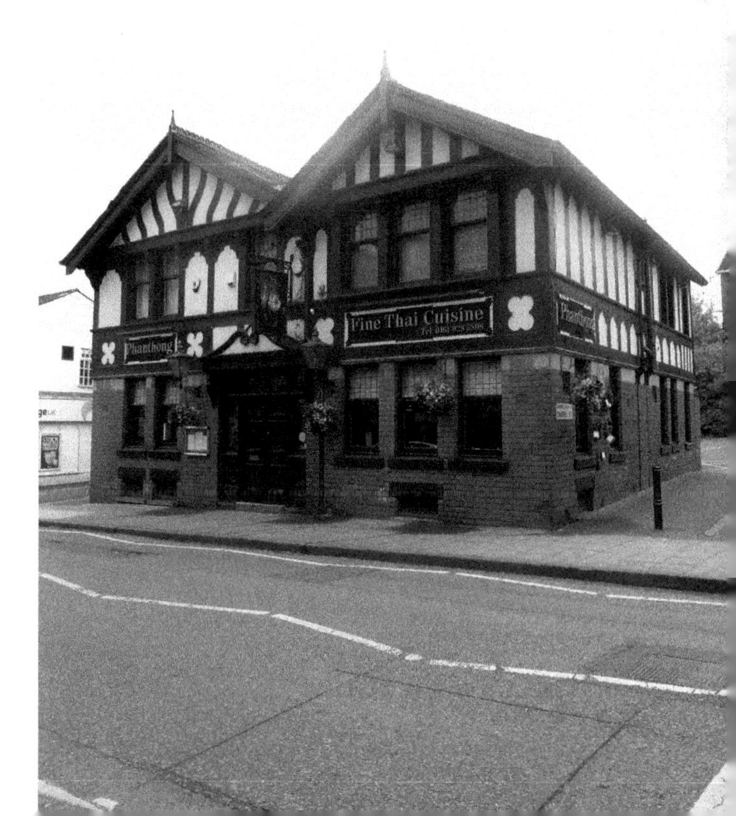

Chapel Street blue plaque from Regent Road.

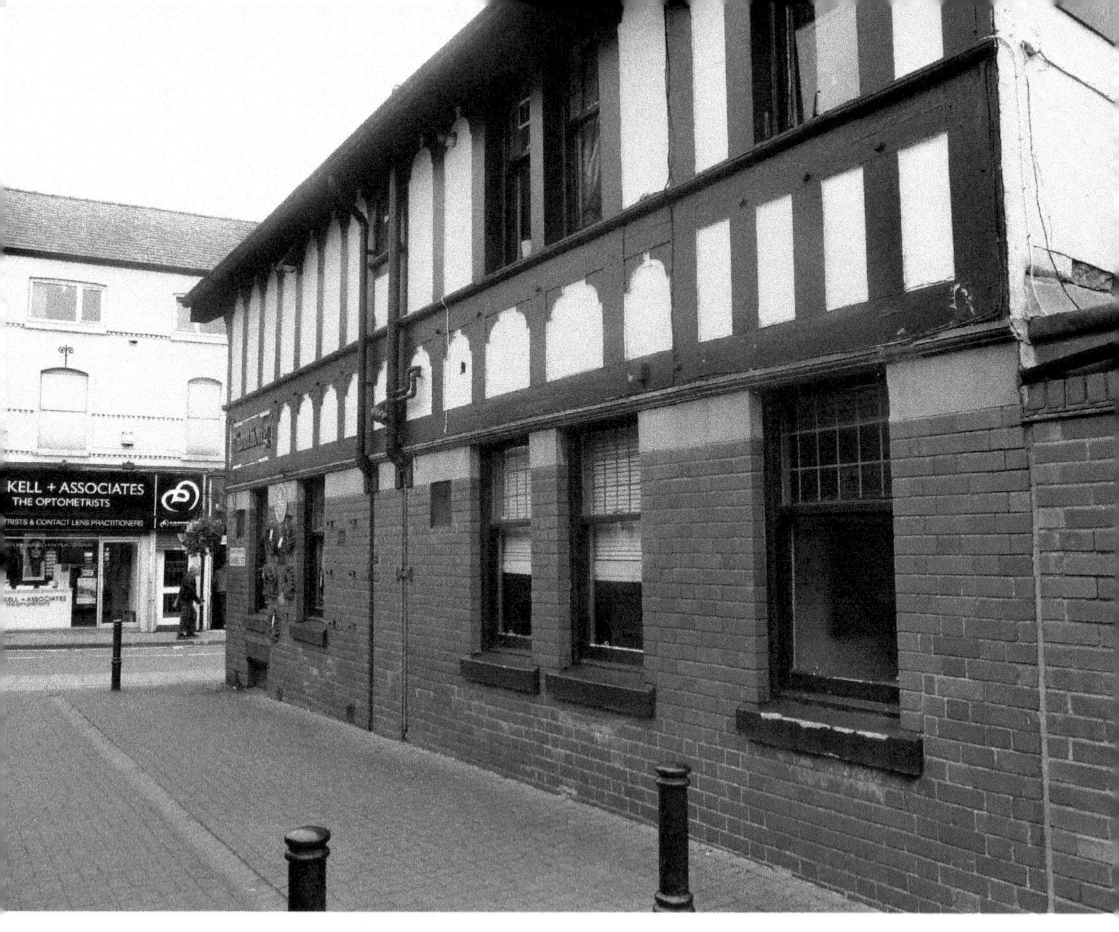

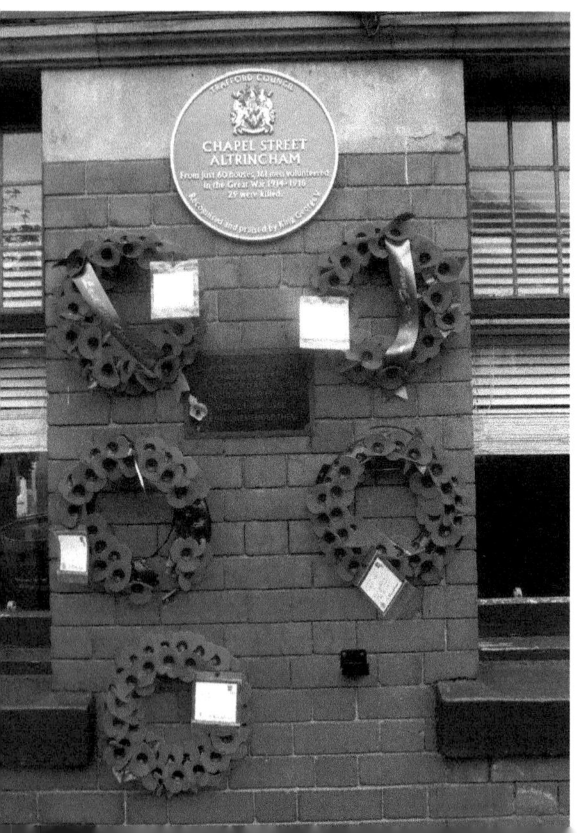

Above: Chapel Street blue plaque looking towards Regent Road.

Left: The Chapel Street blue plaque.

are recorded by Nickson (p. 298): 'Lord Stamford said that no tribute they could pay, and no appreciation they could express, could adequately reflect their feelings of pride and enthusiasm at the honour and distinction which the men whose names were inscribed on the memorial had conferred on their town.' The memorial bore the names of all the men who served in the army and was erected directly overlooking the street, stating, 'In memory of the 161 men of Chapel Street who volunteered and served in the Great War 1914-1918. 29 gave their lives. We will remember them.'

The street was demolished in 1960 to make way for flats, but a blue plaque was erected near the site in 2009 attached to the side of a restaurant. It reads, 'Chapel Street, Altrincham. From just 60 houses 161 men volunteered in the Great War 1914-18. 29 were killed. Recognised and praised by King George V.' George V called Chapel Street the 'bravest little street in England'.

22. Church of St Vincent de Paul, Junction of Bentinck Road and Groby Road, Altrincham

Constructed in 1904–05, the Church of St Vincent is a Roman Catholic church designed by Edmund Kirby of Liverpool in Early English Gothic style. The sole contractor for the construction of the building was M. McDermott. The buildings are in small red Ruabon brick with terracotta dressings, and they have slate roofs and windows without mullions, which are filled with cathedral glass. The church consists of a nave, with a high open-timbered roof, and a clerestory, north and south aisles, a west porch, north and south transepts, and a chancel with a polygonal apse. Gothic arches support

Below left: The Church of St Vincent de Paul, junction of Bentinck Road and Groby Road.

Below right: Close-up of the Church of St Vincent de Paul, Groby Road.

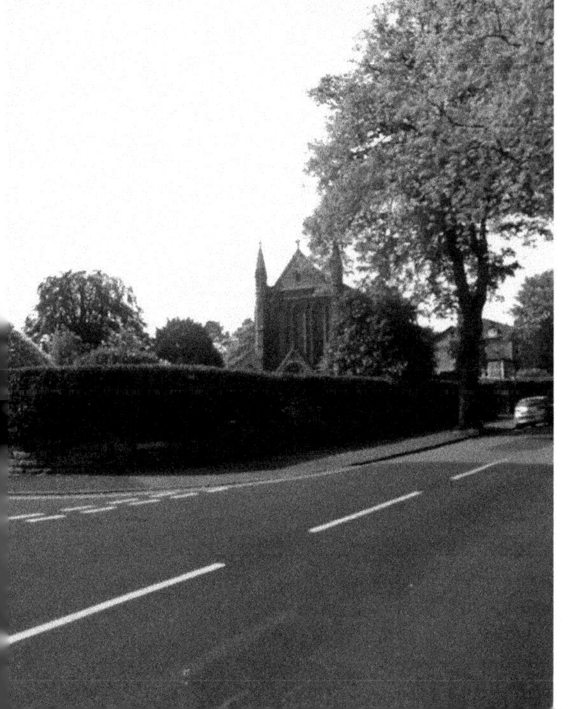

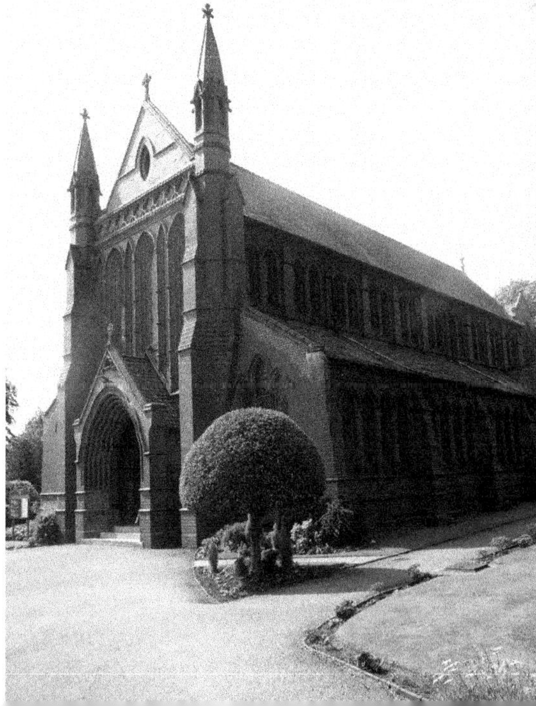

stone capitals, pillars and bases, which separate the nave from the aisles and two side chapels.

The church was originally built to accommodate 500 worshippers. The presbytery was the gift of Peter Kelly, in memory of his wife, and is attached to the south corner. It is in similar materials to the church and has two storeys, a hipped roof, sash windows, a Tudor arched doorway and decoration in diapering. In 1858, the Roman Catholic church of St Vincent de Paul, together with a presbytery, was erected in New Street, opening in 1860. Catholics worshipped here for the next forty-seven years until the church was deemed to be too small for the rapidly expanding congregation. Eventually land was secured at the junction of Bentinck and Groby roads and here a church was built.

On 22 October 1903 the first sod was cut, in order to facilitate the construction of the foundations. The foundation stone was laid on 18 June 1904 in the presence of the mayor and court leet, and the church was opened for worship on Rosary Sunday, 1 October 1905, by the bishop. The rector was the Revd Father Christopher Ryder, the assistant priest being the Revd Father E. D. Kirby. The Revd W. F. Stanley, of Stockport, a former rector, was present to see the end result of the work he had begun five years earlier. In the intervening years many improvements have been made to the church and in September 1909 the forerunner of Loreto Convent, now a grammar school, was founded.

St Vincent de Paul from Groby Road.

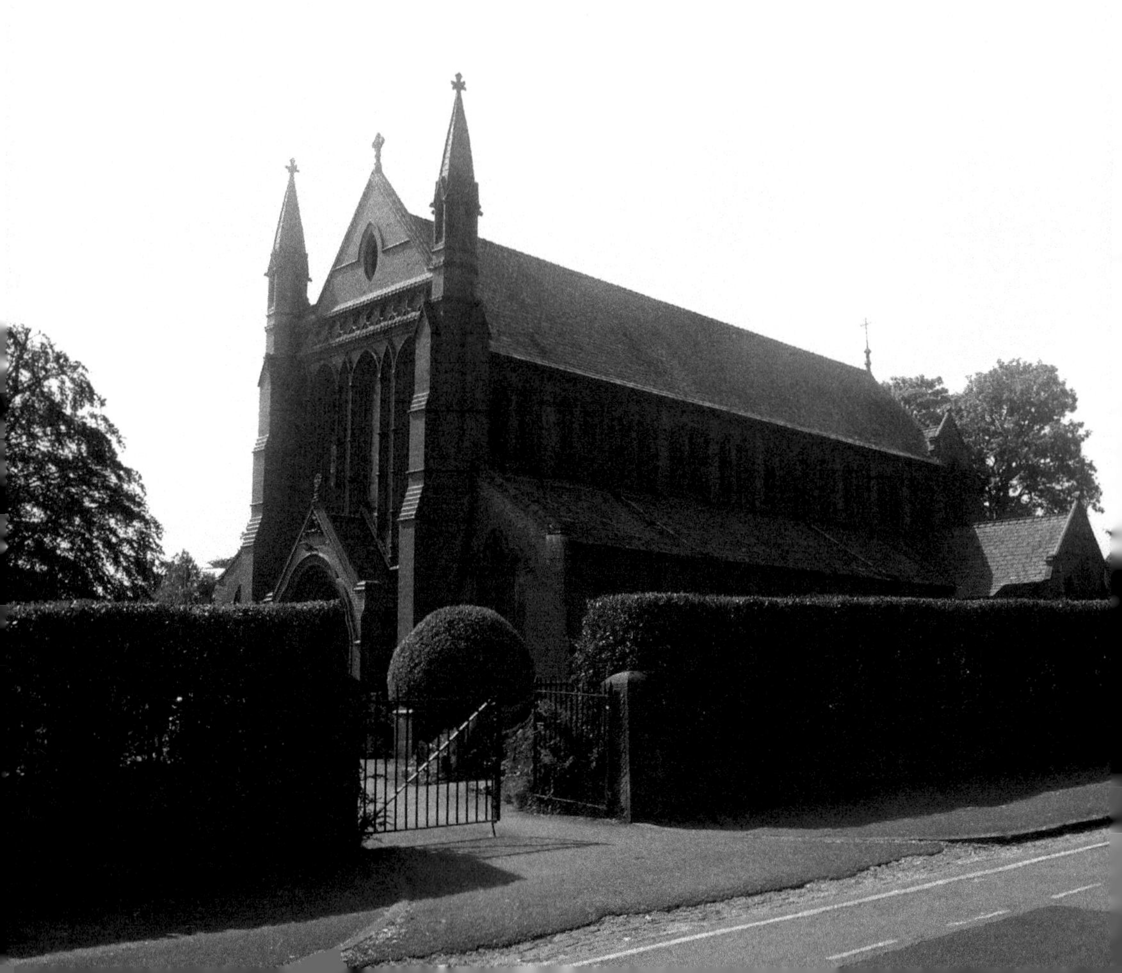

23. Former Barclays Bank, Stamford New Road, Altrincham

This is the birthplace of Ronald Gow (1897–1993), a famous dramatist. The building with a triangular turret was a branch of Martins Bank, which later became a Barclays Bank. The single-storey shops on the right have all been demolished and replaced by a 'mixed-use retail development' linking in to the Goose Green area behind. Altrincham Hospital is now located on Railway Street opposite Regent Road. The building is Grade II listed and dates from 1906. It was built by the Manchester and County Bank and later used for other purposes. It is constructed in sandstone on a plinth, with a dentilled cornice above the ground floor, two string courses, three storeys and three bays. In the right bay is an arched doorway with a fanlight, and Tudor roses in the spandrels. In the upper two floors the central bay is flanked by octagonal pilasters that rise to form pinnacles. Between them at the top is a gable containing a date stone surmounted by a griffin holding a shield. At the ends of the parapet are gargoyles. The blue plaque reads, 'Ronald Gow-Dramatist lived here 1898-1910. Pupil and master at Altrincham County High for Boys. 1937, married actress Dame Wendy Hiller.'

Ronald Gow was born in Heaton Moor, Lancashire, on 1 November 1897 and died on 27 April 1993. Some of his plays were put on in the 1920s by the Altrincham Garrick and in the 1930s two of his full-length pieces were performed in London. One, about Bonnie Prince Charlie, lasted for six weeks at Swiss Cottage. Another, *Gallows Glorious*, lasted for two weeks in the West End and two nights in New York. Gow sent a dramatised version of *Love on the Dole* to the Gaiety Theatre in Manchester. His future wife, Wendy Hiller, whom he married in 1937, played the part of Sally Hardcastle, the play reaching the West End in 1935. Gow adapted Thomas Hardy's *Tess of the D'Urbervilles* in 1946, and further West End adaptations followed in the 1960s.

Below left: Former Barclays Bank, Stamford New Road, showing front elevation.

Below right: Former Barclays Bank, showing passageway to Goose Green on the right.

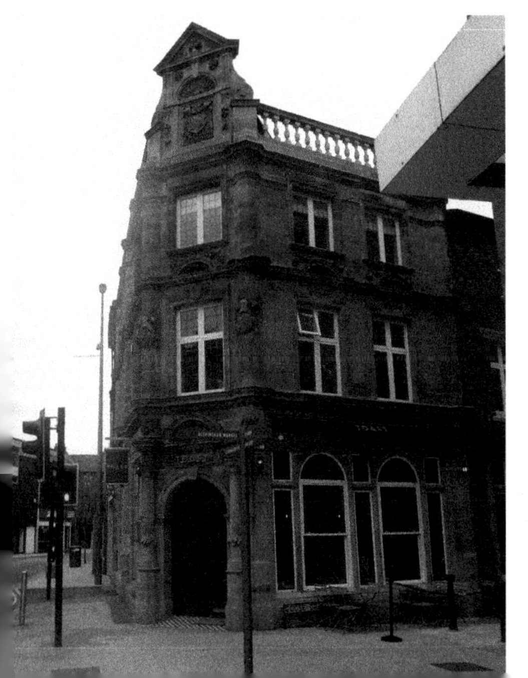

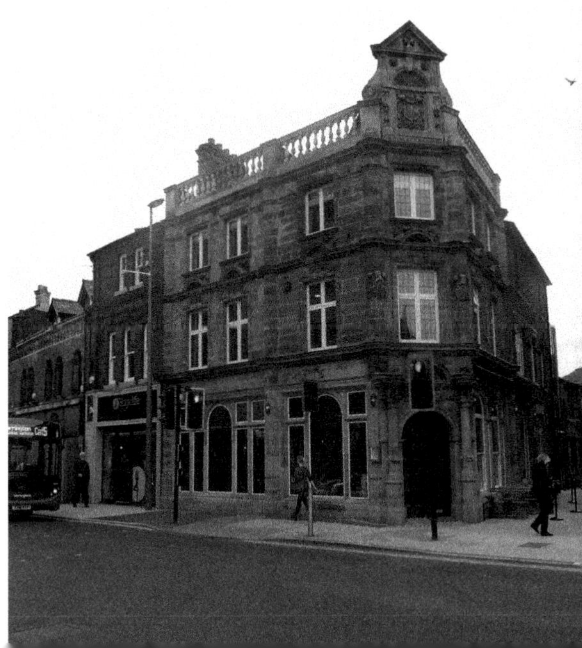

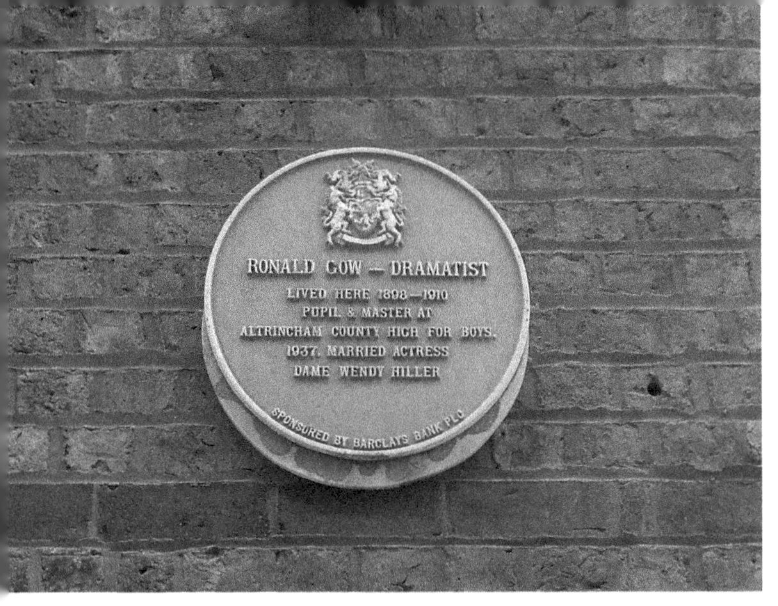

Blue plaque for Ronald Gow, Stamford New Road.

24. Goose Green, Old Cottages, Altrincham

The Green was originally a collection of residential cottages for artisan workers in the early eighteenth century, then moving into the nineteenth century there were several cottages on Goose Green, located at the edge of Hale Moss. During the town centre redevelopment Goose Green was improved and restored, becoming a quiet retail backwater consisting of a few small shops.

Goose Green and old cottages, now retail developments.

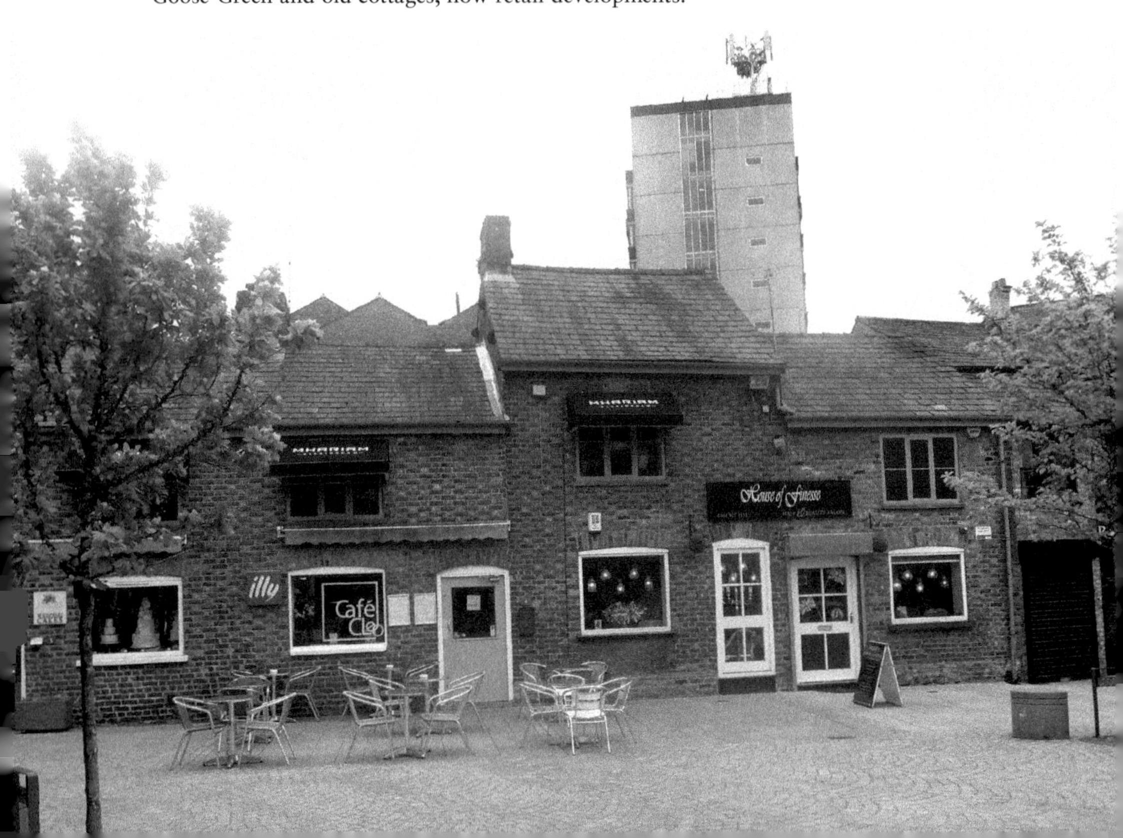

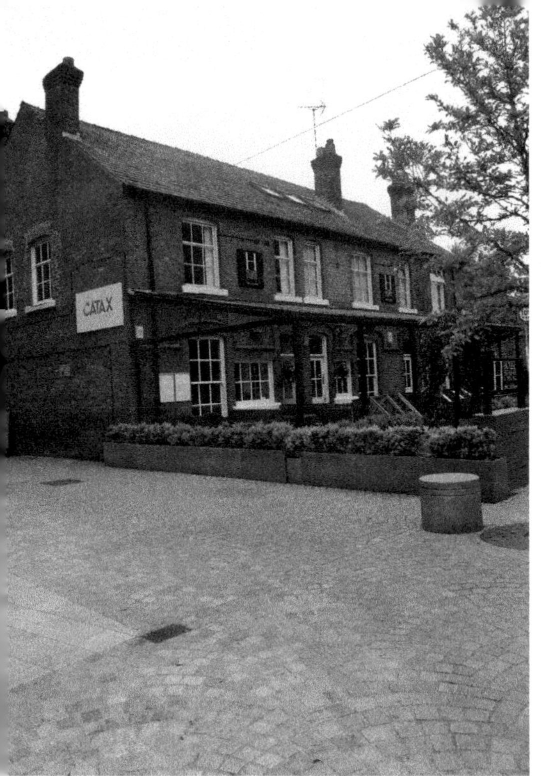

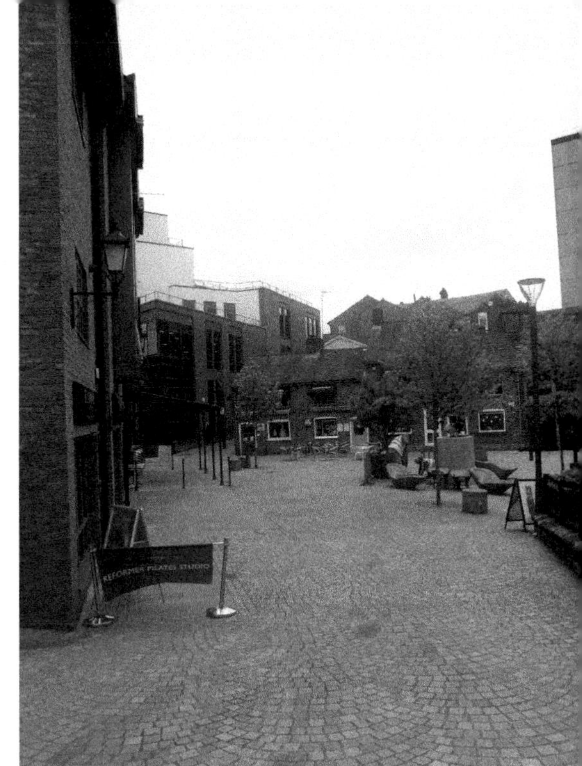

Above left: Goose Green, showing former cottages.

Above right: Goose Green. Modern cafes now front the redesigned Green.

Throughout much of the nineteenth century Goose Green was considered to be an area of working-class dwelling houses. For the whole of this period it retained its cottage-style appearance. Goose Green formed a part of Lower Town, which for the most part housed poorer families in small properties in George Street, the bottom of The Downs and Goose Green. Here there were many small squares and alleyways, which significantly increased the density of Goose Green's local population. More cottages housing the poor began to appear at nearby Pinfold Brow (now Lloyd Street) and Chapel Street. In the 1960s it was popular to demolish larger old houses and replace them with higher density properties, giving a much greater financial return to the building developer. People began to express concern that these modern developments, such as flats constructed on The Downs, did not fit in with the Victorian and Edwardian character of brick houses. This led to the establishment of conservation areas, which included The Downs and Goose Green, in 1973.

Goose Green became isolated from other residential areas in the nineteenth century, with the railway separating it from Pinfold Brow and the development of Stamford New Road in 1880 cutting Goose Green off from the George Street area. Also in this century Goose Green was very densely populated, with most people dwelling in small eighteenth- and nineteenth-century cottage properties, which it was believed could be conserved structurally, if not as houses. Today these renovated structures form a part of the retail district. Statues add focus and make Goose Green a quiet area for recreation.

25. Station Buildings (Stamford House), Stamford New Road, Altrincham

In 1905, J. H. Broun (*Altrincham, A History*, ed. D. Bayliss, 1992) built Station Buildings, an imposing office block. It was one of the first multistorey office blocks in the provinces. He also built Altrincham Post Office and the adjoining shops known as Moss Burn Buildings to the design of a well-known local architect, John McNamara. Station Buildings contained at least eighty-four offices and the building was the first of its type.

Stamford House is a Grade II-listed building, listed on 27 April 1992 and constructed in Edwardian baroque style. It includes Nos 1–13 Moss Lane and was built as commercial buildings with offices over shops. '1904-5 by Charles Heathcote & Sons, for J. H. *Brown* Esq.' (www.britishlistedbuildings.co.uk) Stamford House was built with red brick in Flemish bond and the main elevations are mostly faced with glazed buff terracotta dressings. There is a green slate mansard roof, and brick chimneys also with terracotta dressings. The building is situated on a corner plot, in an L-shaped plan, linked over a wagon entry from Moss Lane. It has three storeys with a basement and an attic storey. There are five matching chimneys. Charles Heathcote was one of the outstanding contemporary Manchester architects and built 'A row of shops with offices above ... in Edwardian Baroque style on a corner site'. In the ground floor are pilasters, a frieze and a cornice, and in the upper floors are giant Ionic pilasters, capitals with foliated pendants, a frieze, and a prominent cornice. The windows are sashes with triple keystones. In the centre of the Stamford New Road front is an open segmental pediment containing a cartouche.

Most of the decorations were factory-made terracotta blocks and it is probable that they were supplied by Shaw's Glazed Brick Co. of Darwen, in Lancashire. They were

Station Buildings (Stamford House), Stamford New Road, *c.* 1915.

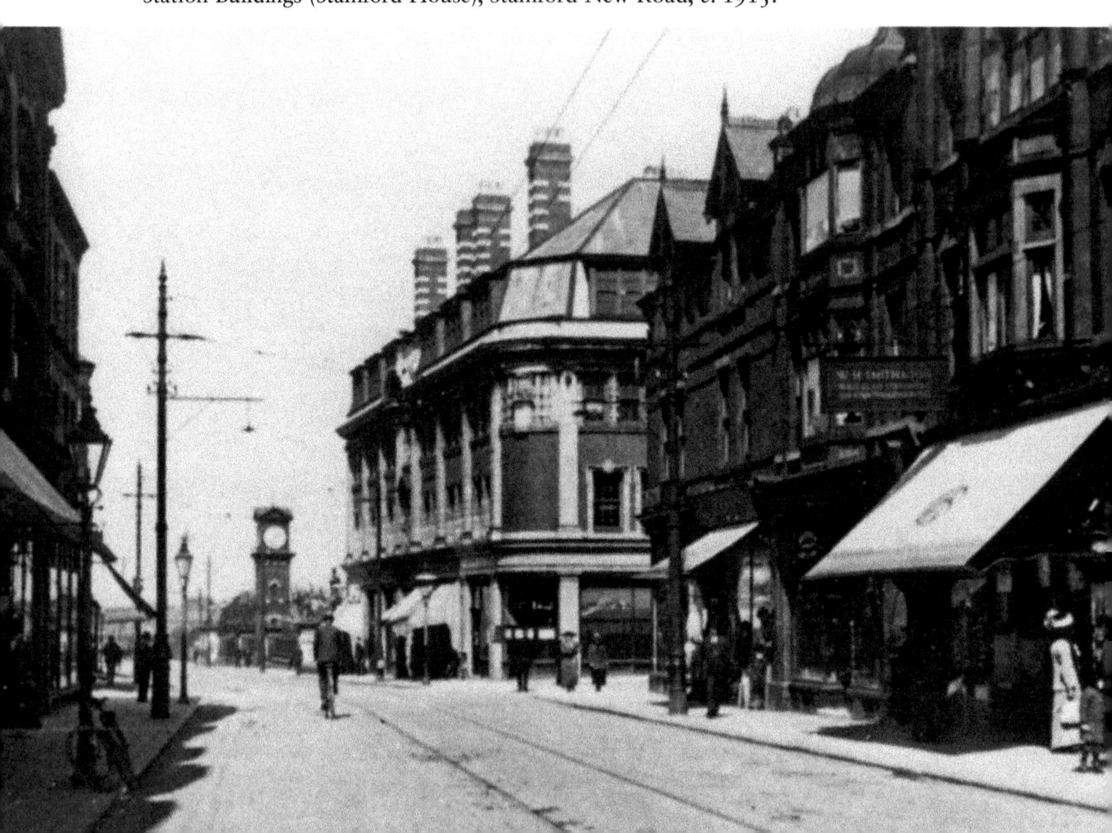

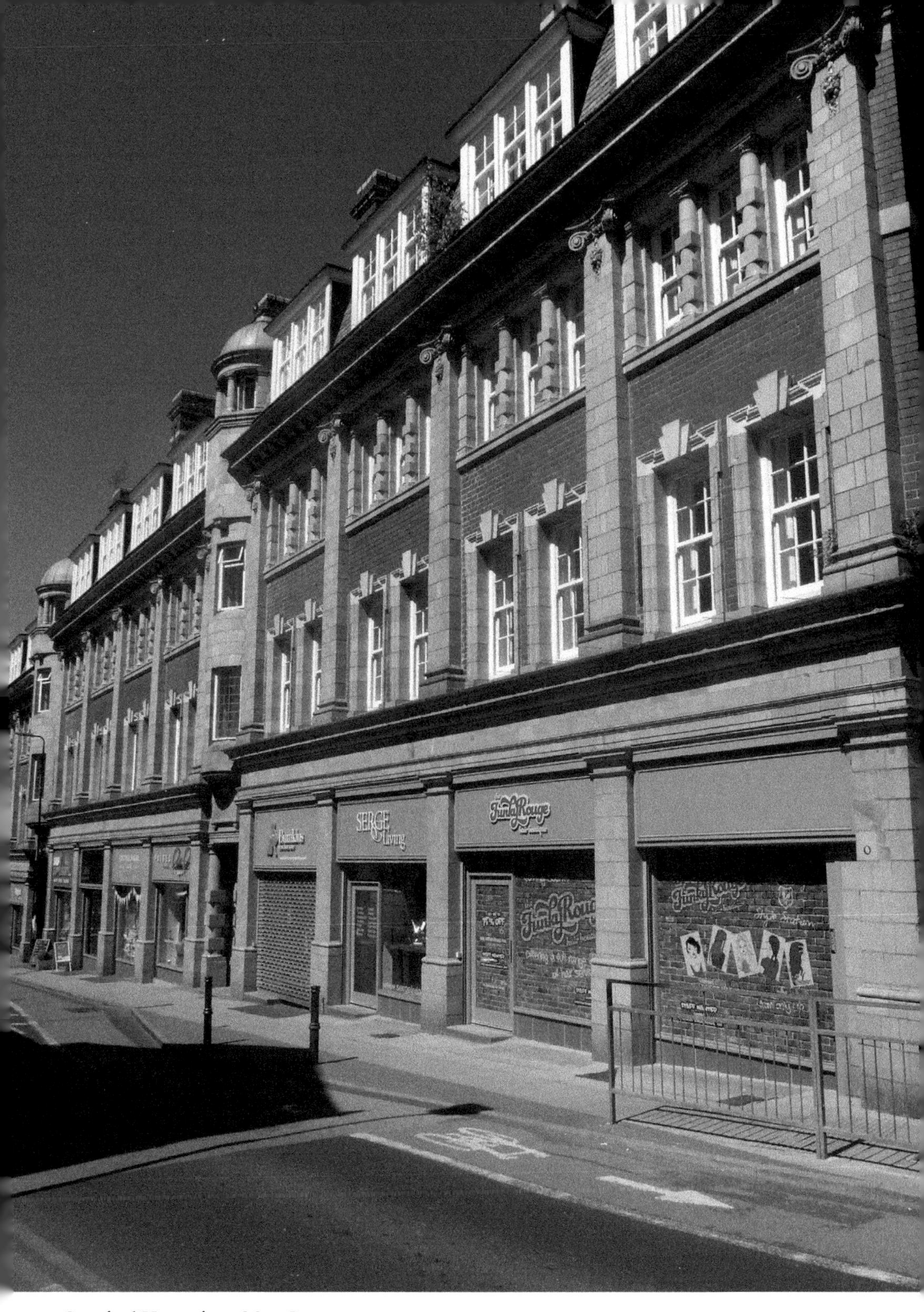

Stamford House from Moss Lane.

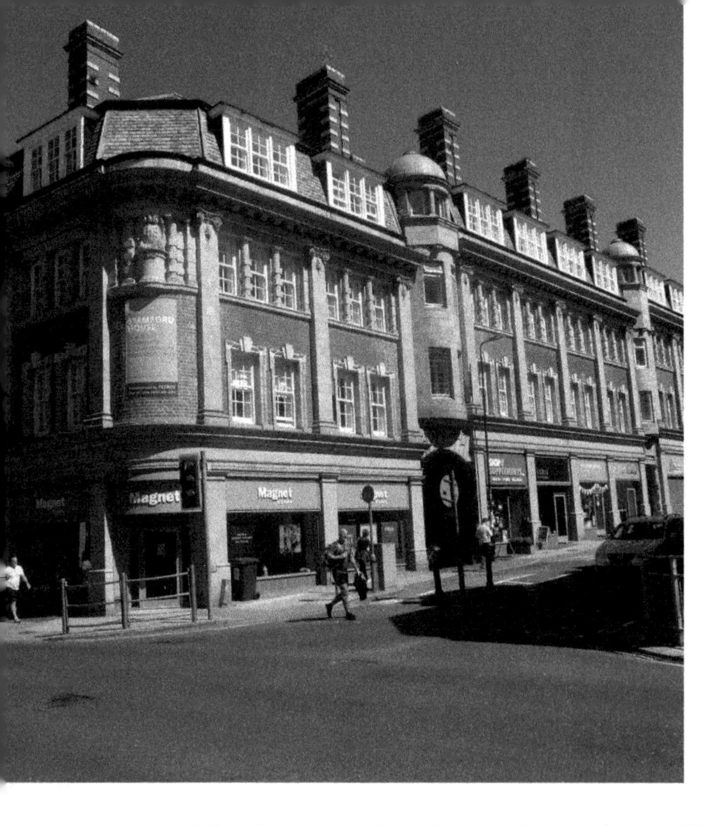

Stamford House, junction of Stamford New Road and Moss Lane, showing carriage entry.

supplying these types of products until around 1980. Their advantage was that they could be reproduced and supplied to the customer many years later if required. Watson's of Ashfield Road were the firm who built Stamford House, but unfortunately they went into liquidation shortly after it was completed.

26. The Station Hotel and Adjoining Retail Premises, Stamford New Road, Altrincham

The Station Hotel is so named due to its proximity to the former Altrincham railway station, now Altrincham Interchange and Metrolink line. The buildings are Grade II listed and of late nineteenth-century construction. They are built of red brick with painted stone dressings to the hotel and some moulded red terracotta ornaments, which have been mirrored on the frontages of Stamford House (Station Buildings) directly opposite. The roof is a slate design and of standard nineteenth-century construction. The Station Hotel is double-fronted, with the retail premises to the right single-fronted. Over the decades there have been various back extensions to the retail premises, which would have undoubtedly been utilised for the various businesses undertaken by the building. The building's style is described as 'eclectic'.

The Station Hotel consists of three storeys and it is almost symmetrical in design. Above the eaves the hotel has an elaborate Dutch gable, with a panel containing the lettering 'Station Hotel'. It originally had a panelled island bar inside with curved corners. The shopfront to the right of the Station Hotel is the original outline of the nineteenth-century building. It is divided into three sections at ground level and has a recessed entrance to the

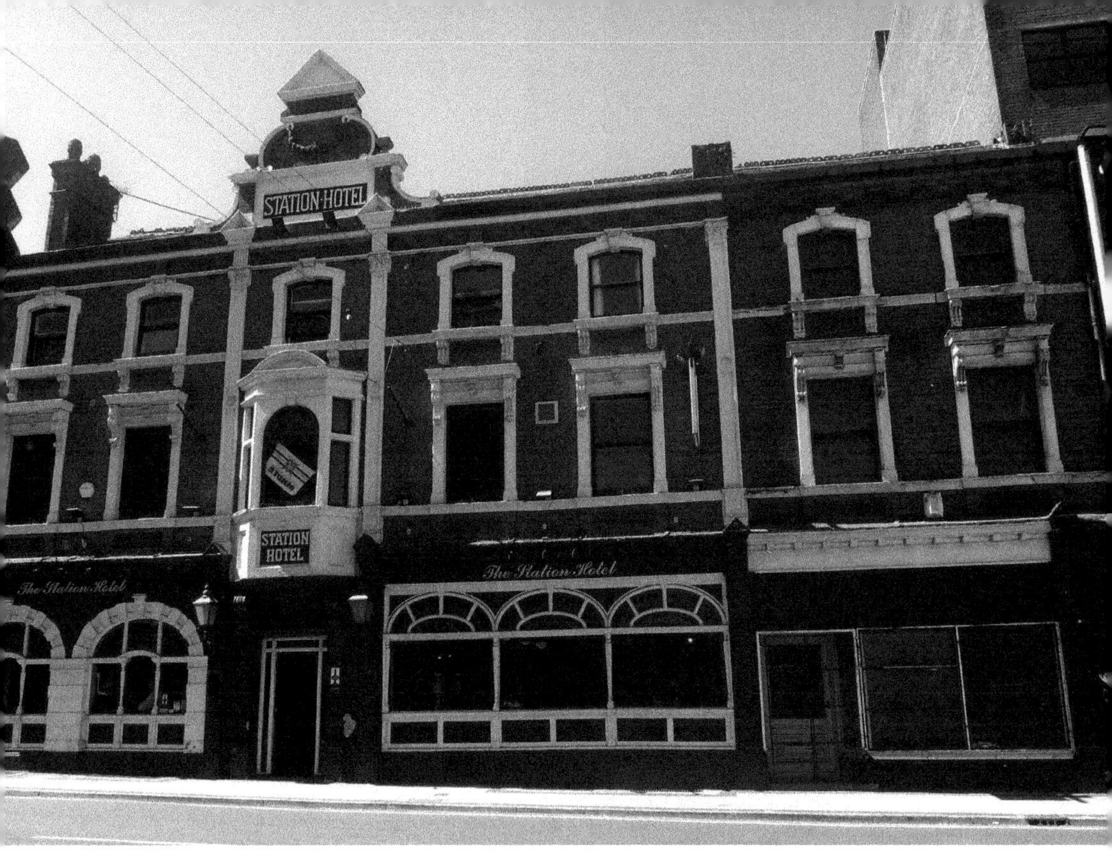

Above: Façade of the Station Hotel and shop, Stamford New Road.

Below left: Side elevation of the Station Hotel, Stamford New Road.

Below right: Station Hotel, Stamford New Road, from Altrincham Interchange.

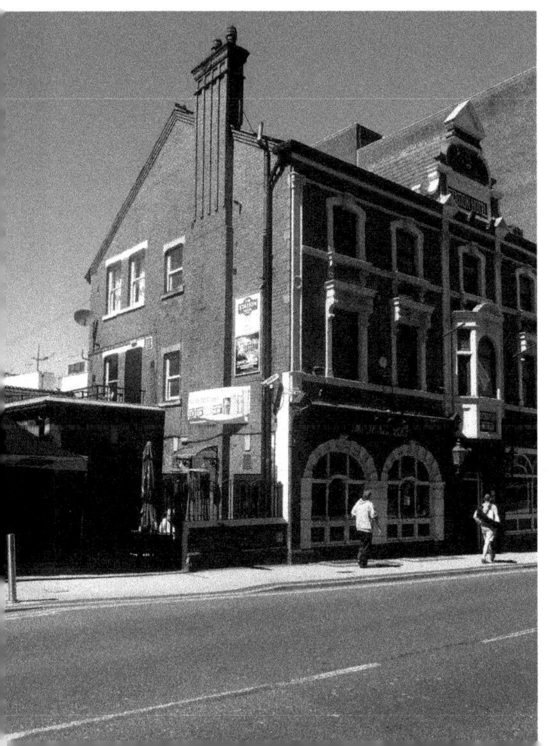

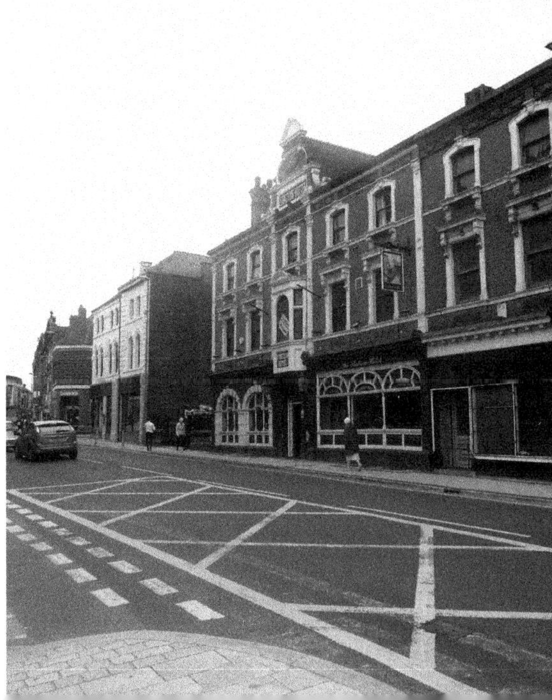

left and plate-glass windows, although it would appear to be vacant at the moment. The upper floors have decoration matching the hotel next door.

The Station Hotel and the adjoining retail premises form a group with the clock tower and Stamford House (Station Buildings) opposite, together marking the northern boundary of the conservation area. These buildings mark the development of this area of Stamford New Road, from the late nineteenth and early twentieth centuries. The Station Hotel, as the name suggests, was built with passengers arriving from the railway station in mind and the conservation area would be their first view of the town on travelling from, or arriving at, the station. Therefore, it was built to be eye-catching and to impress the viewer, and with so many architectural styles it does exactly that.

27. Clock Tower, Altrincham Interchange, Stamford New Road

The clock tower was built on the forecourt of Altrincham station around 1880 and is a Grade II-listed building. It is in brick on a stone plinth, and has a square plan, three stages, a moulded band, a dogtooth band and a cornice on coupled brackets. There is a doorway on the south-east side and a semicircular headed window in the other sides in both lower stages, all with stone surrounds and polychromatic voussoirs. The windows are sashes. In the top stage is a clock face on each side, over which are dentilled pediments.

The town's earliest and first railway station was sited near to the level crossing at Stockport Road. In 1849, Bowdon Station was opened on land fronting Railway Street. The *Venus* was the first engine to work the railway, sixty-five passengers making the inaugural journey in 1849. The station site extended eastwards to a point where it joined

Altrincham Station and Clock Tower, Stamford New Road, *c.* 1910.

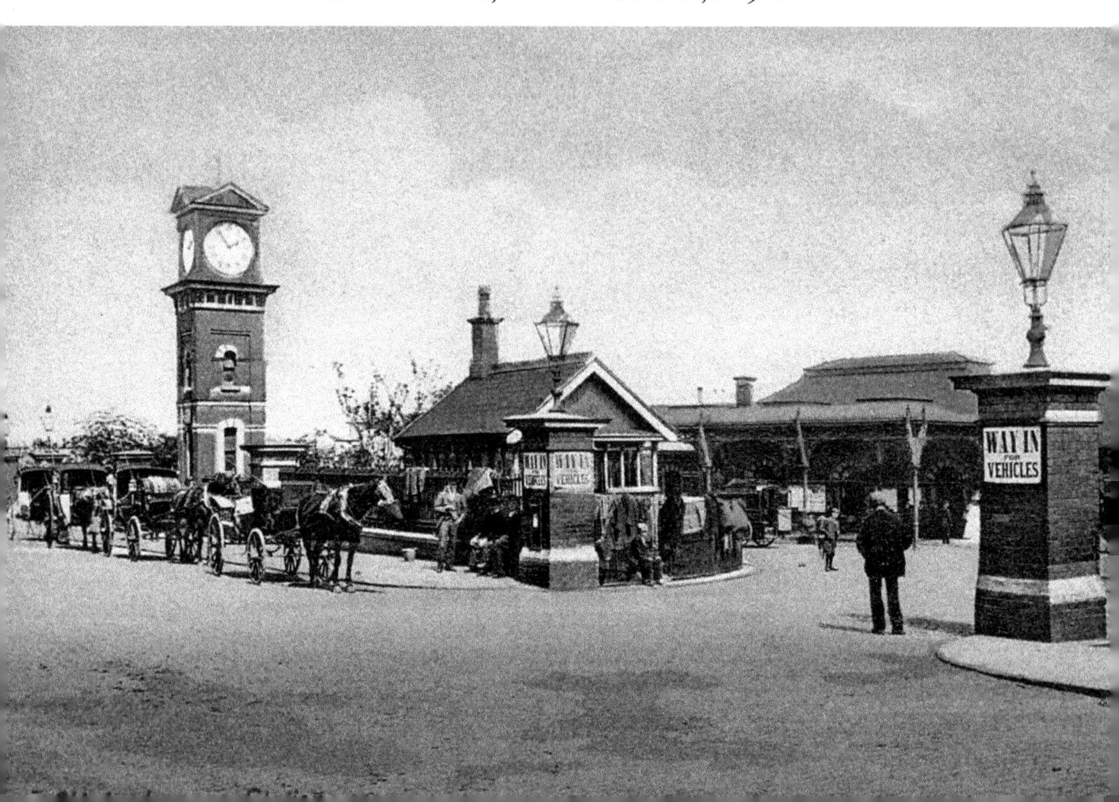

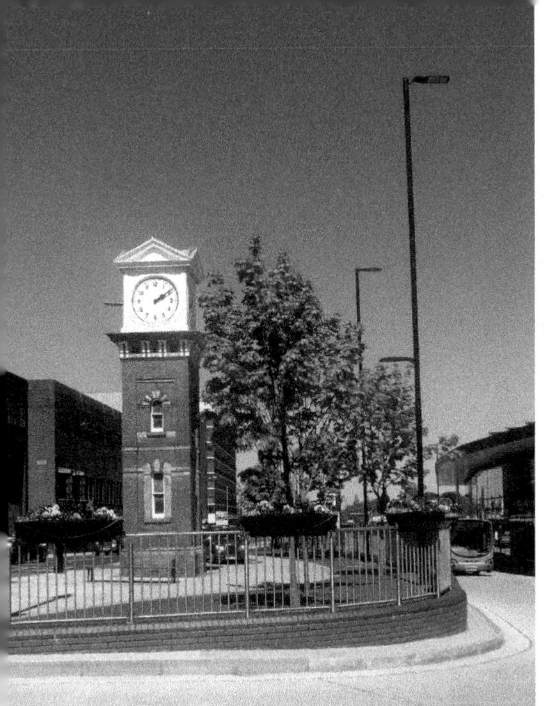

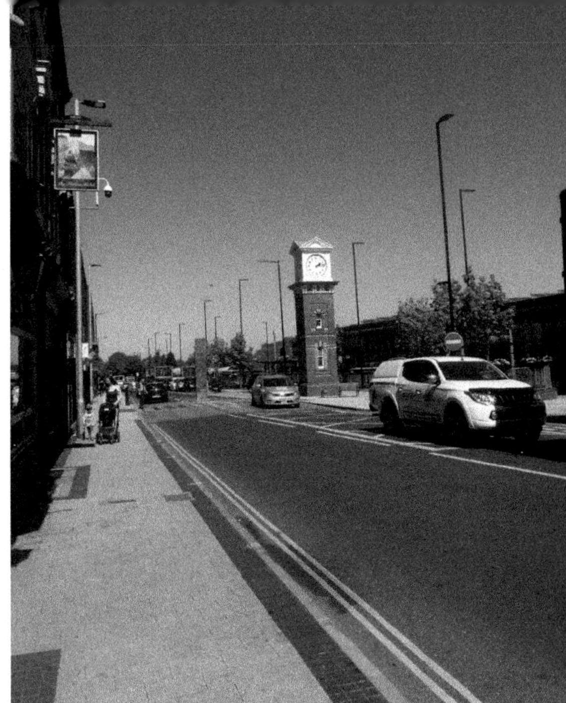

Above left: Clock Tower, Altrincham Interchange, Stamford New Road.

Above right: Clock Tower from the Station Hotel, Stamford New Road.

Hale Moss and was known as the Pinfold (later Lloyd Street.) A row of single-storey shops was erected around 1895 (now the new hospital) along that side of Railway Street. The old station at the rear remained there until around 1965–70, as a carriage repair shed and depot, when it was demolished.

Railway Street was extended into Stamford New Road around 1880 to give access to the new station, with the growth of the town. The station clock tower was constructed at the same time. To achieve access a number of old buildings had to be demolished including Thomas Faulkner's thatched cottage, more than 200 years old (in whose memory the Faulkner's Arms Inn was erected on the opposite side of the road). The adjoining Orange Tree Inn was also demolished at the same time, the name being transferred to the premises opposite the Unicorn Hotel in Old Market Place. On part of what was once the site of the original Orange Tree Inn the Stamford Hotel was built, which was burned down, rebuilt again in Victorian style and finally demolished around 1965 to make way for the Graftons development.

28. Altrincham Interchange, Stamford New Road

When the tramway service ceased in 1931, Manchester South Junction and Altrincham Railway opened to electric trains from London Road, Manchester, to Altrincham, in the same year. The Pioneer system was purpose-built for the electrification of the Altrincham line. It served a rapidly growing residential district between the two destinations. The line was approximately 8.75 miles (14.08 kilometres) in length. The railway served local suburban populations and linked into the national network, including nearby Chester. This was one of many changes to Altrincham's rail services.

The first railway station served Altrincham from 1849–81 and was constructed by the MSJ&AR. It opened in July 1849 and was originally located just south of Stockport Road level crossing, near its junction with Stamford Street. It remained here until 4 April 1881, when Altrincham and Bowdon station, now the Interchange, opened. Bowdon station to the south, at the junction of Railway Street and Lloyd Street, closed at the same time. There are no surviving remains of the Bowdon station site. Gone also are Altrincham's North Signal Box, which opened in April 1908 and was decommissioned 7 July 1991, with South Signal Box decommissioned 14 July 1968.

The station changed its name to Altrincham on 6 May 1974 and in 1975 a new booking office was opened on platform four and work to convert the forecourt on Stamford New Road into a bus station began, with the canopy over the entrance removed. It reopened in November 1976 as Altrincham Interchange. On 15 June 1992 Metrolink opened, with the Interchange later completely redeveloped, officially reopening on 7 December 2014. Other changes include Altrincham goods yard closing on 8 October 1966 and the level crossing closing on 30 October 1978, to be replaced by a bridge carrying the A560 over the railway and Metrolink lines.

Manchester to Altrincham electric trains ceased on 24 December 1991, with platforms one and two later reopening for Metrolink trams. A new roof for platform one was constructed in 2006 and the station clock tower, built in 1880, on Stamford New Road remains as a Grade II-listed structure. Altrincham Interchange has four platforms in total, with two through platforms for services between Manchester Piccadilly and Chester, via Stockport.

Below left: New development at Altrincham Interchange, Stamford New Road.

Below right: Altrincham Interchange from the railway bridge, Moss Lane.

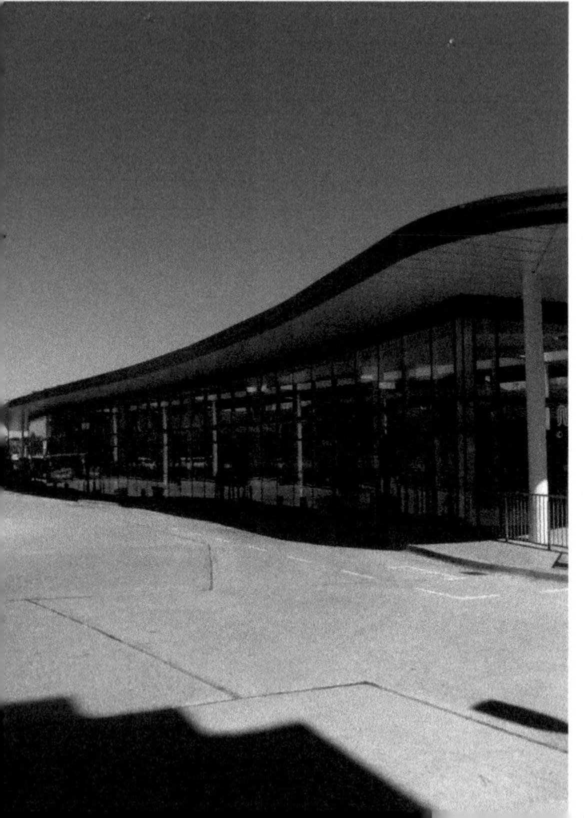

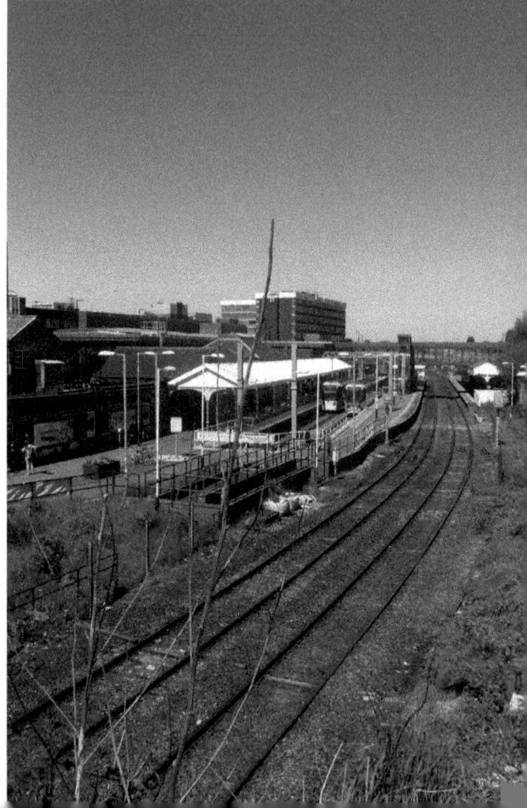

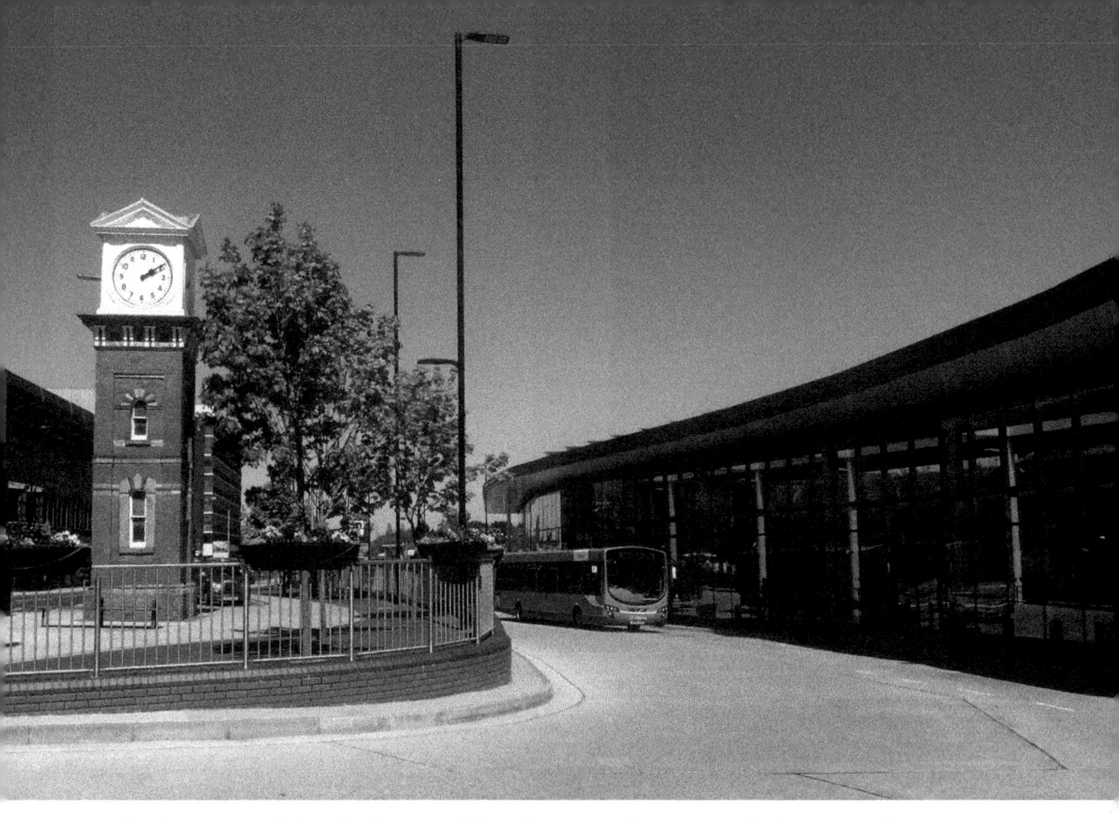

New development and the Clock Tower, Altrincham Interchange, Stamford New Road.

29. Altrincham Ice Dome, Oakfield Road

The concept of an ice rink for the town of Altrincham had been at the forefront of Albert Allen's considerations from the 1940s. Allen was a local businessman and builder, who in 1948 had been collecting signatures on a petition in support of constructing an ice rink in Didsbury, when he met Ken Bailey, who was involved in an ice show. The Didsbury ice rink was never built due to planning difficulties, but Allen brought to fruition his ultimate desire to build an ice rink in Altrincham.

Altrincham Ice Rink opened on 2 December 1960, and 2,000 people attended on the first night. The Grand Ice Gala of the opening night featured an exhibition from Sjoukie Dijkstra, who was the champion of Europe and the world at this time, and who later won a gold medal for her home country, Holland.

At the time of the ice rink's twenty-first birthday, in 1981, there was a visit from the reigning British, European and World Ice Dance Champions, Jane Torvill and Christopher Dean, who later became gold medallists at the Olympic Games. From 1960 the rink was owned and operated by Allen as chairman, with K. N. G. Bailey as managing director, but on 2 February 1987 it was taken over by Derek C. Thompson. At the time the rink supported Altrincham Ice Speed Skating Club and the Aces Ice Hockey Club. Today Altrincham Ice Dome has a capacity of 2,140 seats and up to 300 standing places. It hosts the home fixtures of the Manchester Storm and Altrincham Aces Ice Hockey clubs and Trafford Tornadoes juniors. It is also open to the public and gives lessons. It was previously home to the Manchester Phoenix until there was a legal dispute in 2014–15.

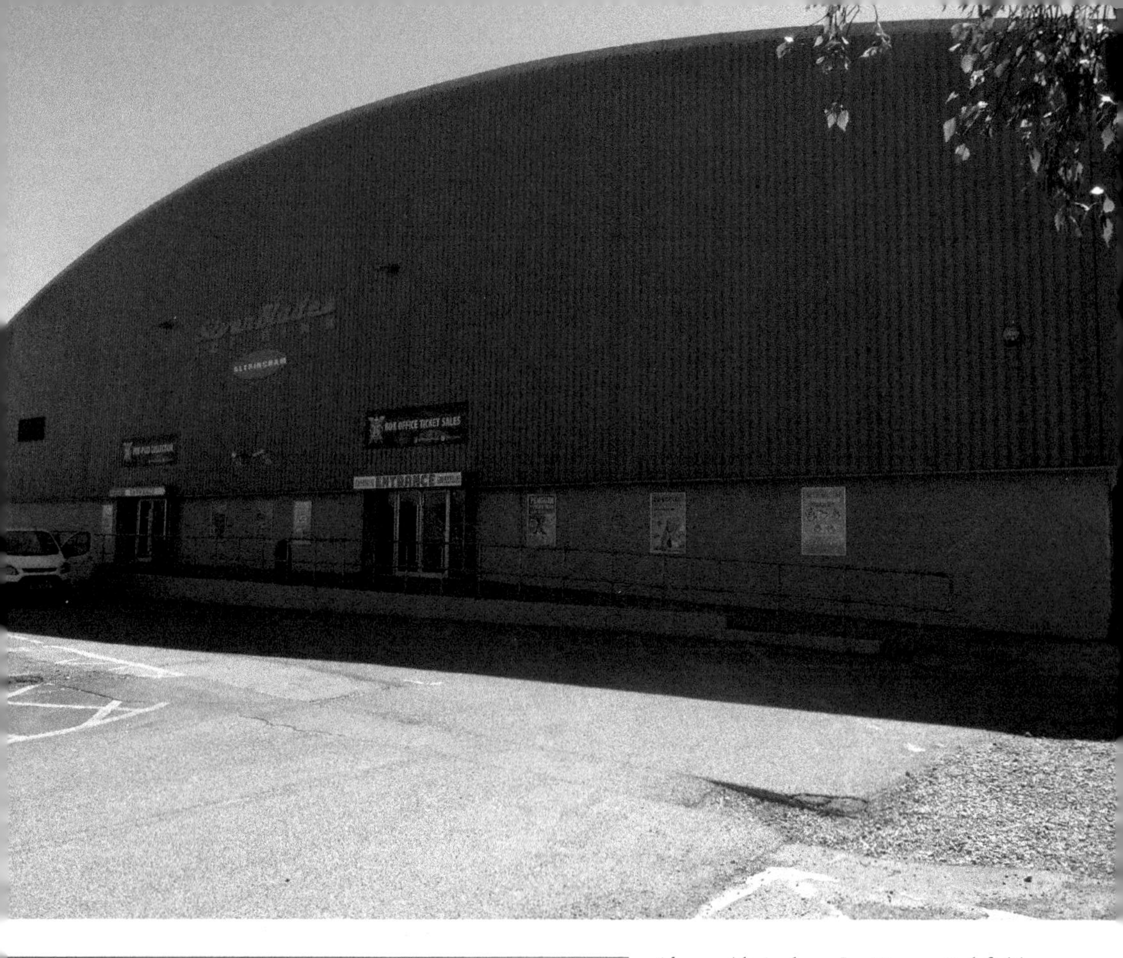

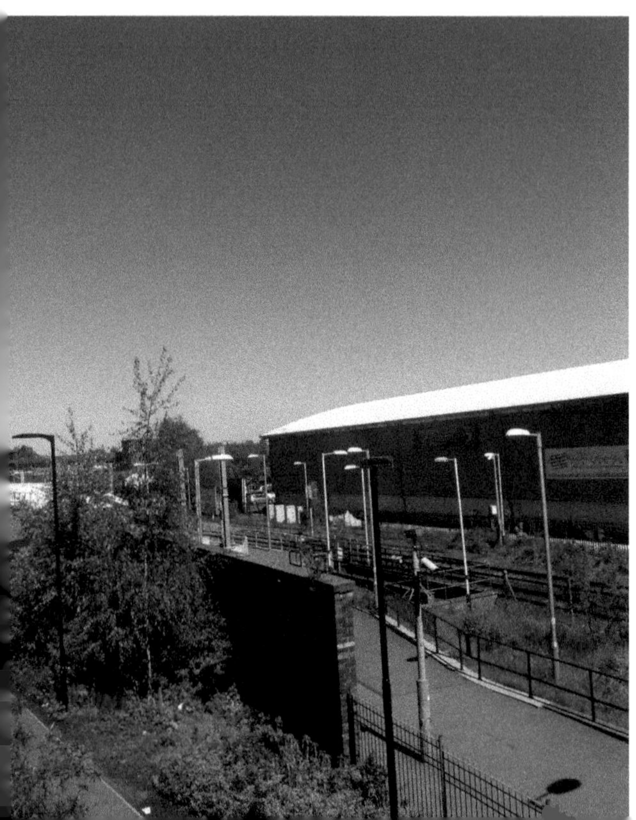

Above: Altrincham Ice Dome, Oakfield Road.

Left: The Ice Dome from Moss Lane.

The Dome replaced Altrincham Ice Rink, which closed in 2003. The Ice Dome is a pre-fabricated structure with a wooden and steel frame, constructed in Finland. Assembly began in August 2006 and cost around £2.5 million. After delays, the first game took place in February 2007 against Basingstoke Bison. Originally built as a semi-permanent structure, the dome is now to be made permanent and will undergo the necessary alterations for this development.

30. Altrincham Football Club, Moss Lane

The football club was founded around 1891 as the Rigby Memorial Club, formed from a local Sunday school. They eventually formed Broadheath FC and were founder members of the Manchester League in 1893. Today, they are the only founder members of the Manchester League still in existence.

Pollit's Field became their home and they changed their name to Altrincham AFC. For the start of the 1910/11 season Altrincham adopted Moss Lane (capacity 6,085) as their headquarters after an agreement with the Urban District Council. Moss Lane was officially opened on 3 September 1910; Macclesfield won 3-1. Altrincham then joined the Lancashire Combination Second Division for season 1911/12 and were promoted at the first attempt. In 1919, they were founder members of the newly formed Cheshire League and won the Cheshire League Cup in 1932/33 and the Cheshire Senior Cup the following year. They were runners-up in the league in 1935/36. Notable post-war achievements included winning the Cheshire League title in back-to-back seasons in the years 1966 and 1967, and they were runners-up in 1968. In 1968, they also became founder members of the newly formed Northern Premier League and went on to establish themselves as one of the leading non-league clubs in the country over the next fifteen years.

Altrincham Football Club, Moss Lane, showing landmark radio mast.

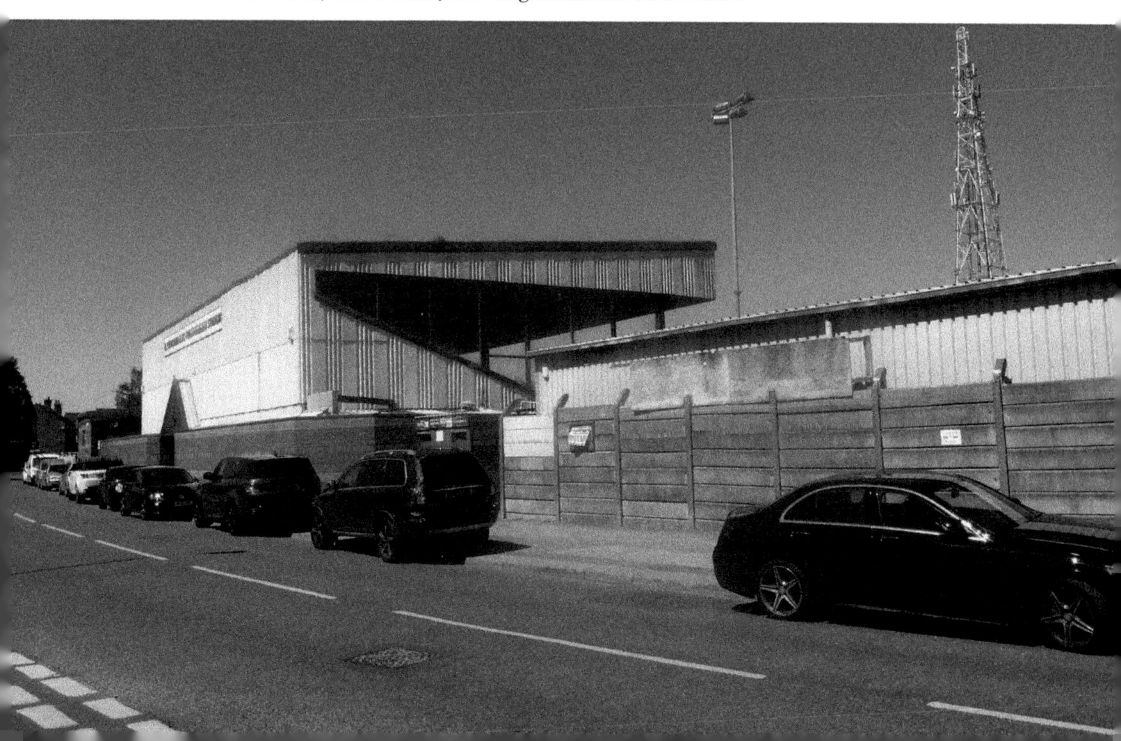

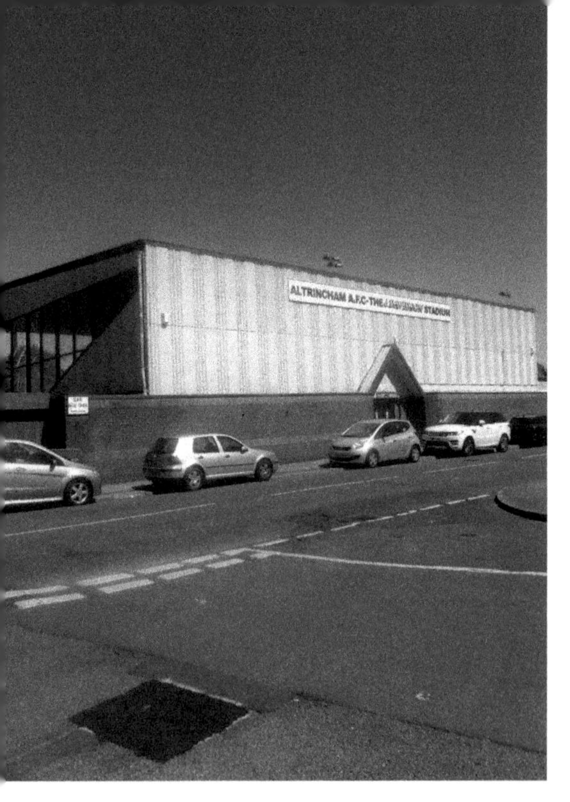

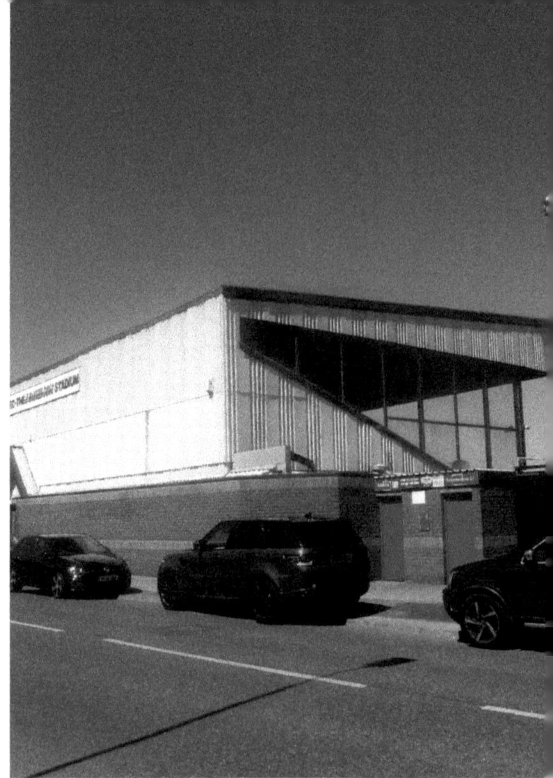

Above left: Altrincham Football Club, Moss Lane.

Above right: Altrincham Football Club's Main Stand, Moss Lane.

The club became well known for their FA Cup exploits and they also won the FA Trophy at Wembley in 1978, the Northern Premier League Cup in 1970 and were the losing finalists in 1974, before finishing runners-up in their final season in the Northern Premier League. In 1979 they were founder members of the Alliance Premier League, winning the title in its first two seasons, as well as the Bob Lord Trophy in 1980/81. They won the FA Trophy in 1986 and continued their FA Cup exploits. However, they were relegated for the first time in 1996/97. The 2017/18 season has seen them gain promotion at the first attempt from the Evo-Stik Premier League back into the Vanarama National League North.

31. Altrincham Garrick Playhouse, Barrington Road

The Altrincham Garrick Society was founded in November 1913 by Walter S. Nixon of Springfield Road. At a meeting in the Trader's Room, on Market Street, 2 December 1913, the Altrincham Society formally came into being, with W. S. Nixon elected as chairman, A.P. Hill as treasurer, and Frank Kenyon as secretary. A permanent headquarters was provided by J. W. Byrom, who offered the use of a large basement under his drapery store at Kingsway. This became the Little Cellar Theatre and committee rooms.

The first play performed by the society was *The Silver Box* by John Galsworthy, at the Public Hall. Encouraged by George Bernard Shaw, the Garrick Playhouse was eventually built. Jack Byrom cut the first sod. Plans to build the Garrick Playhouse were prepared to the designs of T. Harold Hill. This was the first local theatre to be specially built for its

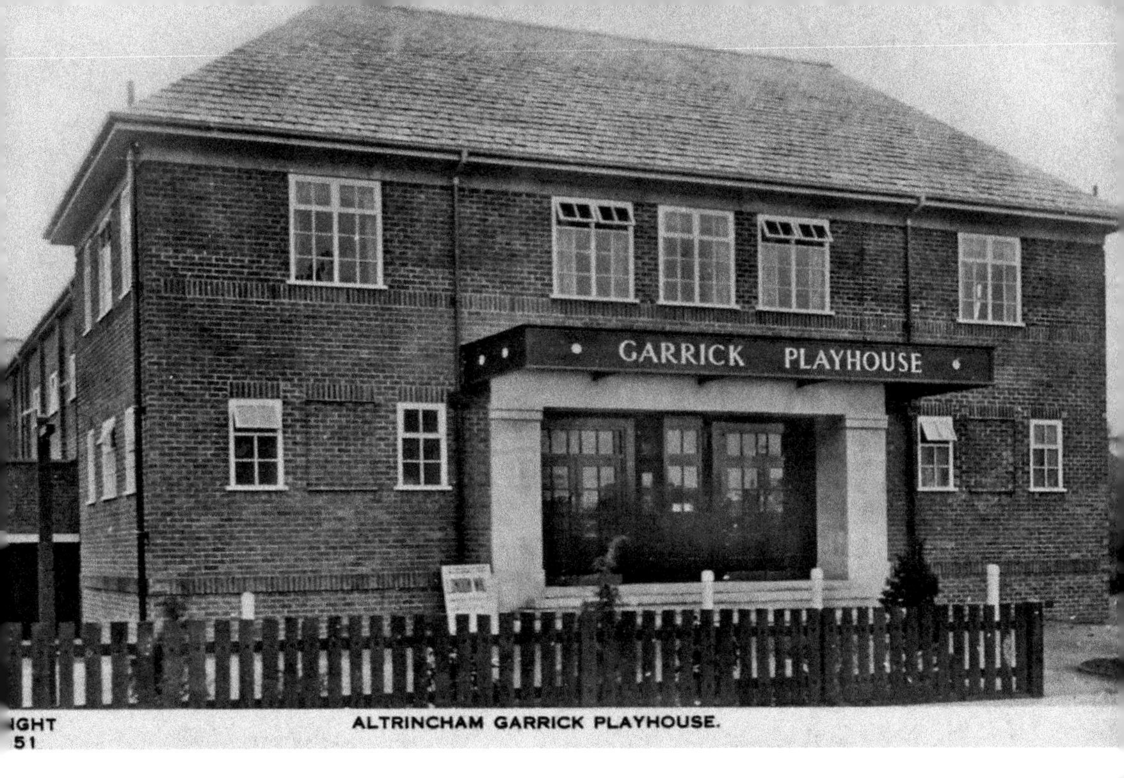

Above: Altrincham Garrick Playhouse, Barrington Road, *c.* 1950.

Right: *As You Are*. March 2–9, 1946. Programme of the Altrincham Garrick Society.

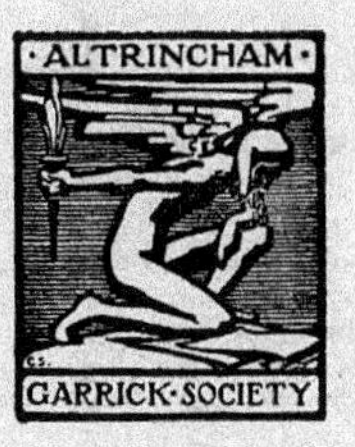

As You Are

By HUGH MILLS & WELLS ROOT.

AT THE PLAYHOUSE,

Saturday to Saturday,
MARCH 2nd to 9th, 1946.

Programme :: Fourpence.

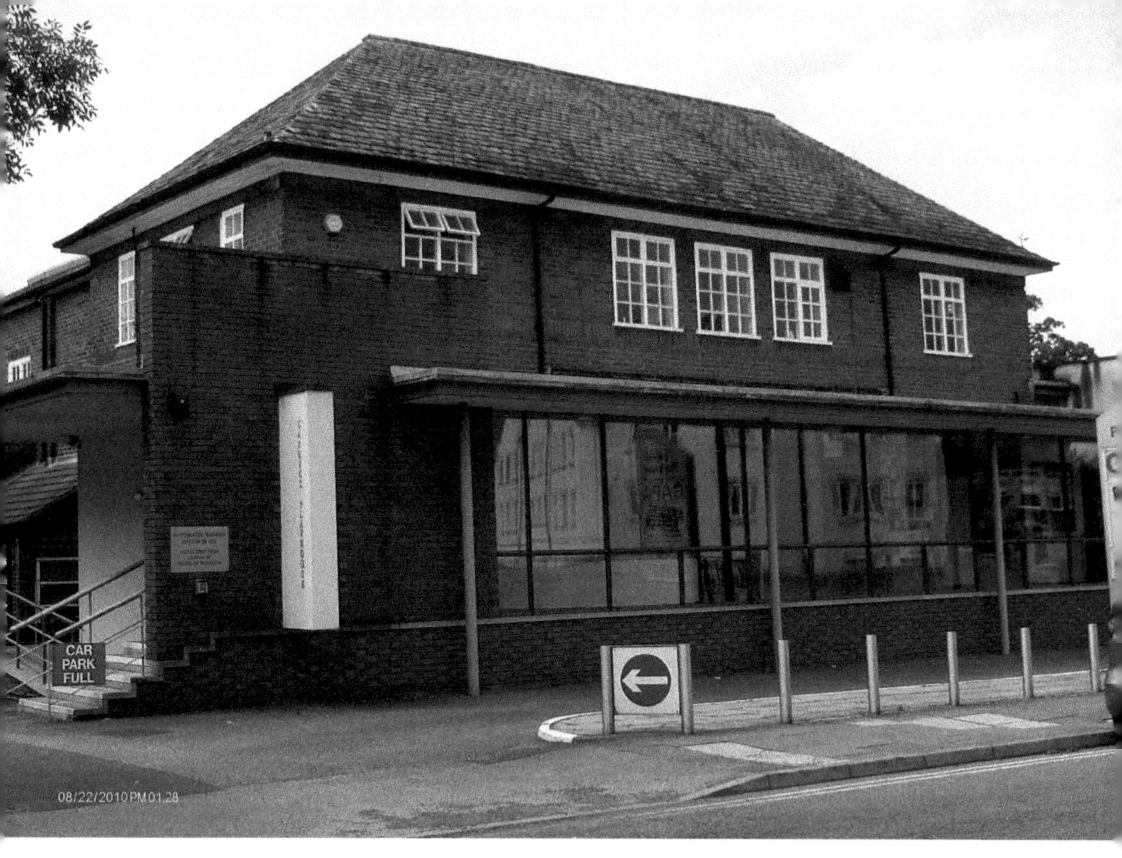

Altrincham Garrick Playhouse, Barrington Road, today.

purpose by any amateur society in Great Britain. It was designed to have a very large stage, slightly wider than that at the Manchester Opera House, with an auditorium of 500 seats. There were large workshops for scenery making, a scenery dock and a rehearsal room and offices. A car park for 300 cars was also part of the plan. It was constructed by Charles Pennington of Hale and opened by the president, P. M. Oliver, on 1 October 1932. The total cost of the construction of the new theatre was around £9,000.

The first play performed was *The Immortal Lady* by Clifford Bax. Some of the plays of local playwright Ronald Gow, which were performed by the society, received their premiere performance in Altrincham. Among other plays performed in its early years were *The Widowing of Mrs. Holroyd* by D. H. Lawrence, which was given its first production by the players. *The Farmer's Wife* by Eden Phillpotts went on to achieve success on the London stage, as did *If Four Walls Told* by Edward Percy. These, among others, helped to establish the company as a leading competitor in the world of theatre. Today the theatre remains an important landmark in the town.

32. Bowdon Parish Church, Stamford Road

There are four districts in this area: Dunham Massey, Warburton, Bowdon and Bowdon Vale, of which Bowdon is the largest ward in the Metropolitan Borough of Trafford (formed in 1974. Bowdon was, before this date, historically a part of Cheshire. From 1894 Bowdon was known as Bowdon Urban District. Prior to this it was Bowdon Local Board, 1864, and then

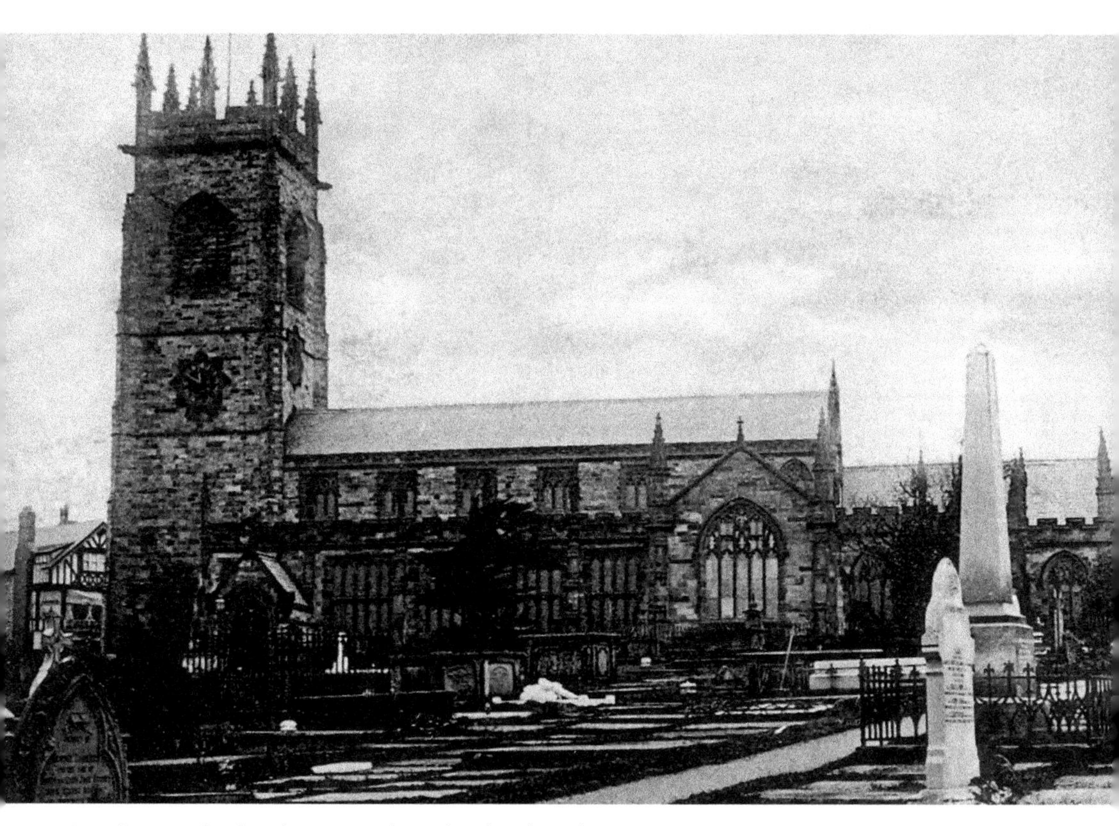

Bowdon Parish Church in 1905, from the churchyard.

Bowdon Urban Sanitary District, 1875–94. The church is sited on an area of higher ground in the centre of the village, with the Griffin public house opposite Bowdon parish church. There has been a church at this location since Saxon times, with a small community established in the seventh century by Archbishop Theodore. A small fragment of an eighth-century Saxon cross has been found here, as well as a fragment of Saxon carving, probably tenth century.

Bowdon is mentioned in the Domesday Book of 1086, with a mill, church and parish priest, at 'Bogedone', which means bow-shaped hill, held by the Norman Hamon de Masci (Massey). In around 1100 the church was rebuilt in stone and in around 1320 a tower and other alterations were added. Effigies with tombs appeared in the church in the fifteenth century. Then in 1510, at the time of Henry VIII, it was partially rebuilt, but not completed. By the early sixteenth century it was fashionable to erect memorial windows, but at Bowdon it was the late sixteenth century before any major changes were made. The new window designs made ideal 'frames' for memorial glass, which was in great demand at the time. Remodelling at this time included a tower housing bells.

In 1856, Archdeacon William Pollock became vicar, which led to the church building of 1510 being demolished in 1858. It was replaced by a new church, which incorporated only a few parts of the old structure. The new church opened on 27 September 1860, costing £12,372 – expensive by nineteenth-century standards and partly due to the quality of the building and its design, which is largely unchanged today. The church is now known as St Mary's with St Luke's.

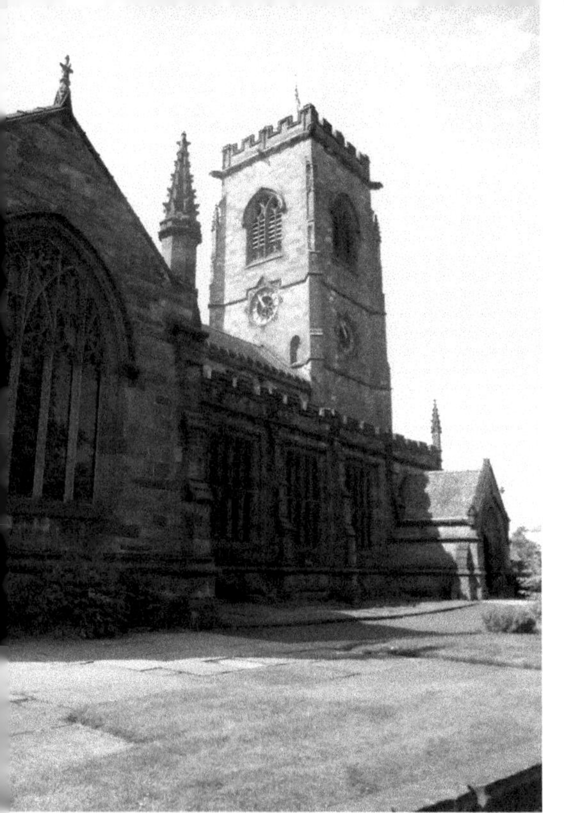

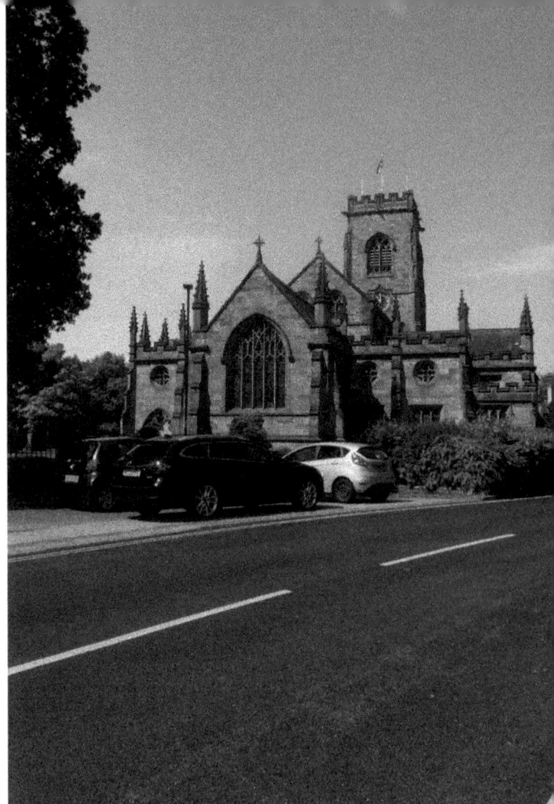

Above left: Bowdon Parish Church from the churchyard looking south.

Above right: Bowdon Parish Church from Stamford Road.

33. Church Brow Cottages, Church Brow, Bowdon

The original photograph dates from around 1904. The right-hand cottage was occupied by a Miss Lightfoot, joint owner with her sister of nearby Lightfoot's Tea Garden. The second cottage was originally one house and was once occupied by Mr Sutton, caretaker at Bowdon Assembly Rooms. Below him lived John Hassall, of Alderley's Farm, Bowdon. In the fifth cottage lived Ann and John Taylor, a teamsman at Alderley's Farm. The cottage below the passage was thatched up to 1914. The Grade II-listed Bowdon Old Forge is also located here.

The cottages along Church Brow were first Grade II listed on 9 August 1979 and are located on the north-west side of Park Road, Bowdon. No. 1 Church Brow is a house constructed in the eighteenth century, with bricks of various types and a sloping slate roof. The original construction of the house is two bays wide by one room deep and two storeys. Sometime in the twentieth century a flat-roofed extension was constructed on the right of the property (now pitched). All the windows have modern casements and there are a total of three windows in the gable, as well as a ridge stack. Nos 5 and 6 Church Brow are two cottages constructed in the eighteenth century, of Flemish bond brickwork and a sloping slate roof. Each cottage is one bay wide with two storeys, and sometime in the twentieth century they originally had extensions to the rear. Each cottage has doors to its right and flat-headed windows to each floor, with twentieth- and twenty-first-century casements. Both

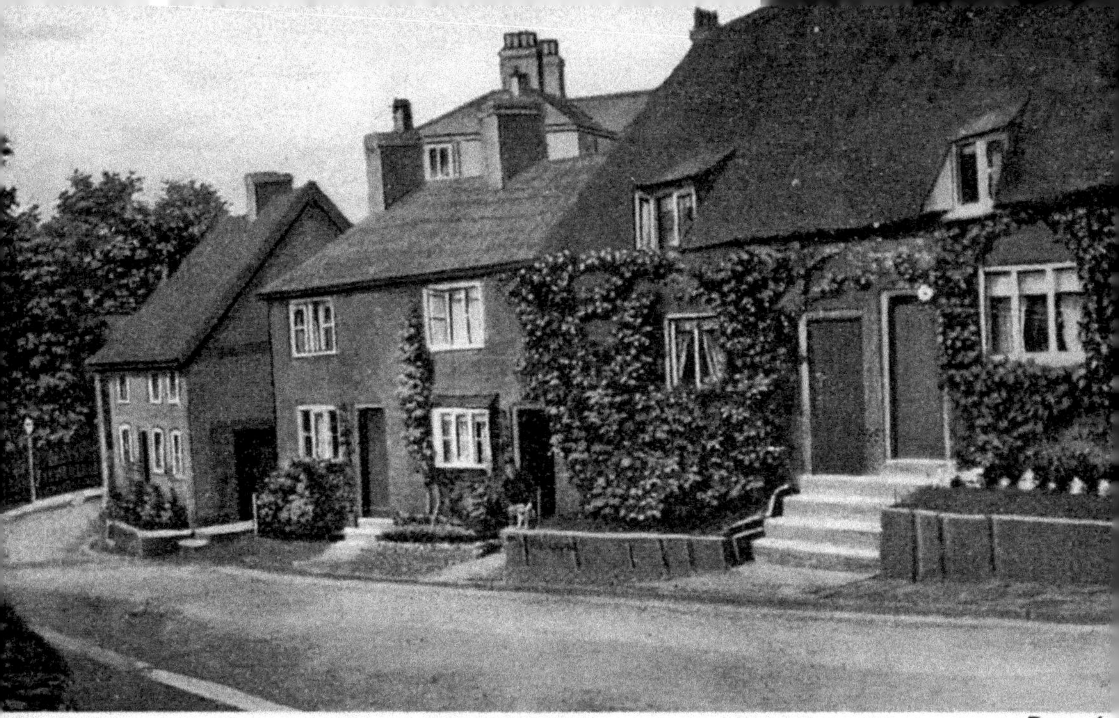

Above: Nos 5 and 6 Church Brow Cottages (centre), Bowdon, in 1904.

Below left: No. 7 Church Brow Cottages and the Old Forge, Bowdon.

Below right: No. 1 Church Brow Cottages, Bowdon.

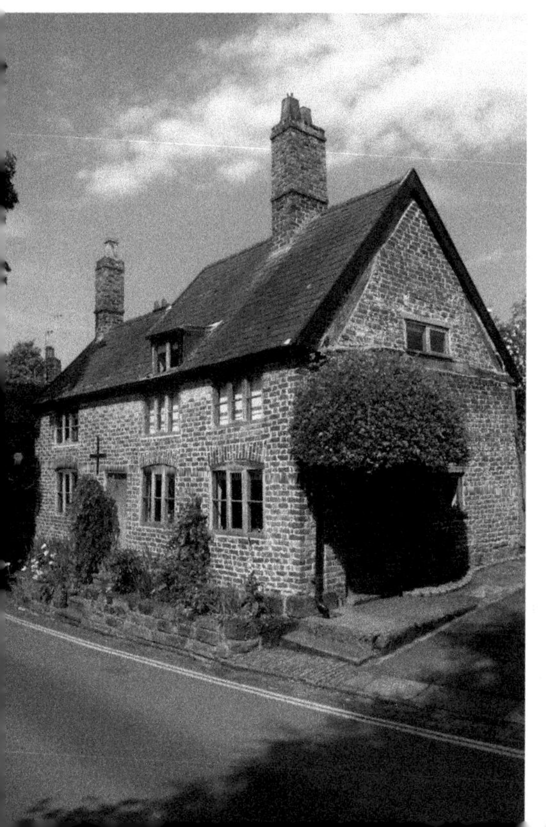

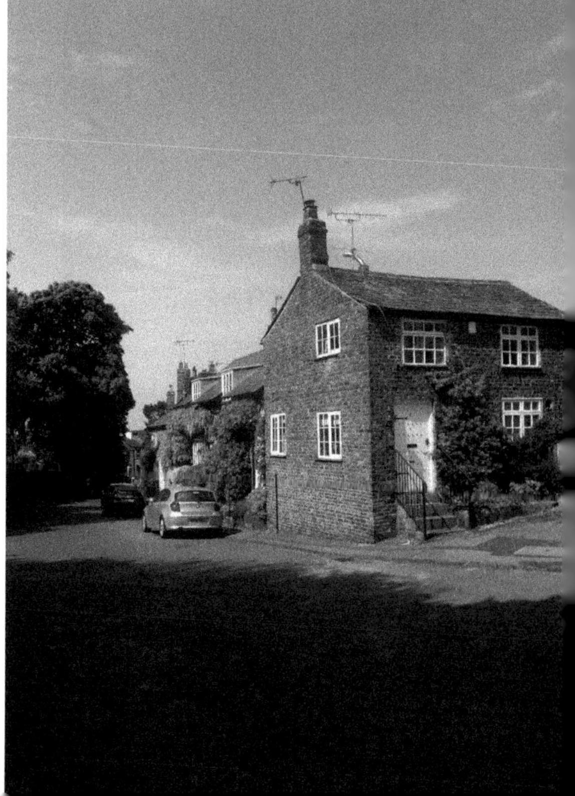

have ridge stacks to the left. No. 7 Church Brow is a house of the eighteenth century, which incorporates earlier work. Flemish bond brickwork is present, as is timber framing, both in the gable (which has an exposed tie-beam truss) and to the rear of the property. Today there is a slate roof, which was originally thatch. The remaining Grade II-listed buildings at Church Brow are Bowdon Old Forge and Nos 8, 9 and 10. These buildings are of brick with slate roofs, the old forge reminding us of Bowdon's former time as an agricultural village.

34. Bowdon Downs Congregational Church, Bowdon Road

Bowdon Downs Congregational Church building is located on the south-west side of Bowdon Road. Built 1847–48 and Grade II listed, it was originally a Congregational church and later a Pentecostal church, and was extended, with transepts and galleries, in 1868. The lecture room was added in 1882 and the west porch in 1921, as a memorial to those church members who fell in the First World War.

The church is in dressed sandstone with a Westmorland slate roof, and consists of a wide nave, north, south and west porches, west gallery, transepts (each with a gallery), a schoolroom, and a vestry. The lecture room and ancillary rooms extend to the south-west along Bowdon Road. Above the west porch is a five-light perpendicular window, small canopied niches and a coped gable with an ornate finial. In the church are three rose windows. The lecture room has one storey, eight bays, three coped gables, and a tall fleche to the lecture hall roof. The interior was constructed with west doors incorporating an iron daisy motif lattice. There were traceried timber screens, two-bay transepts with columns

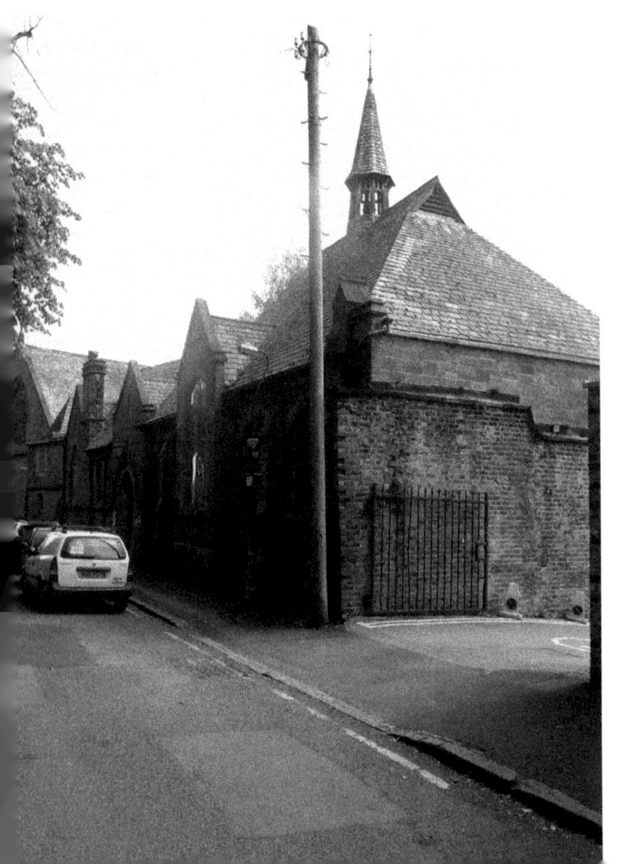

Bowdon Downs Congregational Church, Bowdon Road.

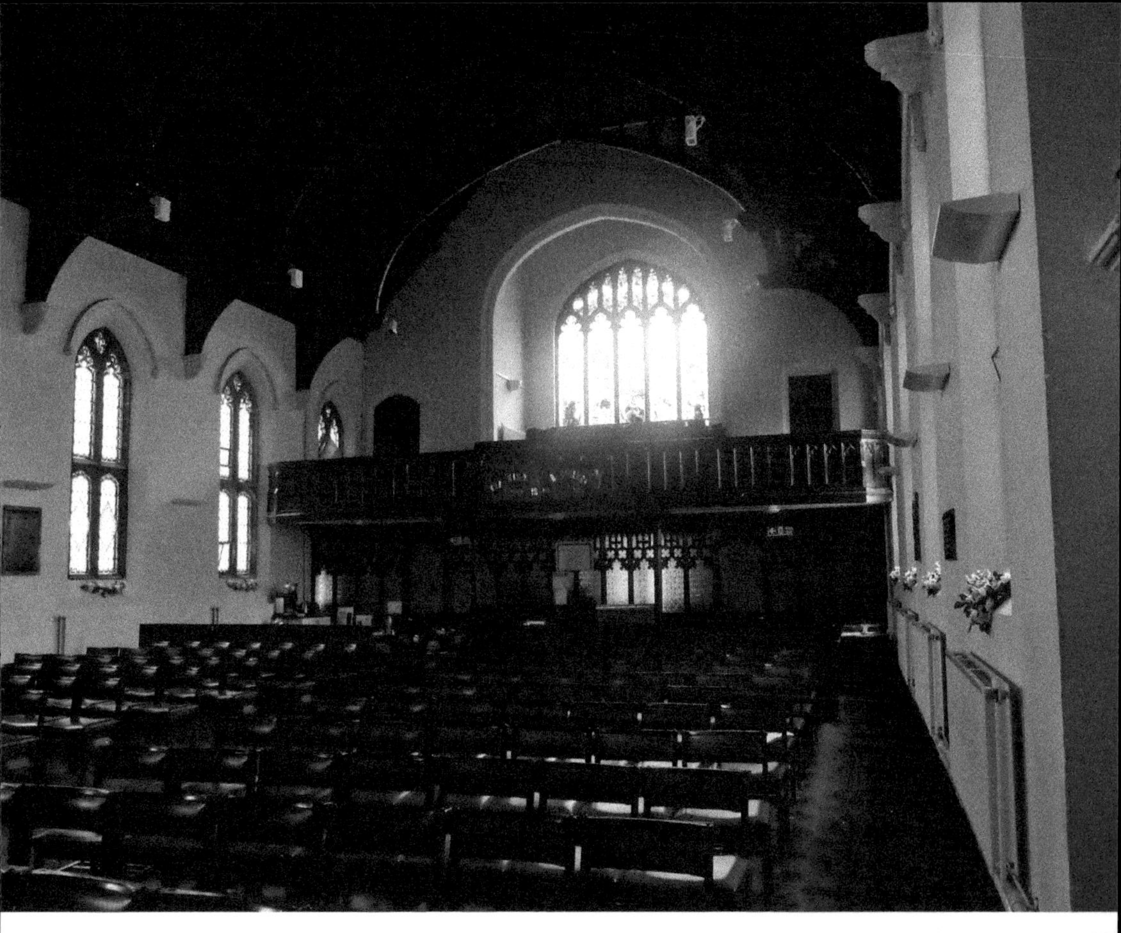

Above: Church interior, showing the West Gallery.

Right: Church interior, showing the transepts with galleries.

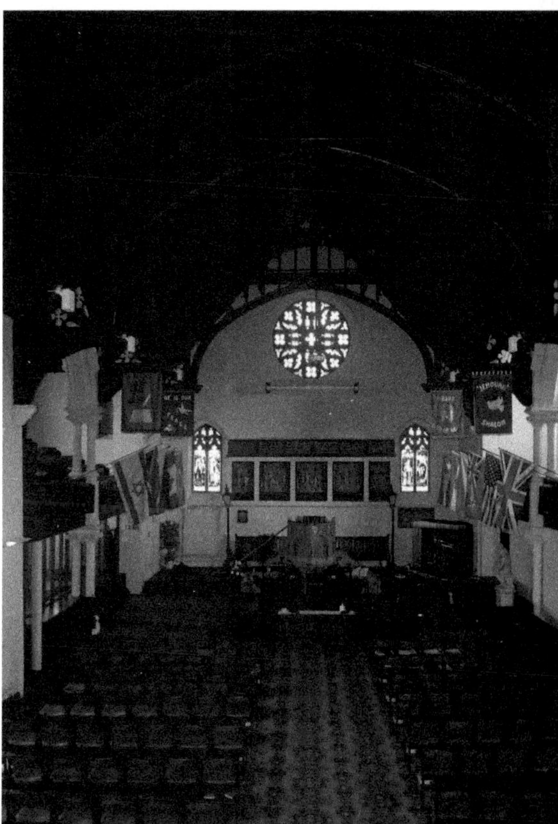

incorporating foliated heads and an arch-braced hammer beam roof. There was also a carved frieze behind the central octagonal stone pulpit designed for, but rejected by, Queen Victoria. A marble statue of Mary and Martha was in memory of Jesse Haworth, 1930. The building has good-quality stained glass throughout, including the lecture hall.

In 1974, the church closed its doors for the last time. In its place was instituted the United Reform church, founded through an amalgamation of other Nonconformist churches and congregations. The decision was taken to use the former Trinity Presbyterian church in Delamer Road as a central headquarters for worship. The then Upper Room Church bought it and it opened for services in November 1978. The iron gateways, in the courtyard and on Bowdon Road, were erected in 1984. Among the members of the Congregational church was the Bowdon-born Cheshire naturalist and author Thomas Alfred Coward. Also a member was Isaac Watts, who was secretary of the Cotton Supply Association, writing its history and editing its journal.

35. St Peter's Church, Ashley Road, Hale

The church was dedicated on 16 June 1892. It was originally a chapel to St Mary's Church (Bowdon) and from 1906 a district church for part of the township of Hale. It was previously served by St Mary's, and St John the Evangelist, Altrincham. The church was needed to serve the growing suburbs of Altrincham. From 2007 to 26 January 2015 Libby Lane was vicar of the combined benefice of St Peter's in Hale and St Elizabeth's in Ashley. She was the first woman to be appointed as a bishop by the Church of England.

On 4 July 1889 it was agreed that a Mission church should be built near Peel Causeway (later Hale) railway station. This was in order to provide for the growing population's

St Peter's Church, Ashley Road, Hale, in 1934.

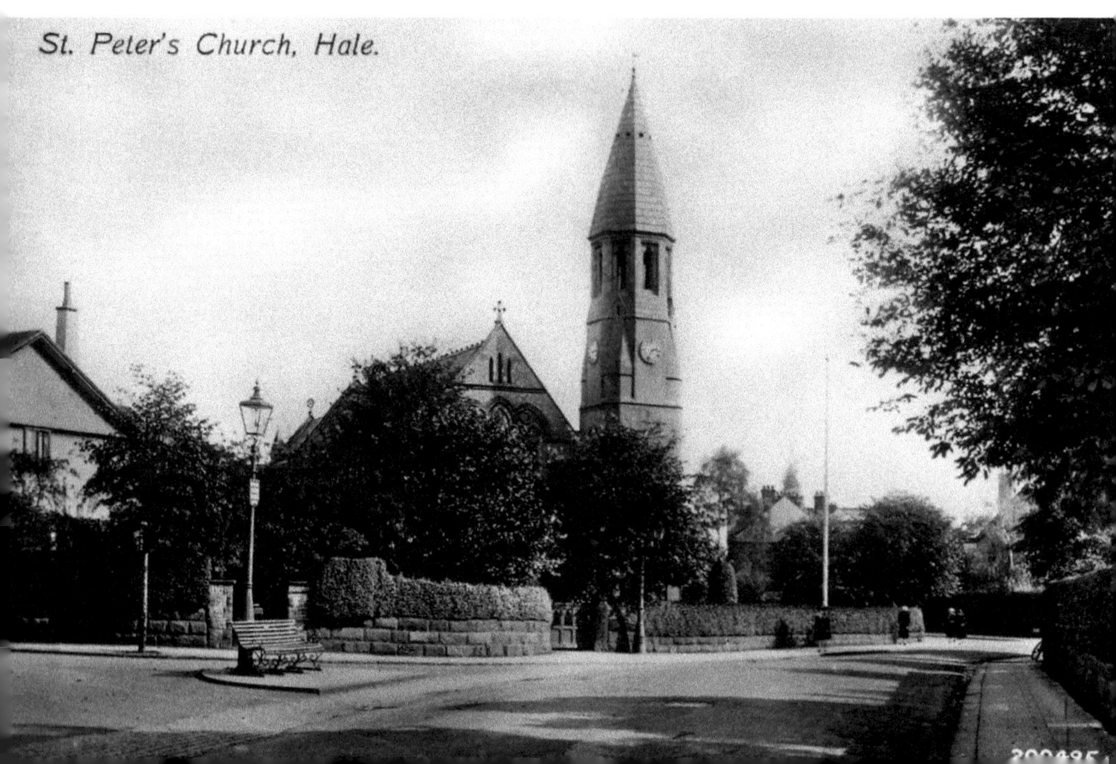

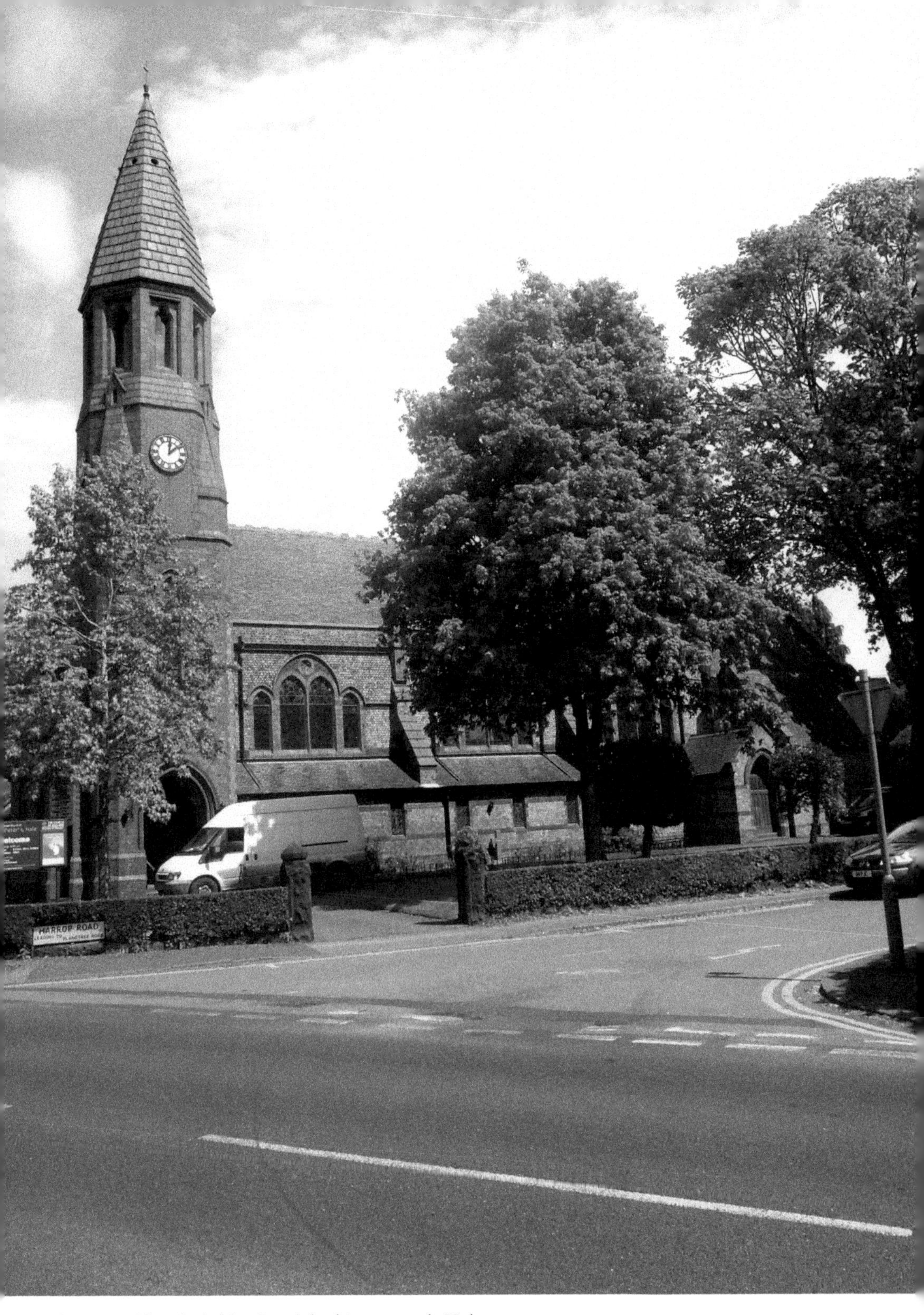

St Peter's Church, Ashley Road, looking towards Hale.

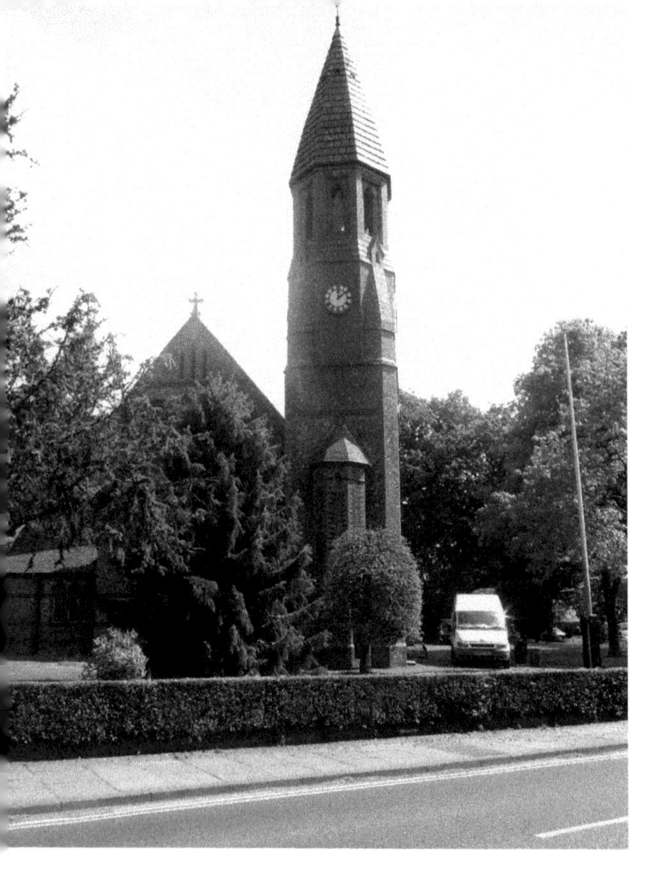

St Peter's Church tower.

spiritual needs. It was agreed that the bulk of the money needed to build a new church would have to be raised by public subscription and a committee of ten was appointed in order to oversee the process. They had discussions with the architects Tate and Popplewell and ideas on how the church would finally look were presented at a meeting in the parish rooms on 14 May 1890, when the plans and drawings were exhibited and detailed.

On 29 November 1890 the foundation stone of the church was laid. Originally £4,165 was the sum thought to be needed for a church to seat 425. The final total was £6,755.15*s*.16*d*. The greatest individual contributions to the church came from the Joynson family. The east and west windows, the bells, the alabaster reredos, panelling in the sanctuary, the sedilia, the credence table, oak doors, block flooring, an open stained wooden roof instead of a plaster one and chairs instead of pews were all influenced by them. There was a carved oak altar and the church was originally planned without a tower, but one was eventually built.

On 16 June 1892 the Lord Bishop of Chester came to dedicate the church and the service was followed by a banquet in the Drill Hall for subscribers. By Easter 1893 all debts were paid and the Revd John Ritson Brunskill was to spend the next thirty-two years in the parish.

36. Christ Church, Junction of Thorley Road and Ridgeway Road, Timperley

Built in 1848–49 and Grade II listed, the church was extended in 1864–65 and altered in 1923. It is of Romanesque style and constructed of red sandstone with a slate roof. It consists of a nave, a porch, north and south transepts, a chancel with an organ chamber and vestry, and a west tower. The tower has three stages, clasping buttresses, dentilled eaves in the bell stage, and a saddleback roof. In the transepts are rose windows.

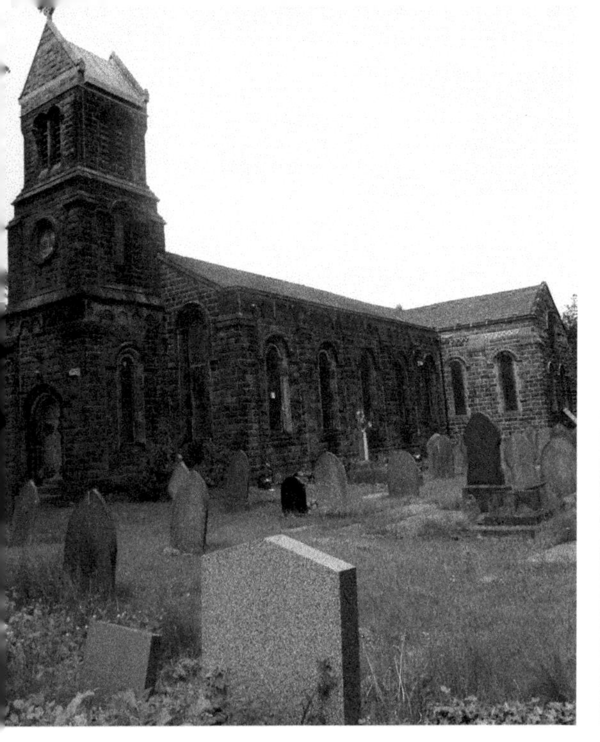

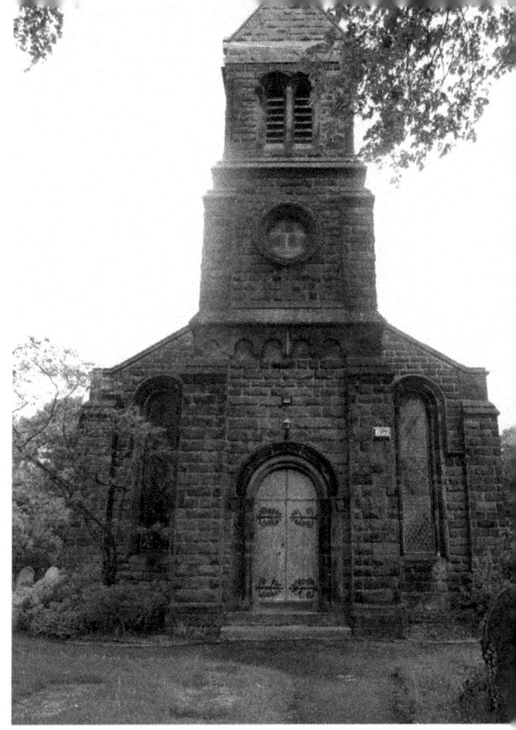

Above left: Christ Church, Timperley, from the churchyard.

Above right: Christ Church, showing the Romanesque tower.

Below: Christ Church from Ridgeway Road.

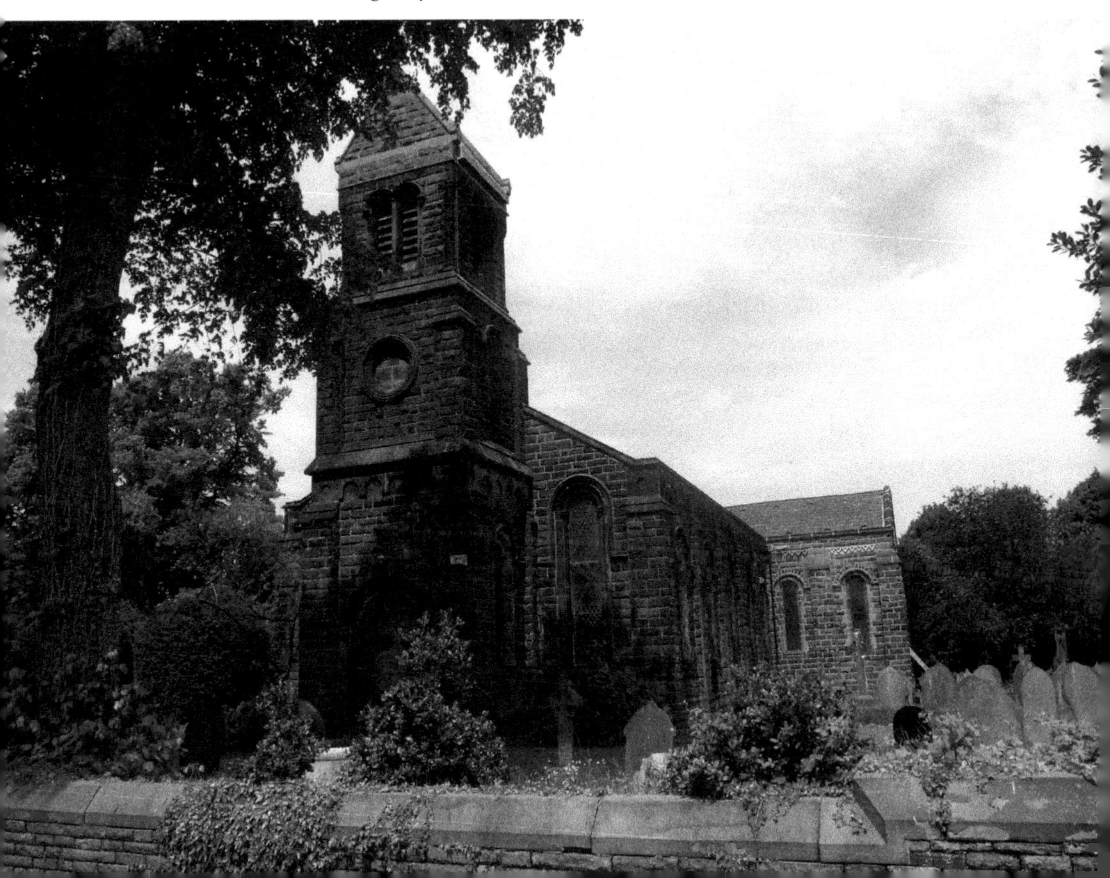

The church is in the deanery of Bowdon, which is part of the diocese of Chester. The parish was formed in 1852, with work starting on the construction of Christ Church in 1848, the foundation stone being laid on 13 November 1848. The church opened one year later, with the first service held on 20 September 1849. It was consecrated on 23 October 1851. All costs of construction were covered by public subscription.

In 1887, the inside of the church walls were lined with terracotta tiles in order to counter the persistent damp, which was affecting the plaster. To cater for the increasing population of Timperley, three chapels of ease were developed in the area. St Andrew's Church was built on Moss Lane in 1932. In 1914, St David's Church was built on Grove Lane, and St Catherine's was opened on Park Road in 1969. In the mid-1990s it was decided that Christ Church would continue as the parish church, with a new church, Holy Cross, built on the site of St Catherine's Church and consecrated on 16 September 2001. St David's closed in 2002.

Modernisation of Christ Church took place in 1987–97, retaining the original box pews. Roof repairs meant that the spire was removed, as it was unsafe, and replaced by a saddleback roof in 2005. In 2006, the final stage of refurbishment saw the pews beneath the gallery removed and the floor levelled. There have been several modern inclusions in this area, with the font being moved from opposite the main door to the corner of the north transept, in order to provide more space.

37. St Alban's Church, Lindsell Road, Broadheath

St Alban's Church was originally part of the large parish of Bowdon St Mary in the eighteenth century, with parishioners having to make their way across fields and footpaths each Sunday. Then in 1799 St George's parish church was built and although closer than Bowdon, there was still around 2 miles for the people of Broadheath to walk each Sunday. When the railway station opened in 1853 it was decided to set up a Mission church in Broadheath, with services being held on a canal boat, located where the Bridgewater Canal passes under Manchester Road.

By 1871 industries were beginning to expand in the Broadheath area and the population grew as a result, so a school was built on Sinderland Road – St Alban's Church School. In 1899, work on the present church began. It was designed by the architects Austin and Paley, of Lancaster. St. Alban's was officially opened on 8 November 1900, although the west end was incomplete and so a temporary wall was constructed until it could be built. The church was not extended to its planned size until work in 2000 had been concluded. In 1902, a vestry and a bell tower were added to the church and in January 1911 the church formed its own parish of St Alban's. The first vicar was the Revd L. W. Thomas. In 1914, the decision was taken to build a vicarage, and this was constructed next to the church. In 1923 the church had electric lights installed, and in 1928 the land close to the church was made into a community area, which included a bowling green and tennis club. The church hall was built in 1935, and this became a home for the Sunday school.

St Alban's Church is a Grade II-listed building and is constructed in red brick with stone dressings. It is roofed in clay tiles. It has a nave with a clerestory, north and south aisles, north and south transepts, a vestry with a pyramidal roof, and a chancel. On the east wall of the north transept is a bell cote with swept coping and grotesque corner figures. The east window has five lights.

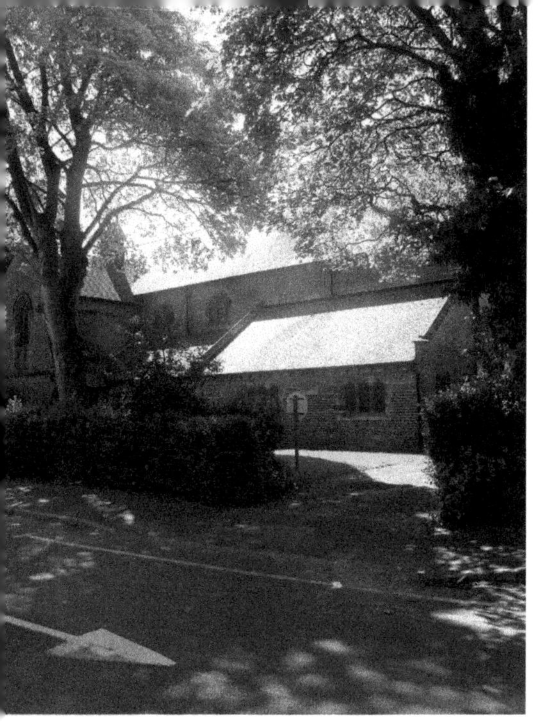

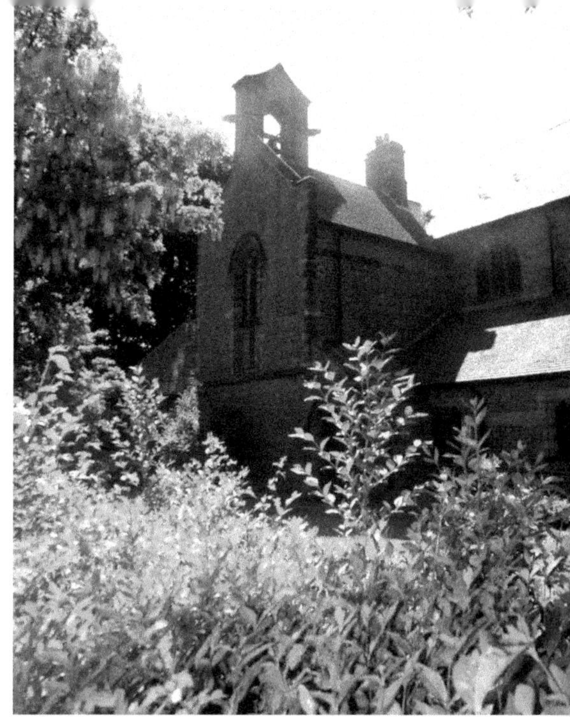

Above left: St Alban's, Broadheath, from Lindsell Road.

Above right: St Alban's, showing the bell cote from Lindsell Road.

Below: St Alban's, showing north transept and bell cote.

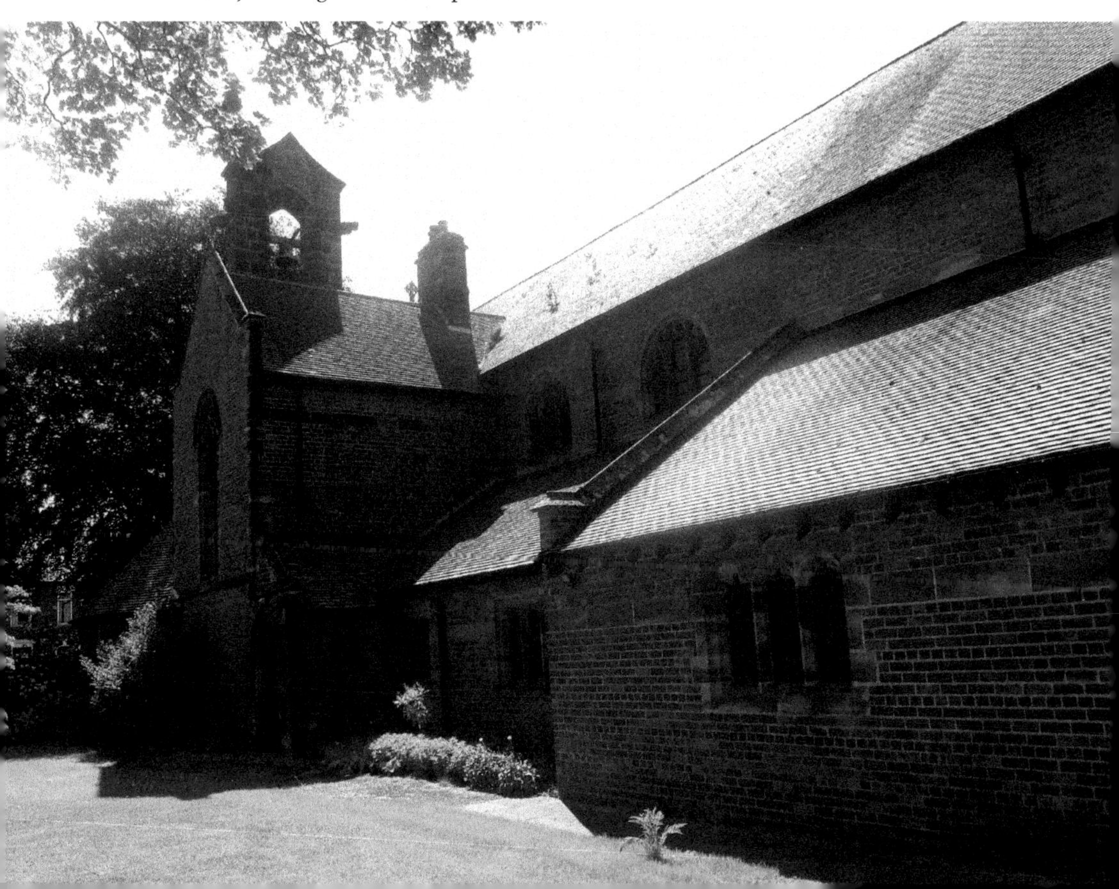

38. Warehouse Adjacent to the Coal Wharf, Bridgewater Canal, Broadheath

Constructed in 1833 and Grade II listed, the warehouse includes an opening containing a branch of the Bridgewater Canal. It is in brick on a stone plinth, with stone dressings, an eaves cornice, a parapet, and roofs of slate and asbestos. It has a square plan, with three storeys and five bays. The central bay projects, and has a pediment with a circular opening and a moulded surround, rusticated quoins and voussoirs and a keystone, above which is a Venetian window with a dated keystone. Elsewhere there are semicircular headed openings and loading bays with hoist canopies. However, many of these features are in danger of being lost due to the dilapidated condition of the building.

The Bridgewater Canal was opened through Broadheath as far as Lymm in 1765. By 1767 the Duke of Bridgewater had built warehouses for corn and coal wharves at Broadheath and the canal had already bridged the River Bollin at Dunham. The whole canal to Runcorn was completed in 1776. Trade on the canal led to the growth and development of Broadheath, and it effectively became the 'port' for Altrincham. There was a sawmill and foundry, a boathouse and warehouse on the north side of the canal, east of Broadheath Bridge. A larger warehouse replaced the existing one in 1833, which was later used as a flour mill.

Broadheath developed its trade in coal, corn, timber, stone and night soil from Manchester, used for market gardening and vegetable growing, while Altrincham benefitted

Warehouse adjacent to former coal wharf, showing modern development (right) and 'opening'.

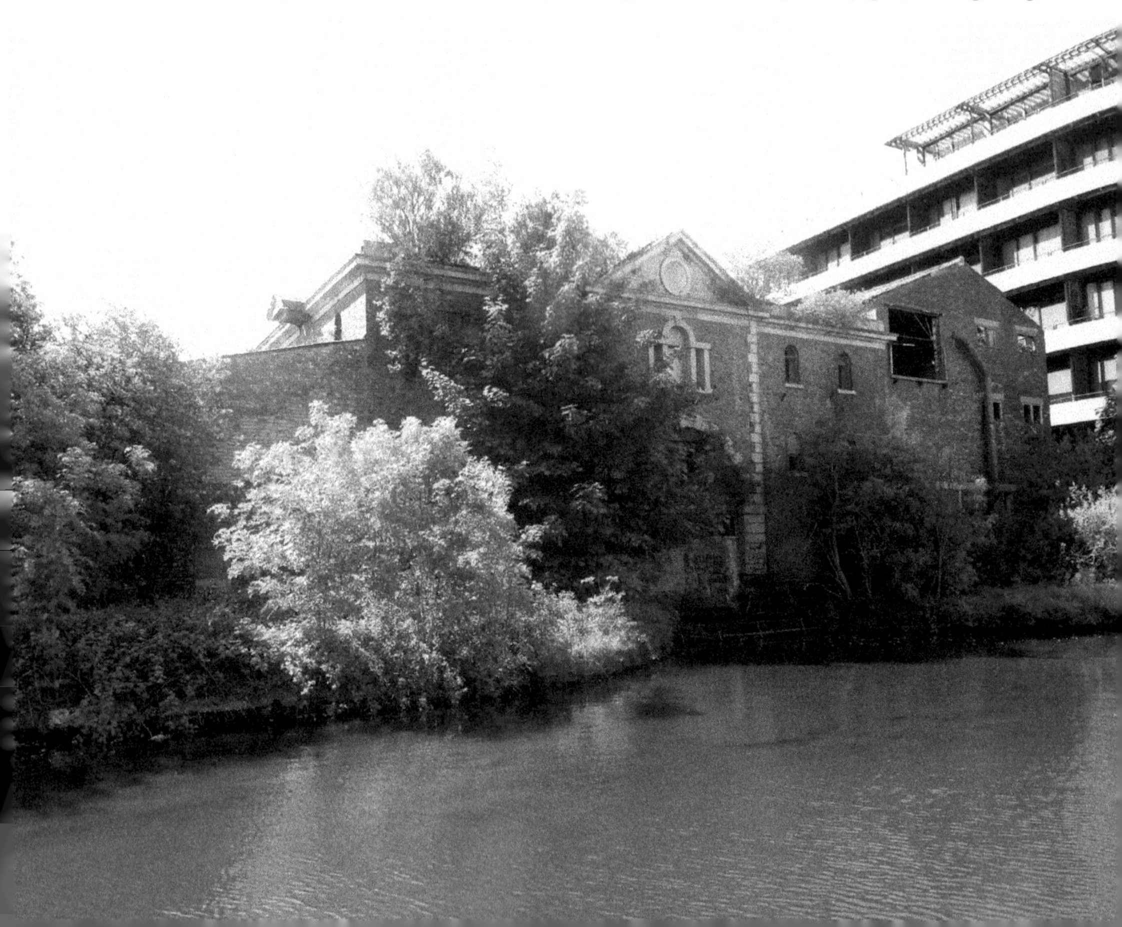

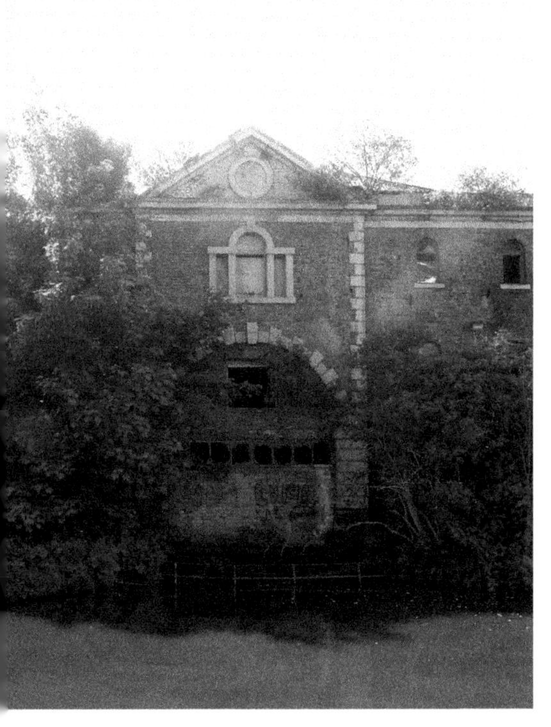

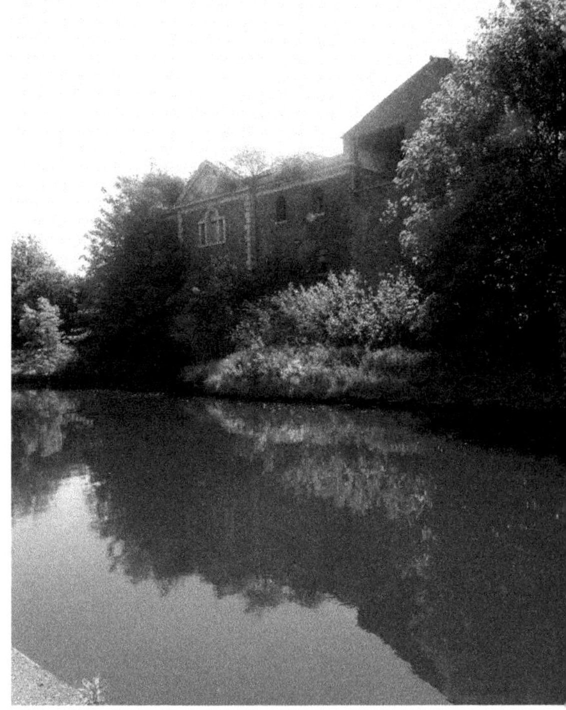

Above left: Warehouse, Bridgewater Canal, showing close-up detail of the Venetian window.

Above right: Warehouse of 1833, Bridgewater Canal, looking towards Broadheath.

from the canal by developing its status as a commuter town, as some of the wealthy used it as a means of transport into Manchester. The canal's status declined with the rise of the railways. In 1846 Lord Francis Egerton, Earl of Ellesmere, agreed for the new railway to Altrincham, opened in 1849, to cross his property in return for 10,000 railway shares and the withdrawal of passenger boats on the canal. The Bridgewater Canal brought trade and prosperity to Broadheath and allowed it to become a flourishing industrial estate. The old coal wharf site has now been developed as an office complex, with the canal now serving leisure activities.

39. Main Office Block, the Linotype Works, Bridgewater Canal, Broadheath

Built in 1897 and Grade II listed, the office block is by Stott & Sons and is in red brick with buff terracotta detailing. It has a symmetrical front, with a main range of two storeys and seven bays, flanked by one- and two-storey ranges. The central bay has an entrance with a segmental head and a six-light fanlight, above which is a mullioned and transomed window and a large rectangular tower with a clock face, a frieze, a moulded cornice, an ornamental metal parapet, and a pyramidal spire. The windows in the upper floor are curved with three lights. Between the bays are piers, and above the upper floor is a dentilled cornice and a deep parapet with recessed panels containing white lettering spelling the name of the company and the date.

Linotype began construction of their building in 1896 and had a major influence on the Broadheath area of the town. They required around 40 acres of land for the undertaking of

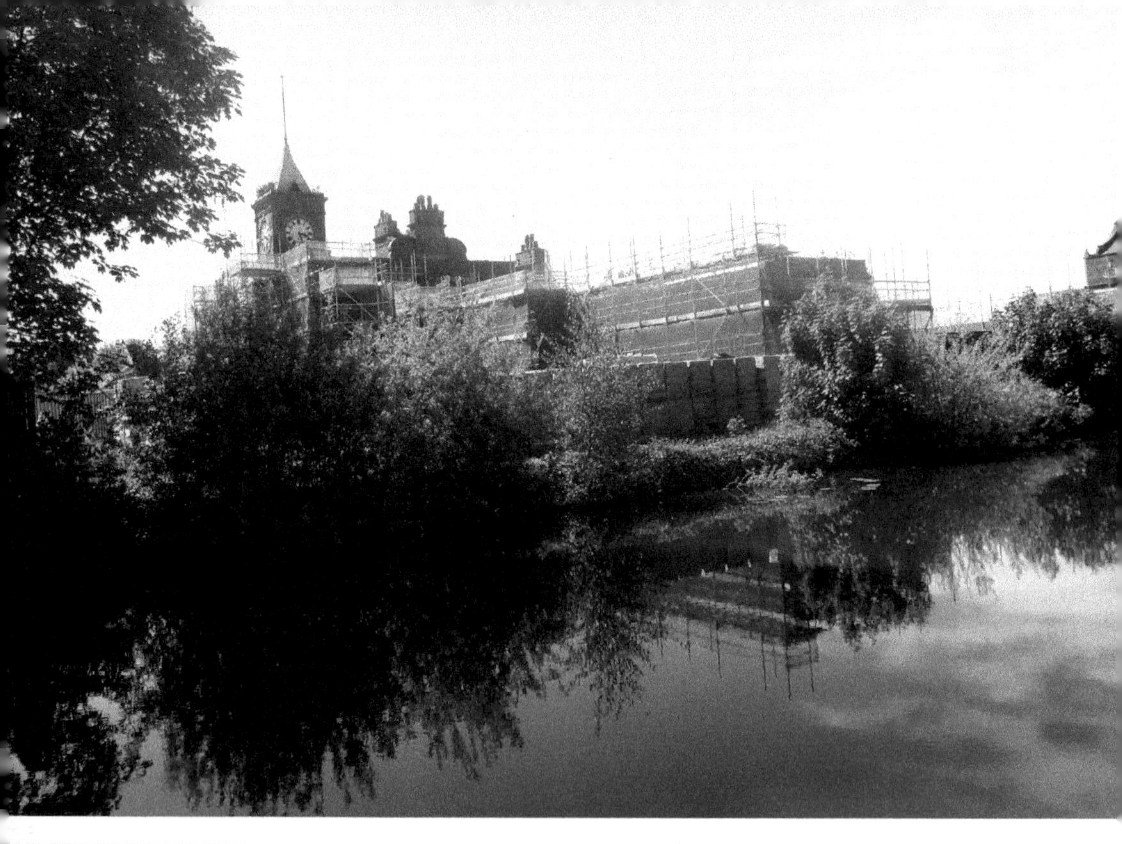

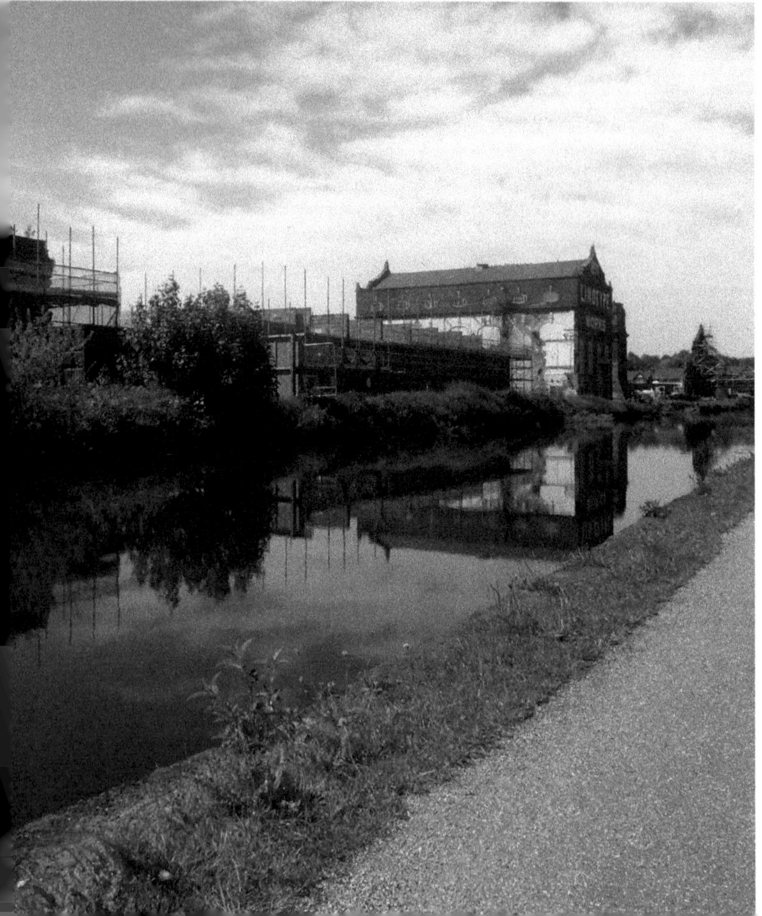

Above: Building work progressing in front of the main Linotype building.

Left: Building work and the Bridgewater Canal at the Linotype site.

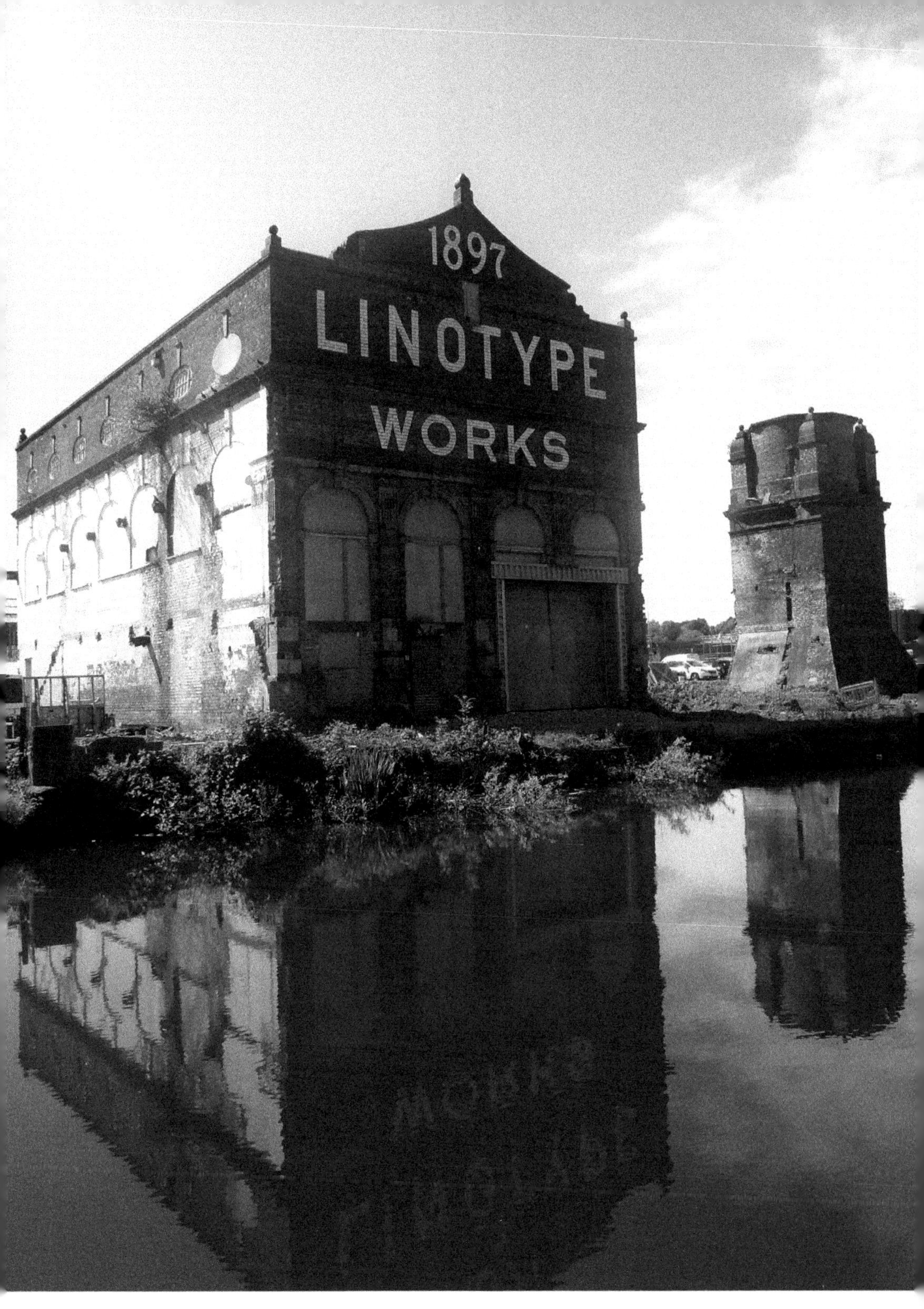

'1897 Linotype Works' on one of the former factory buildings, and chimney remnants.

this scheme, which was sited to the south of the Bridgewater Canal. This conflicted with the ideas of Lord Stamford, whose desire was to limit industrial development to the north side of the canal. Linotype suggested a compromise 'deal' in which they would use just 4 acres of land for their industrial buildings. The remaining 36 acres would be used to develop an innovative housing estate for factory employees while retaining the essential ingredients necessary for a garden suburb, such as tree-lined avenues between the rows of houses.

The design of a tenant's house reflected the status of their employment within the factory. Each road was named after a director of the company. However, there were issues relating to land access, which eventually led to the Broadheath Blockade of the company's entrances to their plant. Local objections also partly led to the abandonment of a power station building project, which would have involved the construction of a very tall chimney. Eventually, the engineering skills required to produce printing machinery was replaced by electronic technology.

40. Seamon's Moss Bridge, Bridgewater Canal, Broadheath

Seamon's Moss Bridge is a Grade II-listed structure and was first listed on 12 July 1985. It is located on Seamon's Road and is a public road bridge over the Bridgewater Canal, which was opened in 1776. John Gilbert (1724–95) was the engineer. John Gilbert was born in Staffordshire and is best known as the canal pioneer who introduced James Brindley to the 3rd Duke of Bridgewater, thus beginning the movement known as 'canal mania'.

Gilbert served the Duke of Bridgewater as his land agent and engineer and, along with his brother Thomas, was an entrepreneur who developed a wide range of industrial and commercial ventures. Gilbert played a significant role in the growth of the canal, being credited with the idea that led to its development; but it is felt by many that his contribution is often overlooked in favour of that of Brindley and the Duke of Bridgewater.

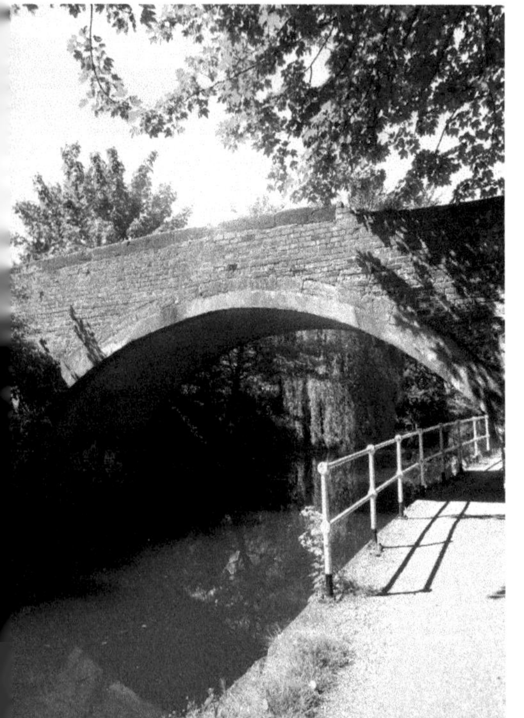

Seamon's Moss Bridge, Bridgewater Canal, looking towards Lymm.

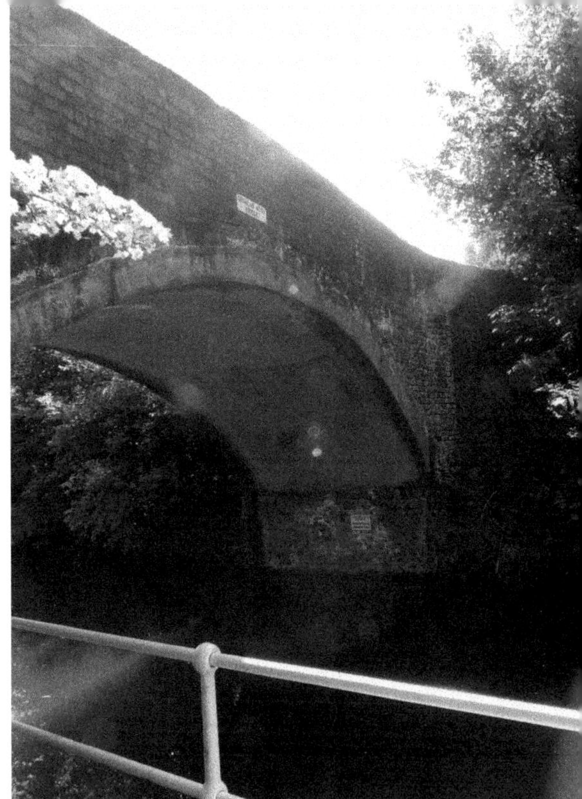

Right: Seamon's Moss Bridge, showing close-up detail of buttress support.

Below: Seamon's Moss Bridge looking towards Broadheath.

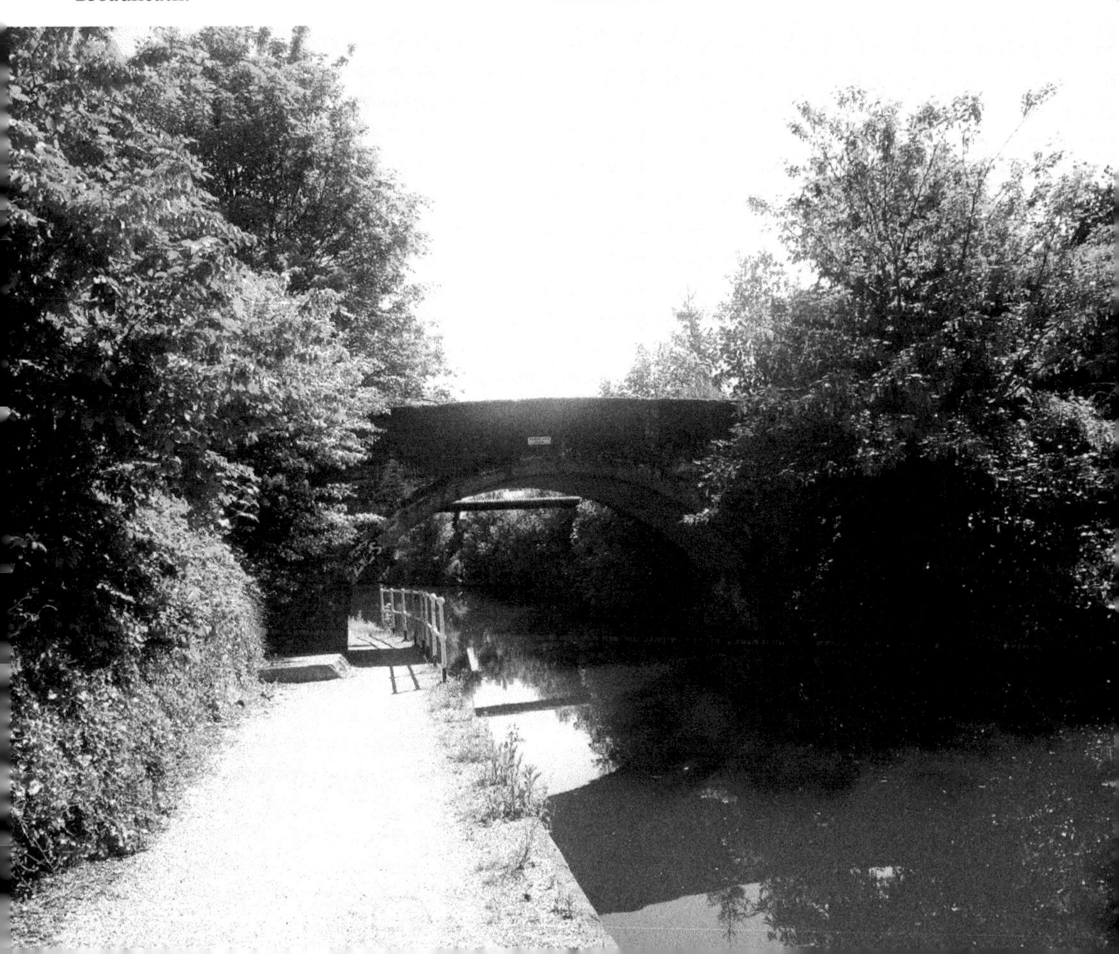

John's brother, Thomas, was working as agent to Lord Gower, brother-in-law of the Duke of Bridgewater. John Gilbert saw the Duke's coal mines at Worsley, leading Gilbert to suggest the idea of a canal in order to drain the mines and transport coal. He was appointed as the Duke's agent around 1758, moving to live in nearby Worsley. Initially he was involved in the preliminary levelling and surveying of the canal. Later James Brindley was appointed as engineer to the canal and the Duke, Gilbert and Brindley supervised the plans together and managed its building from Worsley Old Hall.

The canal is sometimes described as England's first, and was the forerunner of canal networks throughout the country. It was opened on 17 July 1761 and was the first canal in Britain to be built without following an existing watercourse, and so its canal structures form an important historical record. Seamon's Moss Bridge is built of brick with sandstone dressings. The main structure of the bridge consists of a segmental brick arch below a stone band, with stone copings that have been partly replaced by brick. There are also brick buttresses that restrain the side walls.

41. Unitarian Chapel, Dunham Road, Altrincham

In September 1816 the Unitarians of Altrincham opened their first building, sharing their minister with Hale for the next sixty-two years. By 1869 the building on Shaws Lane, demolished in the 1960s, was deemed to be too small, so it was decided to construct a new place of worship. Altrincham Unitarian chapel was built in 1872, replacing the earlier chapel of 1814/16. It was opened by the Revd William Gaskell, husband of the famous novelist Elizabeth. Its architect was Thomas Worthington, some of whose relatives were long-term members of the chapel's congregation. It was built at a cost of £3,054. The three

Unitarian Chapel, Dunham Road, *c.* 1910.

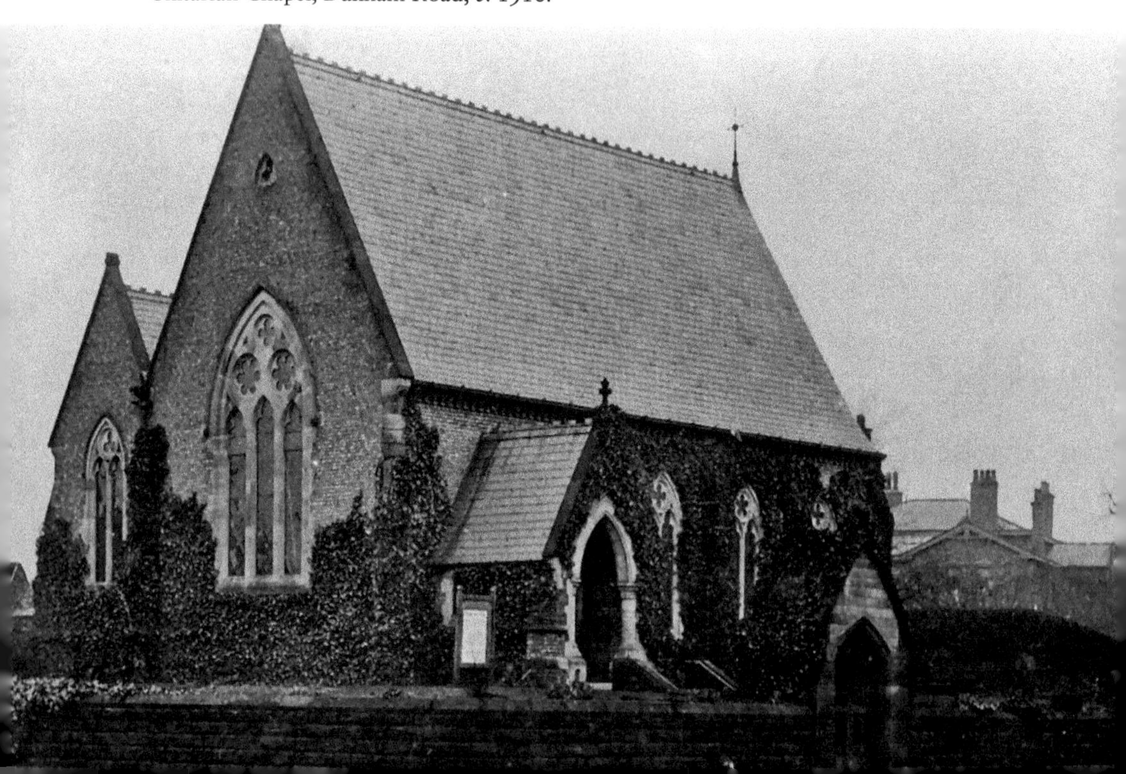

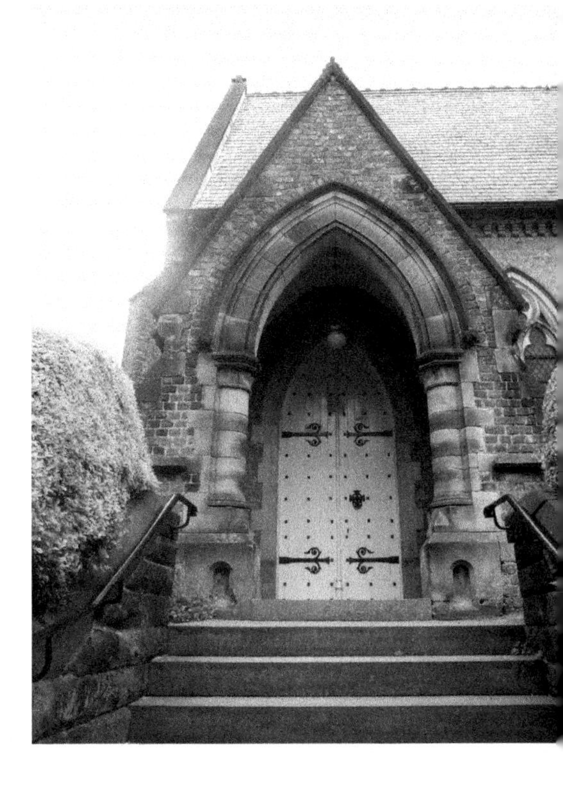

Unitarian Chapel, Dunham Road entrance.

stained-glass memorial windows at the front of the chapel were a later addition. The original windows, displaying flowers, plants and the seasons, are on the south side of the chapel. Further additions included, in 1875, a Sunday school and chapel keeper's house, on Sylvan Grove. In 1883 an organ was presented by James Worthington and in 1890 a series of stained-glass windows were installed. In 1884 the large schoolroom was built and in 1899 the parsonage was constructed. These buildings were all located at one site. The chapel, located on the busy Dunham Road, is close to Old Market Place.

42. Denzell House, Dunham Road, Bowdon

Denzell House is a Grade II-listed building constructed of rock-faced stone with ashlar dressings and a coloured tile roof. The house was built in 1874 for Robert Scott by Clegg & Knowles of Manchester, noted for their palazzo warehouse designs in the city. It cost £18,000 to build, on 10 acres of land sold by the 7th Earl of Stamford in 1874. It is built on a two-storey rectangular plan with an entrance and *porte cochere* to the north-west and a conservatory to the south-east. The entrance hall leads to a central corridor, with rooms on either side. This is repeated at first-floor level. The exterior is described as 'eclectic Jacobean, Gothic and Italianate style'. There are also Tudor-style chimney stacks and steeply pitched roofs with crested ridge tiles.

In 1904, the house was sold to Samuel Lamb, who established the gardens. After his death in 1936, his children gave the house and its grounds to Bowdon Urban District Council. A park from 1938, the house became a residential adult education college, then an evacuation centre for expectant mothers during the Second World War. It was an annex to Altrincham General Hospital until 1979, and a hospital for the elderly before closing in 1987. After lying empty, the building was renovated into offices.

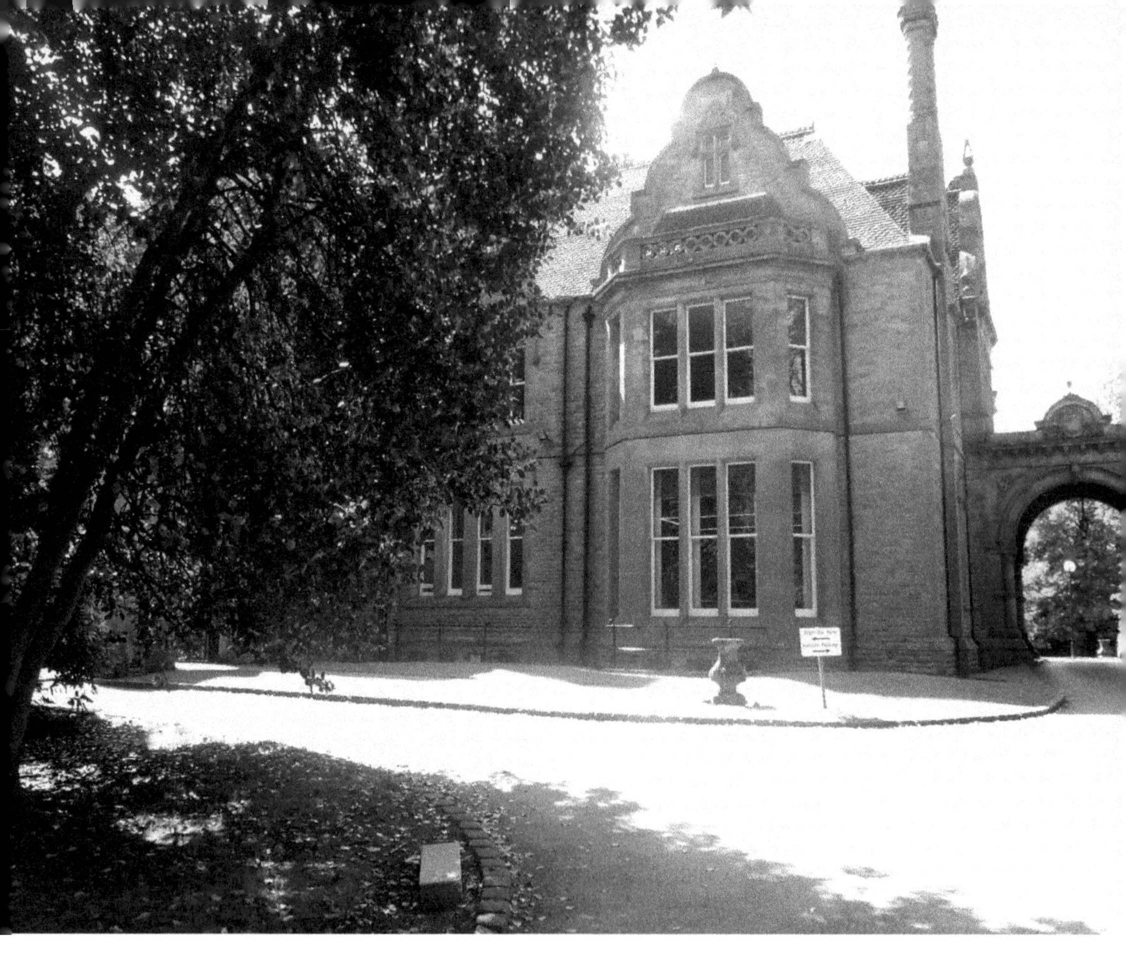

Denzell House and Gardens, Dunham Road, showing *Porte Cochere.*

43. The Motor House, Dunham Massey Hall

In 1855 the 7th Earl of Stamford, George Harry Grey, married his second wife, Catherine Cox, a former circus performer. They were subsequently shunned by Cheshire society and left Dunham, taking paintings, furniture and silver with them. The hall was left empty for fifty years. In 1906, the 9th Earl, William Grey, returned with his wife, Penelope Theobald, and their children, Lady Jane Grey and the future Earl Roger. In what became known as the 'Homecoming', cheering crowds greeted them as their carriage travelled through Hale, Altrincham and on to Dunham Massey.

Of course, in the intervening fifty years the hall would have required some upgrading and renovation and many changes were made in the remaining years of the Edwardian period. The Motor House is a response to this modernisation process, in an era when motor transport was just beginning to challenge the supremacy of horsepower. There is also a stable block to the left of the Motor House, in similar design.

In 1915, the hall underwent yet further changes when it became the Stamford Military Hospital. The saloon was converted into a ward, with around fifty-three hospital beds. Nurses, including Lady Jane Grey, treated nearly 300 patients at Dunham Massey.

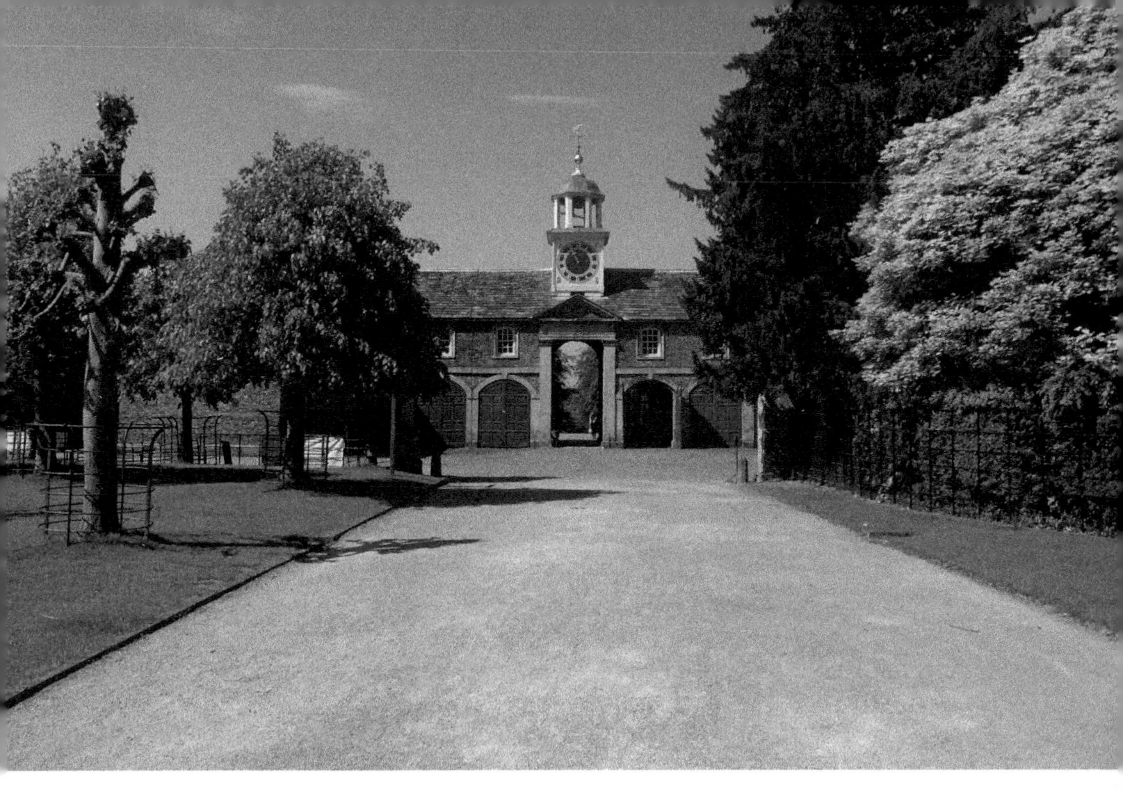

The Motor House, Dunham Hall, Dunham Massey.

44. Former Stamford Estate Office and National Trust Shop, No. 18 High Street, Altrincham

The building is Grade II listed and dates from the late eighteenth century. The office is in brick on a stone plinth with a sill band, a modillion eaves cornice, and a hipped stone-slate roof. There are two storeys, a symmetrical front of four bays, and a one-bay extension to the left. The original central two bays project slightly under a pediment. The doorway has

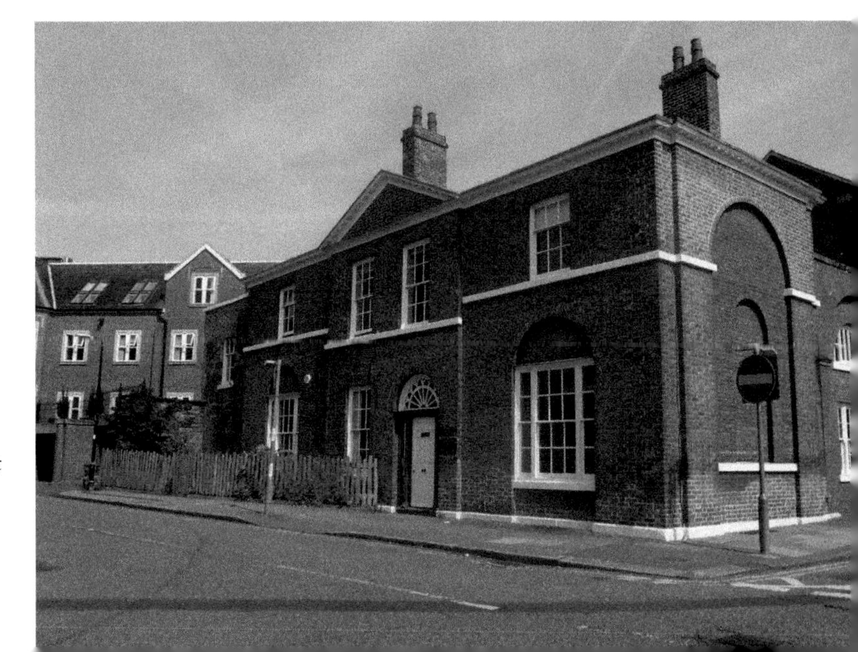

Former Stamford Estate Office, showing coach entrance on Market Street (right).

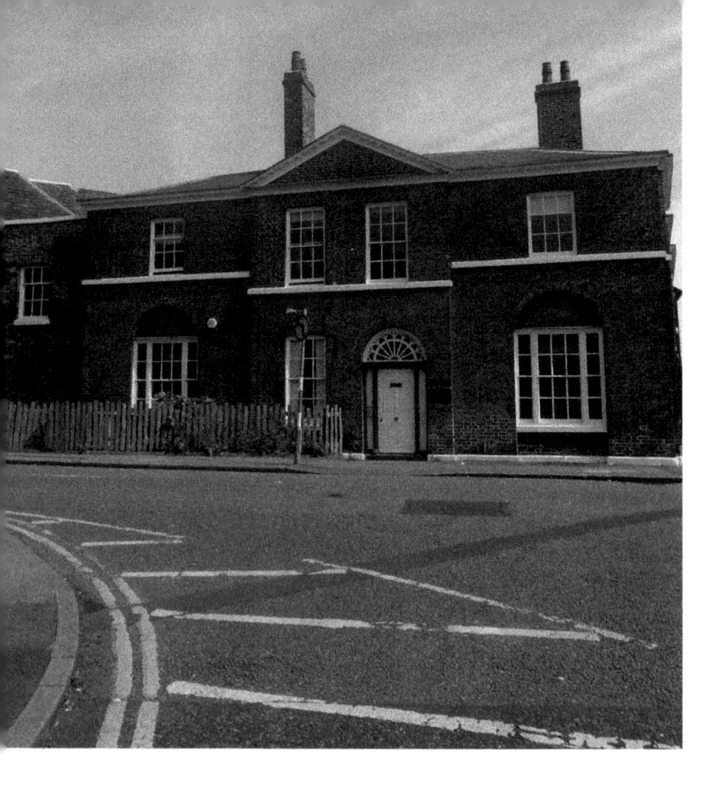

Front elevation of the former Stamford Estate Office, No. 18 High Street, Altrincham.

fluted three-quarter columns, side lights, and a decorative fanlight. In the right return is a blocked carriage entrance, with a semicircular head and a parapet above. This was located at the rear of the building and opened into Market Street.

The former Stamford Estates Office was built around 1780 and is a former gentleman's dwelling. It was later used as a solicitor's office until Lord Stamford made it his estate office. Its design is very similar to the Georgian houses on the Downs and it is constructed in Flemish bond brick. The main entrance, with its fluted columns on either side, leads into a large foyer and a semi-elliptical staircase leading to the upper floor. From one of the upstairs rooms there is access to a storeroom, which is barrel vaulted. Here, the Worthington's, Lord Stamford's stewards, kept the papers of the Stamford Estates.

45. Old Houses, Lower George Street, Altrincham

Lower George Street was originally known as Well Street, with the sixteenth-century thatched cottages shown here, opposite the old library and the police lock-ups, which date from 1838. A well, known as 'Big Well', was located at Well Lane, later known as Victoria Street. Nickson (p. 141) tells us that 'There was a well at the bottom of Victoria Street, then known as Well Lane, and as it was the chief source for the supply of water to this part of the town it was known as the Big Well. This was the centre at which all the town gossip was turned over, and it was not unusual to see a dozen women grouped about the well in the early morning with pails and jugs.'

One of the cottages was occupied by William Ashley, an Overseer of the Parish. All these structures were demolished in the late 1970s when Petros Developments built the modern shopping centre. They are indicative of a long-gone rural age, which Nickson (p. 139) describes thus: 'Until the middle part of the last century, the features of the district were chiefly pastoral. Emerald meadows, rustling cornfields and pleasant orchards spread on every side, and in the topmost boughs of a leafy wood, was a colony of crows.'

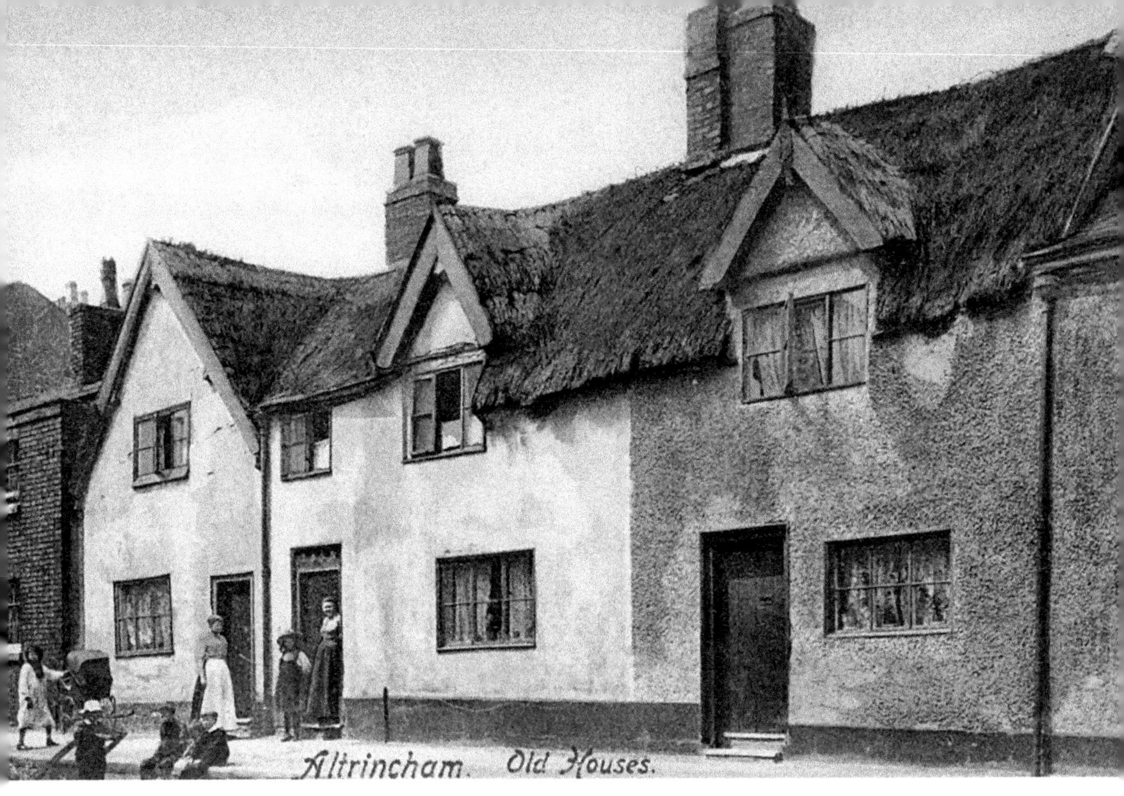

Above: Old Cottages, Lower George Street, Altrincham, 1905.

Right: New development along Lower George Street.

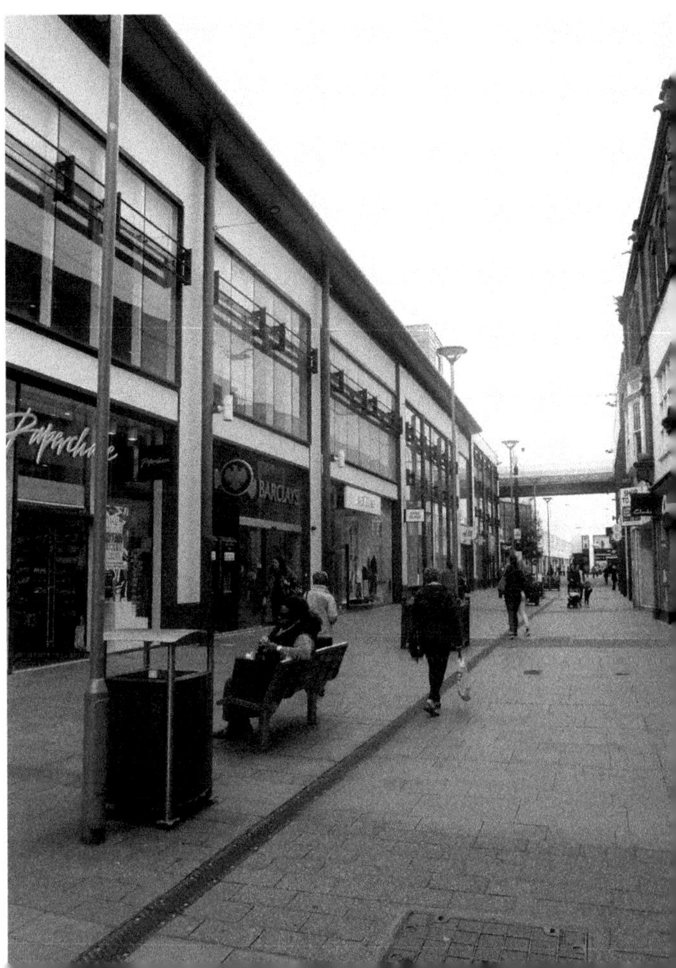

46. Church of St John the Evangelist, Junction of St John's Road and Ashley Road, Altrincham

Built in 1865–66 on land provided by Lord Stamford, opening on 14 December 1866, the site was previously the location of farm buildings, shippons and stables used by Ralph Pickstone, with a farmhouse immediately opposite. The church stands on an elevated site, with its spire visible from Ashley Road. It was initially used as a chapel to Altrincham St George. In 1867, it became the district church for parts of the townships of Altrincham, Dunham Massey and Hale, with further boundary changes on 31 July 1906. The church, designed by J. Medland Taylor in Early English Gothic style, is of stone and has slate roofs with coped gables. The design of the font and pulpit are particularly indicative of his style. St John's consists of a nave with a clerestory, north and south aisles, a west porch, north and south transepts, a chancel with a polygonal apse, a vestry and an organ chamber, and south-west steeple. The steeple has a three-stage tower, with buttresses, lancet windows, and a broach spire with gabled lucarnes. It was originally built to seat 920, costing £7,000. The school, parish hall and vicarage, which adjoined the church, complemented its design. The church has some notable stained-glass windows, particularly the east window, located behind the altar.

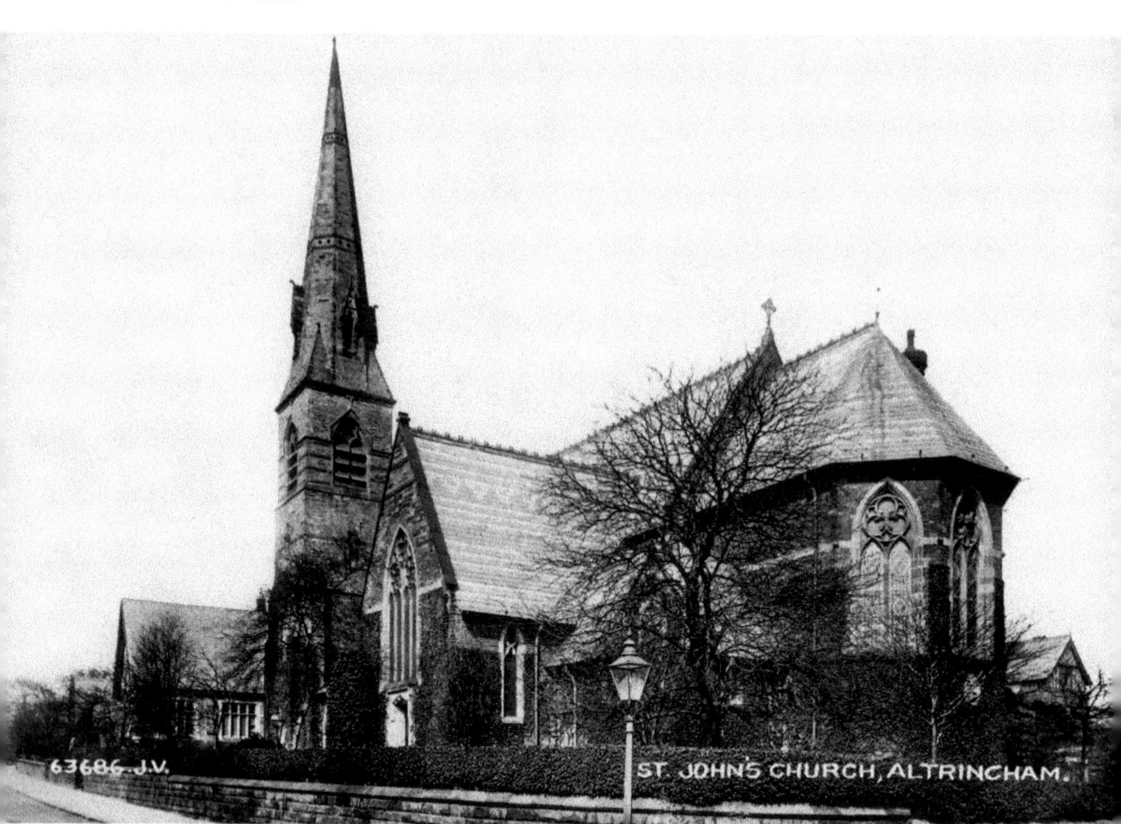

St John's Church from Ashley Road, *c.* 1910.

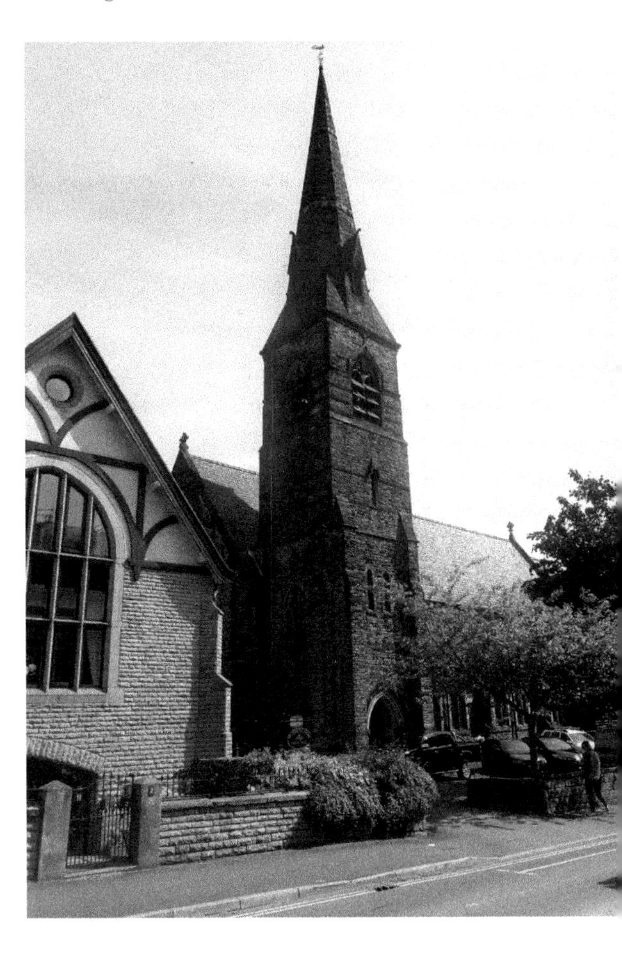

St John's Church from St John's Road, former church buildings (left).

47. The Old Post Office, Stamford New Road, Altrincham

Altrincham Post Office is on the left, where there was a gas lamp on the pavement outside the entrance. It was built by J. H. Brown (Nickson) (J.H. Broun), including the adjoining block of shops, from the designs of John McNamara, a well-known local architect. In 1905, Charles Heathcote and Sons built Station Buildings (far right) for J. H. Brown, adjoining Altrincham station and now Stamford House. Grade II listed, together with the Station Hotel, opposite, and the Clock Tower, they mark the northern boundary of the conservation area. The Old Post Office is of the same substantial construction and exterior design as Stamford House, Altrincham station, the Station Hotel and the Clock Tower. As such it blends very effectively into the backdrop of Altrincham's Stamford New Road. It has been updated for modern commercial and retail use, its size and solidity lending it perfectly to this task. Nickson describes construction along this part of Stamford New Road in the latter part of the nineteenth century as a 'wave of building' (p. 95). He goes on to say that 'to-day there is not a single trace of the gardens which, as late as 1890, bordered both sides of the road'. These buildings were 'a typical example of the rapid progress Altrincham was making'.

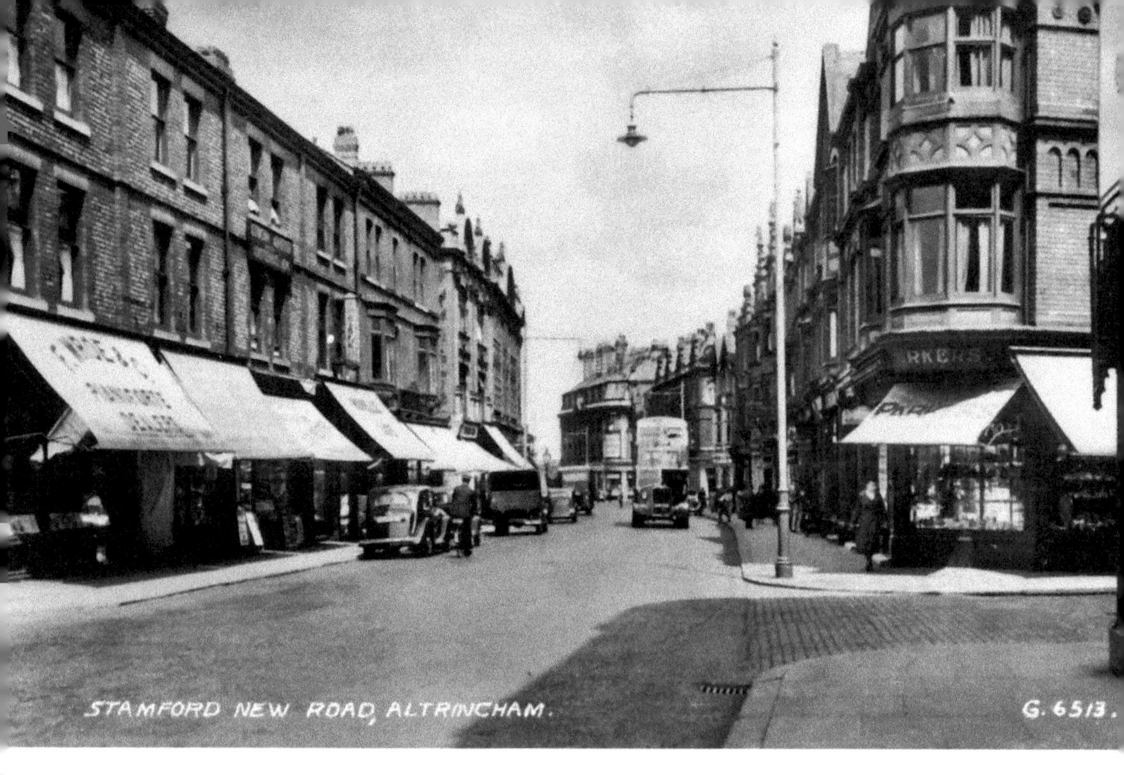

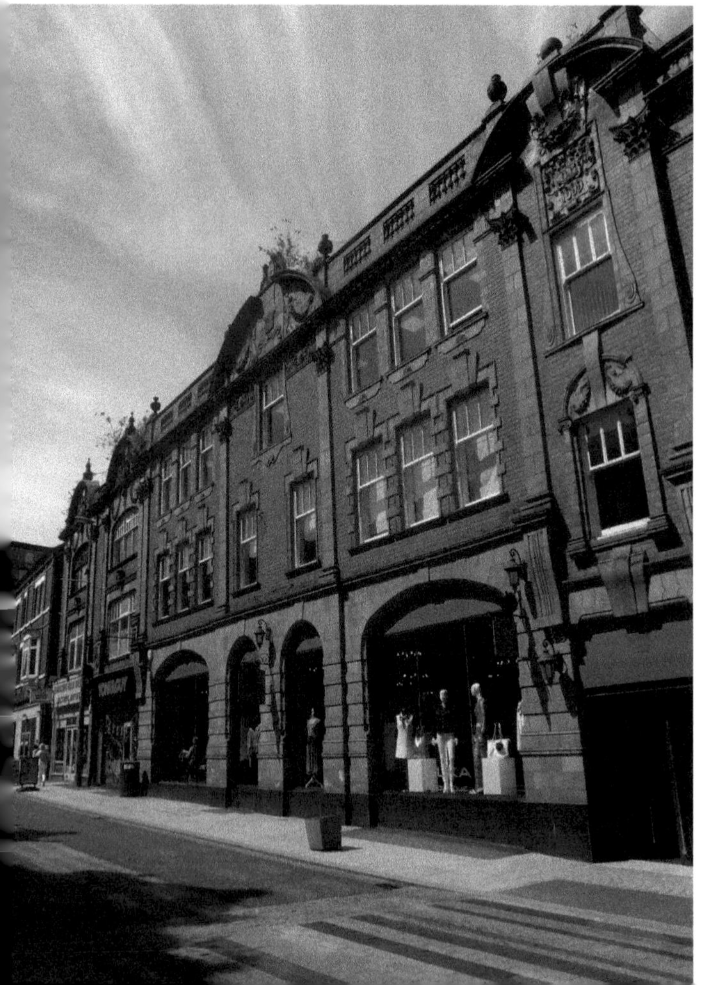

Above: The Old Post Office (far left), Stamford New Road, *c*. 1950.

Left: Former Post Office, Stamford New Road, 2018.

48. Church Bank, Langham Road, Bowdon

Captain Edward Kinder Bradbury (1881–1914) was awarded a VC for action on 1 September 1914. His blue plaque reads, 'Captain Edward Kinder Bradbury (1881-1914) Born at Church Bank, Bowdon. Awarded the Victoria Cross for bravery in the First World War 1914-1918. September 1st 1914, Nery, France.'

Captain Edward Kinder Bradbury belonged to L Battery, The Royal Field Artillery. He died at the age of thirty-three and is buried at Nery Communal Cemetery. He obtained his commission in South Africa during the Anglo-Boer War of 1899–1902. He joined the Royal Artillery as a second lieutenant in 1900 and was promoted to full lieutenant in April 1901. In January 1902 he was seconded for service with the Imperial Yeomanry in the Second Boer War, serving as a lieutenant with the 31st Battalion. He received his captaincy in 1910 and became an adjutant in February 1912. His VC was for gallantry and ability in organising the defence of L Battery in extreme circumstances at Nery on 1 September 1914. He was killed during the 'Retreat from Mons'. Both he and other members of his battery were severely wounded but continued to engage the German offensive. Five VCs, two DCMs and a French Order of Merit were won in this engagement.

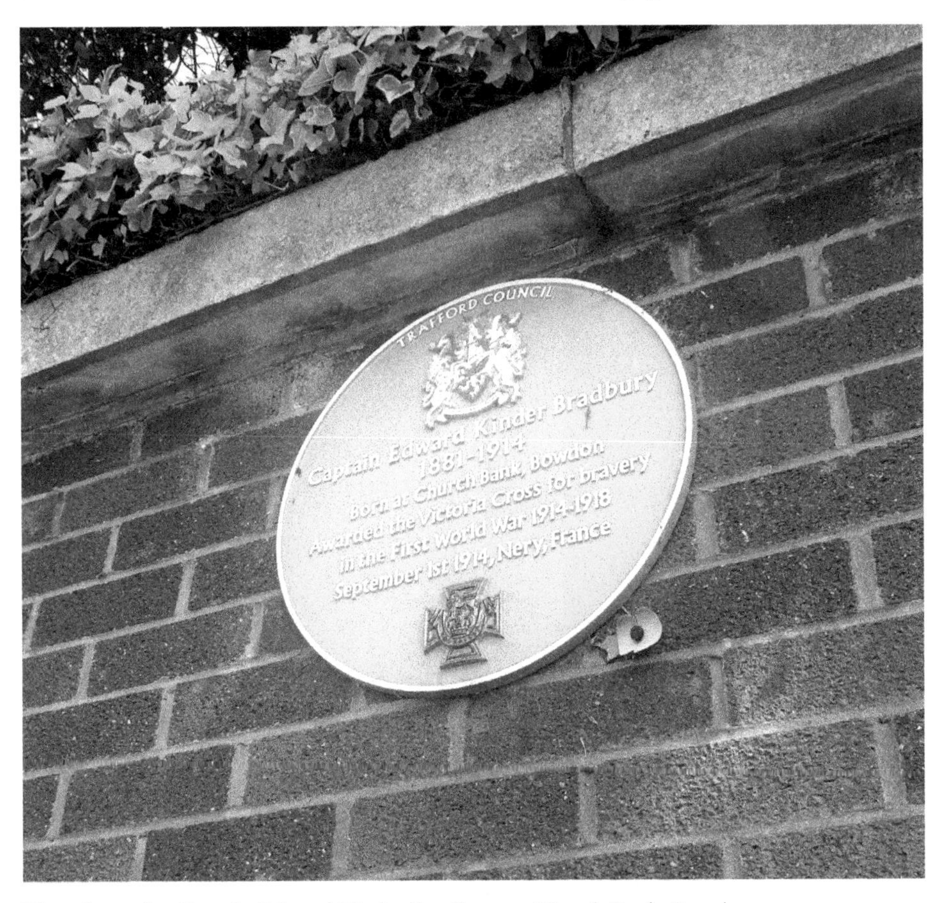

Blue plaque for Captain Edward Kinder Bradbury at Church Bank, Bowdon.

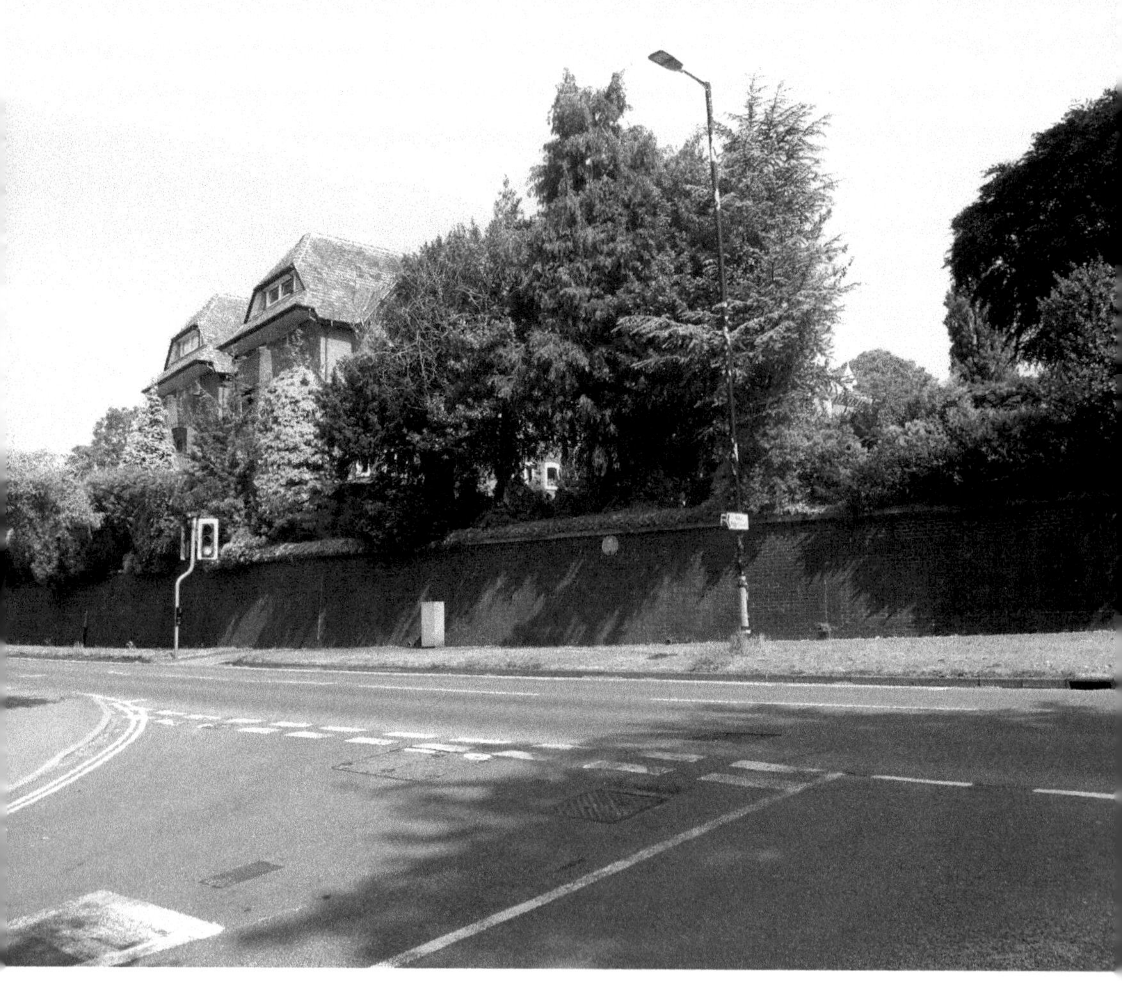

View of Langham Road, Bowdon, location of the blue plaque.

49. St Alban's Vicarage, Lindsell Road, Broadheath

Built in 1914 and Grade II listed, the vicarage is in brick with sandstone dressings and a clay tile roof. There are two storeys with attics, and five bays. Above the doorway is a segmental-arched fanlight, the windows are mullioned and transomed, and the roof has a hipped dormer window. The fifth bay is corbelled out at the upper floor. In the left gable end is a two-storey canted bay window, and at the rear are two more dormer windows.

In the late 1890s the development of Broadheath as an industrial area of Altrincham made the necessity of building a new church all the more important. This was swiftly erected, with the dedication ceremony taking place on 8 November 1900, conducted by the Bishop of Chester. The church cost in excess of £5,000 and is built in the decorated style of architecture. Local bricks were used for external facings and bricks and moulded terracotta from Northwich were used for the interior. The arcades, except the arches and the dressings of the windows and doors, are of Runcorn flecked stone. The contractors were Stelfox & Son, of Northwich, with the masonry work carried out by G. Rathbone, also of Northwich. St Alban's parish became independent from St George's on the induction of the Revd L. W. Thomas on 30 January 1911.

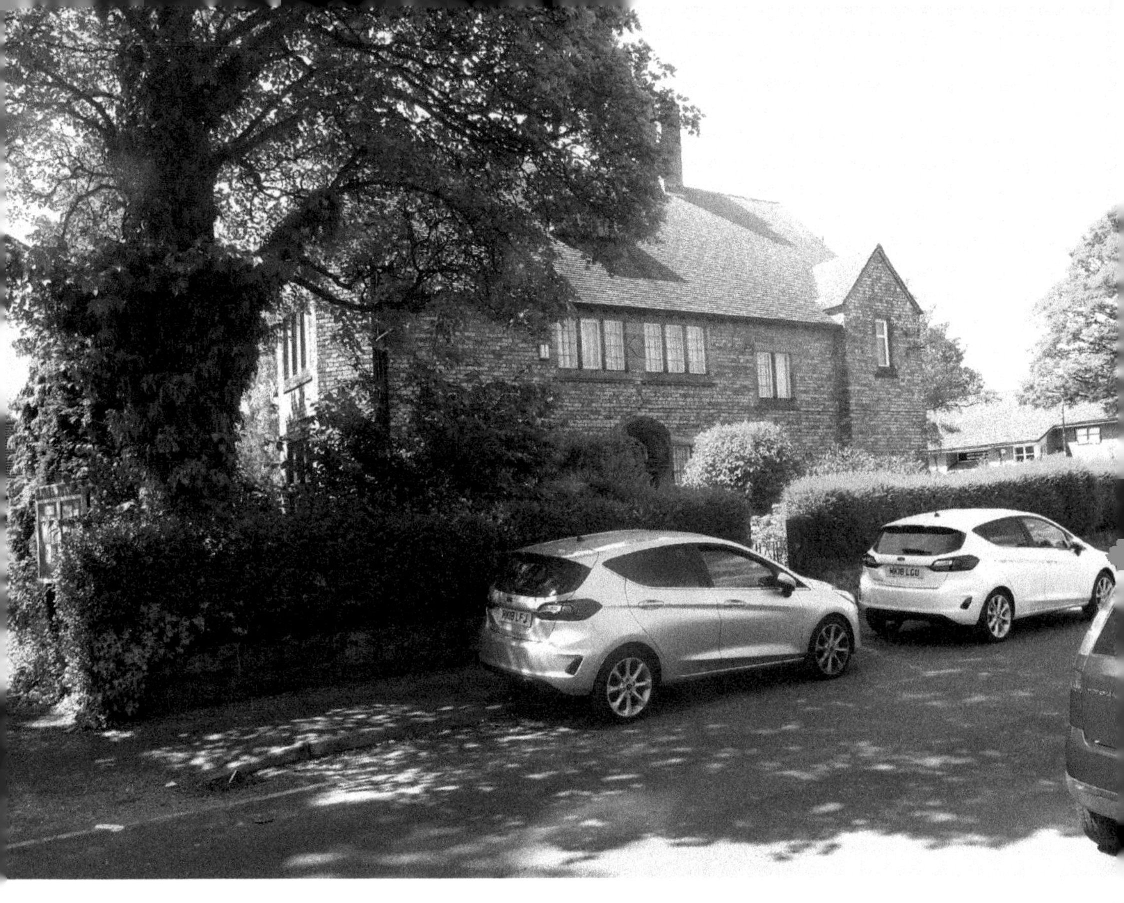

Above: St Alban's Vicarage from Lindsell Road.

Right: St Alban's Vicarage, showing hipped dormer window.

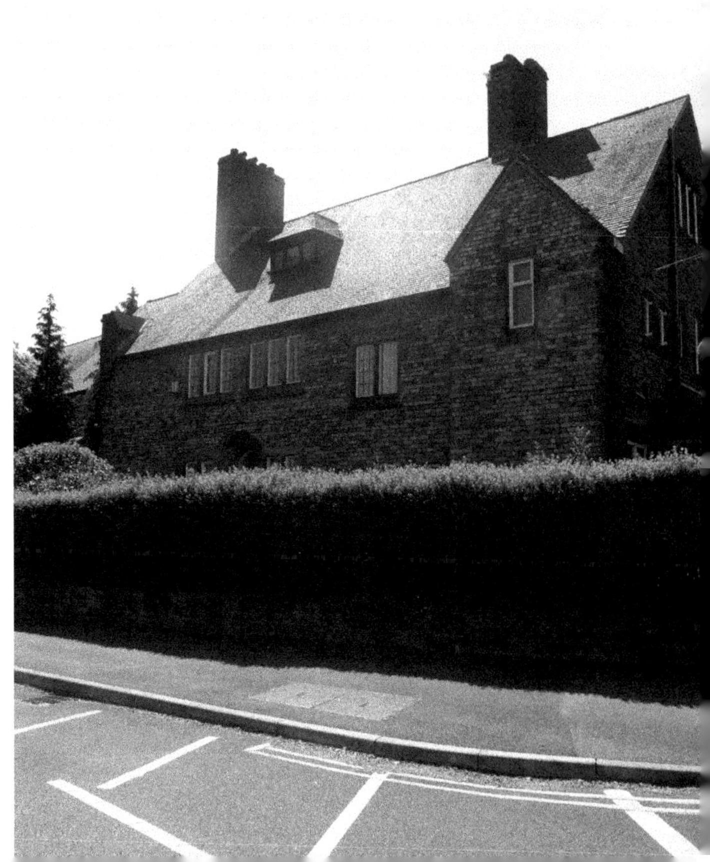

50. The Railway Inn Public House, Manchester Road, Broadheath

Built in the mid-nineteenth century, around the time that the railway line opened in 1853, and Grade II listed, The Railway Inn is of red and purple brick, with a Welsh slate roof, two storeys and three bays. The off-centre doorway has a moulded surround, a semicircular head, and a fanlight. The windows are sashes with 'segmental arched heads'.

The name of the public house is a constant reminder to motor traffic passing on the busy Manchester Road that there was once a railway line and railway station at this point. Broadheath railway station served the northern part of Altrincham and opened on 1 November 1853, closing on 10 September 1962 for passengers and closing completely on 28 December 1964. It was built by the Warrington & Altrincham Junction Railway, although renamed the Warrington & Stockport Railway shortly before the station opened. It was situated on an embankment west of the A56, beneath George Richards Way and behind the Railway Inn. The name of the railway station changed again to Broadheath (Altrincham) in November 1856. Trains served Manchester to the north and Lymm and Warrington Arpley to the south. Today, this remains a busy location, with a retail park on the site of the station.

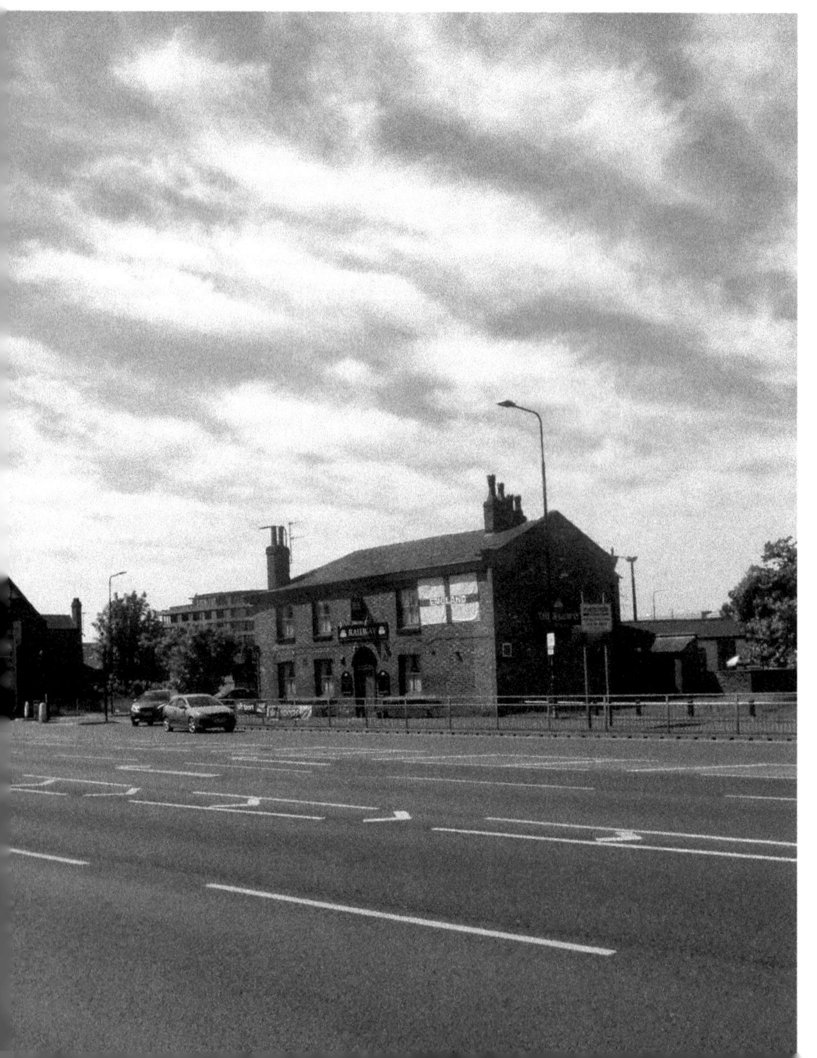

View of the Railway Inn from Manchester Road.

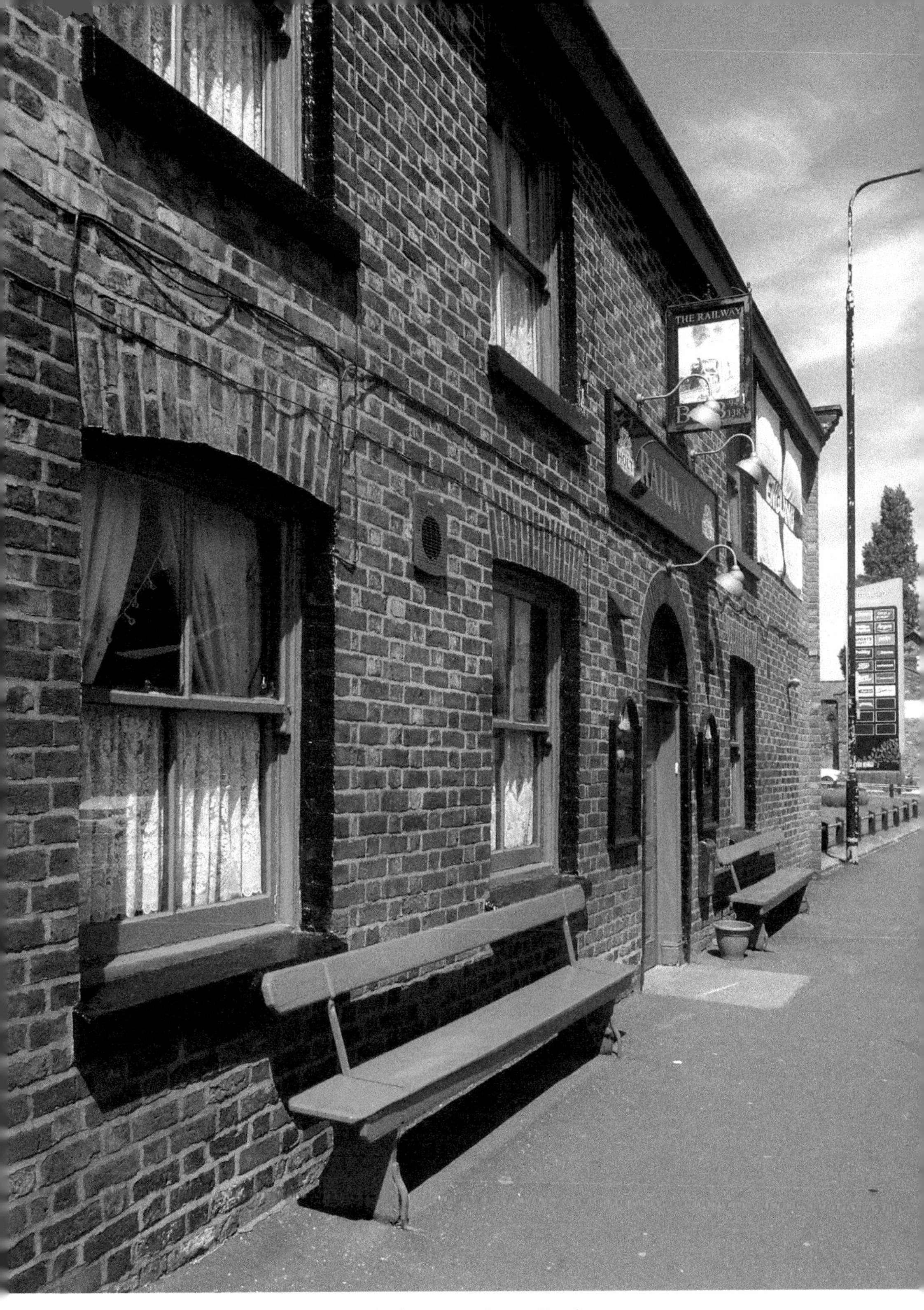

Close-up detail of the Railway Inn overlooking Manchester Road.

Sources

Bamford, F., *Mansions and Men of Dunham Massey, from Errant Earl to Red Dean* (Altrincham: Local History Press, 1991)
Bayliss, D., ed. *Altrincham a History* (Timperley: Willow Publishing, 1992)
Bridgewater Canal www.bridgewatercanal.co.uk/history
Dickens, S., 'Parklands, Dunham Massey and the Families of William and Thomas Berry, Blacking Manufacturers', *Altrincham History Society Occasional Paper*. No. 24. 2012.
Dickens, S., 'Parklands, Dunham Massey and the Families of William and Thomas Berry', *Altrincham Through Time* (Stroud: Amberley, 2016)
Dunham Massey www.nationaltrust.org.uk/dunham-massey
Listed Buildings in Trafford www.britishlistedbuildings.co.uk
Morrison, B. D., *Looking Back at Altrincham* (Timperley: Willow Publishing, 1980)
Nickson, C., *Bygone Altrincham: Traditions and History* (Altrincham: Mackie & Co., 1935)

Many thanks to Mick Smith of Bowdon Downs Congregational Church.